'The Streetcl

It seeped
into his body,
Society,
Absolved
Sacred
Sanctified
Possessed
Society,
    . . . Like a flood of dark crows into the fibres of
        his inner tree,
and taking his place
Made him a suicide.

For it is the anatomical logic of modern man
never to be able to live, nor think about living,
but as a man possessed.

Antonin Artaud,
'Van Gogh, le Suicidé de la Société'.

Nicole Ward Jouve

'The Streetcleaner'

The Yorkshire Ripper Case on Trial

Marion Boyars   London   New York

Paperback edition published in
Great Britain and the United States in 1988 by
Marion Boyars Publishers
24 Lacy Road, London SW15 1NL
26 East 33rd Street, New York, N.Y. 10016

Originally published in cloth in 1986 by
Marion Boyars Publishers

Distributed in the United States by
Kampmann & Company Inc, New York

Distributed in Australia by
Wild and Woolley, Glebe, N.S.W.

Distributed in Canada by Book Center Inc, Montreal

© Nicole Ward Jouve, 1986

ISBN 0-7145-2847-1 Cloth
ISBN 0-7145-2884-6 Paperback

British Library Cataloguing in Publication Data

Ward Jouve, Nicole
    'The streetcleaner': the Yorkshire Ripper case on trial
    1. Sutcliffe, Peter, *1946–*   2. Murder—England,
    Northern   3. Women—England, Northern—Crimes
    against
    I. Title
    364.1'523'0924   HV6248.S6/

Library of Congress Cataloging in Publication Data

Ward Jouve, Nicole.
    'The streetcleaner.'
Bibliography: p.
    1. Sutcliffe, Peter.   2. Crime and criminals—
    England—Biography.   3. Murder—England—Case studies.
    4. Victims of crimes—England—Case studies.   I. Title.
    HV6248.S69W38   1986   364.1'523'0924[B]   85-26924

Printed and bound in Great Britain by
Biddles Ltd, Guildford and King's Lynn

Contents

The Case of the Yorkshire Ripper

On a morning in October 1975, in a playing field in the area of Chapeltown, Leeds, the body of a blonde woman was found by a milkman on his round. Her blouse and jacket had been torn open, the bra pushed up to expose her breasts, and the trousers dragged down around the knees. She had died of two massive blows to the head dealt with a hammer, and received fourteen stab wounds in the chest and stomach, and one in the neck. Her name was Wilma McCann, and she had been murdered a hundred yards from her home. Classed by the police as a 'good-time girl', she was separated from her husband, and a mother of four. Two of the children had been found at dawn by a neighbour, waiting at the bus stop for their mother who had failed to return home that night.

Far from being what is known as a 'fish-and-chips job' — the one-off murder of a prostitute after closing-time — the murder of Wilma McCann turned out to be the first of an appalling series of killings and attacks by a man the media called the Yorkshire Ripper, and who was to become known as one of the most dangerous mass-murderers of our time. Between July 1975 and January 1981, he left thirteen women dead, and seven grievously wounded. The man seemed to strike exclusively in the cities, in the north of England, inside the West-Yorkshire/Lancashire quadrangle. Most of the attacks took place in

Leeds, or Bradford, two in Halifax, two also in Manchester and Huddersfield, one in Keighley and another one, it was thought, in Preston. The killer's methods were remarkably consistent, though he departed from them a few times. He either picked up his victims by car and drove them to a quiet corner, where he would invite them out, or entice them into the back of the car, and hit them as their heads were lowered; or he would lie in wait and creep up from behind. He would then hit them on the back of the head with a hammer, then, as with Wilma McCann, expose part of their bodies, throw away or arrange some of their clothes, and stab them repeatedly with a knife or a screwdriver. As the killings multiplied, the violence of the stabbing increased. Some of the victims were stabbed more than forty times, so forcibly sometimes that their insides came out. The man tried to decapitate one of his victims; he pierced the eye of another. The police would not release details as to the manner of the killings. Horrible as the actual mutilations were, the unsavoury speculations which the police secrecy gave rise to were worse.

The first few recognized victims were prostitutes, or regarded as such by the police. Fear of the ubiquitous killer remained restricted to prostitute areas: there would be a wave of terror, women would be particularly cautious for a while, or disappear from the streets altogether. Then, as memory of the last attack receded, though some precautionary measures would remain (such as one woman taking down the number of a car her friend got into), things went back to normal: there was no public outcry. The murder, however, on 26 June 1977, of a 16-year-old shop-assistant, Jayne MacDonald, as she was walking home on a Saturday night after having been out with her boy-friend, raised widespread indignation. The scale of the police enquiry was much increased. It was to be stepped up again and again, encouragement being given first by Labour Home Secretary Merlyn Rees, then by his Conservative successor, William Whitelaw, as 'respectable' women increasingly became the targets: a bank clerk, a secretary, an office assistant and students from Leeds and Bradford Universities. Towards 1979-1980, panic spread throughout the north of England. All women in the area came to feel they were potential victims. They became frightened to go out at night. Female students were advised by University authorities not to do so. Everywhere men saw their women home.

The police had a number of clues right from the start: the blood group, from traces of semen left on the back of one of the victims, together with boot and tyre prints. Some of the survivors gave descriptions of their assailant: one or two of the photokits turned out to be remarkably accurate. In fact the police came very close to nailing the man, when, in October 1977, a brand-new five-pound note was found in the bag of a Manchester victim, a woman called Jean Jordan. The bag had fallen in some bushes during the struggle she had put up against her assailant. He had returned to the still undiscovered body a week later, looking for the bag, evidently realizing what powerful evidence the new note might be; and he had failed to find it. The Manchester police, part of the Lancashire Constabulary, had the note and were following the trail that would lead them into the Bradford area, West Yorkshire. And after much searching, they had finally narrowed down to 300 the number of possible recipients of the new note. The firms they had concentrated on included W.T.Clark's, an engineering contractors which in fact employed the killer, who was questioned several times, and then let go.

At the time there seemed no way for the police to capture their man unless he struck again, and they could catch him red-handed: prostitutes were used as unwilling live bait in some areas of Leeds and Bradford. A gigantic manhunt, the largest of its kind ever to take place in Great Britain, and the first to make use of computers and advertising on a large scale, was mounted. But the whole enquiry began to go hopelessly astray when the Ripper squad received, and decided to consider as authentic, letters and a cassette tape from a man who called himself 'Jack'. He had a Sunderland accent, which seemed to place him outside the West Yorkshire and Lancashire area where the murders were taking place, and into the Wearside area, near Newcastle, up north. Or so the experts thought. The huge enquiry into Wearside yielded nothing, and none of the survivors had mentioned a Sunderland accent. Yet that clue went on being regarded as vital, and when the real killer, a truck-driver called Peter Sutcliffe, was finally arrested, it turned out he had been questioned by the police several times, not just in relation to the new five-pound note, but to his car being sighted frequently by the TV cameras which had been installed in some red-light districts: and that he had been eliminated on account of his Yorkshire accent.

Sutcliffe was caught only by accident. He had moved outside his usual territory, into Sheffield, South Yorkshire. He was about to kill the prostitute he had picked up, a Jamaican called Ava Reivers, when two young policemen interrupted him on a routine verification. The number plate on the man's Rover was the wrong one, and he was taken to the police station for further questioning and simply charged with theft of a car number plate. It was while he was being questioned that one of the policemen who had arrested him remembered that Sutcliffe had gone to relieve himself behind some bushes. He went back to the spot and found a hammer and a screwdriver. Confronted with the discovery of the tools, and his wife having failed to confirm one of his alibis, Sutcliffe said calmly, 'I think you are leading up to the Yorkshire Ripper. That's me'.

There was considerable surprise at who the now self-confessed killer turned out to be. He had been imagined as an unmarried social outcast, a monster. He was a family man, happily married or so it seemed, with a good job, a mortgage on a nice house in a nice area of Bradford, a courteous manner, a soft voice. The trial took place in May 1981 at the Old Bailey in London, safely away from the area where it had all happened. The defence and the prosecution were agreed upon the plea of manslaughter on the grounds of diminished responsibility, the man suffering from schizophrenic paranoia according to the unanimous diagnosis of the psychiatrists who had seen him in jail. The judge instructing the case, Judge Boreham, however, refused that plea of not guilty to murder, and insisted on an open trial by jury. Sutcliffe was found guilty of multiple murder and sentenced to life, to serve a minimum of thirty years. He was placed in a maximum security prison on the Isle of Wight. While he was there, he was attacked and badly slashed in the face by a co-detainee, at whose trial he appeared as prosecution witness, wearing a cross round his neck, and voicing manifestly genuine outrage at the unprovoked attack of which he had been a victim. Since then, he has been transferred to Broadmoor, the psychiatric hospital on the mainland, his behaviour having become so disturbed that he was now a threat to the other inmates.

FOCUS

THE KILLING GROUND

9 May 1976 Marcella Claxton — ATTACKED

14 December 1977 Marilyn Moore — ATTACKED

24 September 1980 Upadhya Bandara — ATTACKED

31 January - 3 February 1978 Helen Rytka — MURDERED

5 November 1980 Theresa Sykes — ATTACKED

1 October 1977 Jean Jordan — MURDERED

17 May 1978 Vera Millward — MURDERED

20/22 November 1975 Joan Harrison — MURDERED

4/5 April 1979 Josephine Whitaker — MURDERED

15 August 1975 Olive Smelt — ATTACKED

4/5 July 1975 Anna Rogulskyj — ATTACKED

29 January 1976 Emily Jackson — MURDERED

26 June 1977 Jayne MacDonald — MURDERED

30 October 1975 Wilma McCann — MURDERED

17 November 1980 Jacqueline Hill — MURDERED

5/6 February 1977 Irene Richardson — MURDERED

20/21 August 1980 Marguerite Walls — MURDERED

2/3 September 1979 Barbara Leach — MURDERED

10 July 1977 Maureen Long — ATTACKED

21 January - 26 March 1978 Vartan Pearson — MURDERED

23 April 1977 Patricia Atkinson — MURDERED

THE MISSING LINK?

LEEDS

BRADFORD

MANCHESTER

PRESTON

PENNINES

HALIFAX

HUDDERSFIELD

KEIGHLEY

Bingley

CHAPELTOWN RED-LIGHT AREA

CITY CENTRE

ROUNDHAY PARK

RED-LIGHT AREA

CITY CENTRE

SUTCLIFFE'S HOUSE

HEATON

T & W H CLARK Sutcliffe's employers

N

2½ miles

3 miles

> IN THIS TRUCK IS A MAN
> WHOSE LATENT GENIUS IF
> UNLEASHED WOULD ROCK THE
> NATION, WHOSE DYNAMIC ENERGY
> WOULD OVERPOWER THOSE
> AROUND HIM: BETTER LET
> HIM SLEEP?

Acknowledgments

Photograph of Zapolski's tomb © *Bradford Telegraph* by permission of *Telegraph* and *Argus*

Sunday Times photograph of Zapolski's tomb © David Bailey by permission of *The Sunday Times*

'The Geography of Terror' chart © *The Sunday Times* by permission of *The Sunday Times*

Part One

Voices

One

The Thread and the Web

Like all women living in Yorkshire at the time of the 'Ripper' murders, I was fascinated. When you are fascinated, you just can't help looking at the very thing you want to avoid. It's got under your skin. Even when you close your eyes, won't read the papers, refuse to discuss it, join in the wave of indignation and fear that follows each new murder, it still materializes within you. I remember being haunted by an image, after the body of the second victim was discovered. The papers spoke of a derelict blind alley, where such women go. I 'saw' a woman lying on a mound of dirt, and the mound became a slagheap. Later, when the last few women were killed and panic had really set in, when Yorkshire Universities organized relays of buses and cars to see all female students home at night, and you didn't dare let your daughter go to the fair or even cross the village street in the dark, my particular fear focused on having to get coal from the shed after sundown. I thought that somebody was prowling round there, ready to bash me on the head: as I bent to shovel coke into the scuttle my back and neck bristled. Black on black mound, coal in the dark, the most unseeable thing there is. Taking a torch didn't help: it simply made me more visible.

Three or four times, as chance would have it, professional or administrative duties took me to Bradford or through

Huddersfield and Manchester straight after a murder. It was as if my own life insisted on mixing me up with it. It altered my way of looking at all that urban waste, the signs of the recession everywhere. You couldn't help wondering what connections there were between the socio-economic dereliction which much of the geography expressed, and the type of violence which was at work in the nooks and crannies of those landscapes. I felt personally affronted. I, a French woman, had settled in Yorkshire, because myths like the Brontës, spaces like the moors, had appealed to me as deeply nurturing, promising freedom and scope. Now, other places and a new myth that were uncomfortably close to those I loved, were threatening murder. The place was spelling death to me as a woman. It was willing you dead.

I had to reclaim those landscapes. I had to understand what was happening. I was obliged to do so: part of me was at stake.

Is this 'Ripper Country'?

> 'On a return journey (from York) to Bradford, Sutcliffe made a detour to Chapeltown, Leeds. Asked why, he remarked, "This is Ripper country" '.[1]

The moors. In the 18th century, people called them 'bleak'. Bleak: stark. That wonderful hard 'k', that has something terminal about it. The surface is bare like high mountain slopes where the tree-line stops. Their colour too makes you think of high mountains. Darker hues though: bog brown, rust brown, purple as well as the whitish shimmer of dry grass. Their appeal perhaps comes from this illusion of sudden, magical heights: you haven't climbed much, you can see the green patchy dales at your feet. And yet you'd think you were on the roof of the world. You feel violence in the wind, cleanliness in the smells: clear springs, the scent of peat, of heather, of moss so spongy, so intricate, it makes you think of deep sea reefs. Rocks, stonewalls. On the moors you can see the bones of the earth.

You are close to what is most real — most essential: the oldest, that which lasts longest.

Their surface is exquisite to the foot: spongy, springy. You can throw yourself into high heather and your fall is like a dream, cushioned as if by heaps of mattresses. You look at the sky: it is vast as silence. A long way ahead, the shrill, pearly cry of a grouse, then the tumult of its flight.

They are the places in the north where I now live which most remind me of the *garrigue* of my provençal childhood. Smoother: the heather does not scratch your legs, the level peat does not twist your ankles. Harder: neither sun nor heady scents, but wind, snow. Entire days are clouded by mists and fogs. On clear days, as far as the eye can see, the heather, reddish-brown in winter, pink or purple in summer. Green or tawny ferns. Red-mottled with brown, purple-spotted with green, endlessly. You think of infinity there; as when you are by the sea.

You think of freedom too. Men from time to time set fire to the heather. They leave after them charcoal patches whose blackened stumps look like a miniature forest ravaged by fire. Later, tender green shoots sprout, grazed by sheep. Free lands, which only fire can till.

When I first came to England, a foreign schoolgirl on an exchange visit, my hosts took me from Halifax to Haworth. Driving over those moorlands, reading Emily Brontë poems, I fell in love with the place. It had a lot to do with my adopting it.

I could not think of Brady and Hindley and their secret moorland cemetery. I felt sullied. What had always meant cleanliness and expanse had been violated. Then time and the wind and the heather won. The silence washed over the sickness.

With Sutcliffe it was a close shave. His first recorded attack was in Keighley, a few miles down the road from Haworth — on the edge of the moors. Always, he struck in the thick of cities, but also he always lived, and killed, along the Aire valley. The valley along which, as some commentators have noted, Mrs Gaskell travelled when she came to see The Reverend Brontë after Charlotte's death. Who knows but that Heathcliff also followed it, walking towards the thickening cities, when he disappeared from *Wuthering Heights* — vanished from the text — to go and seek his fortunes?

Sutcliffe steered clear of the moors. Just.

Sheffield 1979. Travelling down the M1. As we were nearing the city, and all the time of our by-passing it, the sun was hidden by the mist. The wind must have been blowing against us. Columns of steam or smoke, all bent northwards at a sharp angle, joined chimneys and cooling towers to the ceiling of mist. None of it seemed to be moving. It was as if a pall had been hanging over the city, and all the city could do was join in with it. On many factories, red on white, 'For Sale' signs. Who could want them?

Oct. 1979. Bradford. A month ago, Barbara Leach was murdered here, I thought, as I was walking out of the station. I lost myself, wandered into a huge bus depot. Rows and rows of buses, tall, still, empty. I fancied I heard steps. Got desperate; sweated; started running. Everything in the town centre seems oversize: splendid squares overlooking the valley, and hardly anyone about. Spaghetti junctions that force you to use underground pedestrian crossings, often deserted. Many men alone. I must have been a bit unhinged, I thought they all looked odd. Unemployed men, probably, killing time wandering about. Idle mill chimneys everywhere on the horizon. Woollens, textiles, carpets, they've all been hit. Do all the women who live here keep wondering, 'is that *him*?' every time a stranger comes near?

Beautiful, dark stone 18th century houses round the University buildings. Some of them derelict. Many students live there. Grass grows between the cobblestones. Barbara Leach was found in a leafy alley between such houses. The elders must have been covered in berries, the wild poppies still in bloom. Some rubbish-dumps in those alleys too, and much interesting-looking junk. Or so I thought till I remembered that she'd been found near a dustbin, hidden under a carpet.

June 1980. Travelled by train from Leeds to Liverpool. Had forgotten how the area is built up practically all the way through. A sprawling, barely-interrupted city from West Yorkshire to the Irish sea, where immigrants used to sail for America, and where Mr. Earnshaw discovers Heathcliff the gipsy. Even the valleys, those with wool mills at the bottom near the river, have tiers of terraced houses up the hill. You can see the moors through the archways between some of those houses. What a contrast to the modern blocks of flats, dirty red — or dirty white painted brick, windows uniform, paintwork monotonous, in their patches of concrete. You're all alone, and you've got no privacy.

Sharp-edged gravel on the rail-tracks, stained rusty rails. Purple and red rose-bay willow-herb grows on the embankments, straggly and luscious. It's made me think of Helen Rytka, how her body was found in a wooded patch close to a rail-track. How you could scream, and the noise of a passing train drown your voice.

Ugly high-rise. Ugly council houses. The beautiful architecture is that of the Victorian temples to industry, the town halls and factories and warehouses, crenellated tops, gothic arches, gloomy grandeur. Most of them empty: at least those you see from a train window. The paint on the windows, those incredible English colours, turquoise, ox-blood, indigo, has flaked off; the metal turned rusty. Rust has dripped in uneven streaks down the façades. The windows are dirt-blind, or broken. Zig-zagging gutters: rusty labyrinths. The wind trusses the leaves of the trees, elders, acacias, sycamores; they shine a greyish white.

Unbelievable that there could be so many warehouses, empty, blackened, as you emerge from tunnel after tunnel into a new valley. So much ugly or dilapidated housing. Car tips. Heaps of broken rails. Pieces of waste ground. You're in the kingdom of rust and soot. The only dynamism is that of wild vegetation, grass growing along the gravel on the rail tracks, thistles crowning the lone wall of what must have been a level-crossing station, its triangular top still mourning its roof. The occasional gold of a field. Dandelions, buttercups. The mauve shimmer of tall grass. A huge slagheap has been reclaimed by greenness. Elders, everywhere.

The only real moment of life, a passing sea-breeze, is Manchester Victoria station. Factory chimneys, church steeples, parallel to each other, thrusting into the sky. Forests of signs. The platform is edged with a wrought-iron banister, painted apricot and plum. You'd think you were at the opera. Beer temples, breweries spewing smoke; breweries are among the few thriving industries. But then, as you edge out of Manchester, it all starts again: car tips, several stories high, a block of flats overlooking a cemetery, rows of houses with boarded windows and punctured roofs, a blue tank, three-quarters rusty, scaffoldings, rusty, abandoned road-works with a huge embankment of freshly turned earth, a good place to bury someone.

Immigrants. A Pakistani woman ignores me studiously. Stiff, middle-aged, rather pretty. On the left, a dark young man, curly hair cropped close, is reading an Arabic newspaper. A student. Further along, an African, portly, gentle-looking, a bonnet on her conked hair.

Why do people buy such ugly clothes? It's not the poverty: poorer people, in India, in Africa, dress so much better. It's the ugliness of the ready-made. Dingy parkas and baggy trousers in dull colours, the heavy shoes. Ugliness is an affliction, and only the pieces of waste ground are beautiful. The pieces which the wilderness manages to reclaim, in the crannies of all that urban seediness. And that is where, for the last five years, the Ripper has been killing.

The metal hearts are grinding to a halt. In their place, a man hammers at female flesh.

September 1980. How different it looks from the M62. The thick, aggressive traffic. Three lanes both ways, two of them filled with trucks thundering away. The crossing of the Pennines is breath-taking: dun, curving expanses, then up and down, the lovely wooded valleys crested with houses, steeples and chimneys rising in the blue morning mist — only, you can't admire much of it because the traffic is pelting past you, vicious juggernauts glued to your back bumper looming over you and flashing their lights if you're in the second lane and not moving fast enough. Traffic so dense, pace so fast, the landscape is a dream: dream-like, too, the sudden ease of access to all the towns: Leeds — Bradford — Dewsbury — Halifax — Huddersfield — the Pennines, and then Manchester and its drove of worker towns. Further on it says 'Preston' . . . All these towns: places where murders are taking place. The ease of access from the M62. The dream-like pace of the M62. Does he drive down the M62 when . . .

The one murder-free spot, Dewsbury, the place where he'll be committed for trial.

November 1980. Visits to my friend Polly who's had an eye operation at the General Infirmary, Leeds. Was I upset at seeing Polly with her eye bandaged and her bruised cheek — or was it that her eye made me think of the perforated eye of Jacqueline Hill? Four days ago . . . close to the University, a churchyard, some abandoned chapels, half-derelict churches. Shattered stained glass, jagged edges: a place where the mind is being assaulted by images of tearing and staining and soiling. Looking up at a grimy steeple, at first only the face of the clock, lunar white, seems clean. Till I noticed that the black of the hands and the Roman numbers were the same black as the rest of the church: here time marks itself as dirt.

Predictably I lost my way. Harehills, besieged by demolition sites, caterpillar tractors riding roughshod over bulldozed walls. Bypasses, motorways, are biting into the broken-down tenements, some of them handsome. Attractive terraced houses up the hill, most of them empty, windows boarded up. Leprous corner shops. In one, the collapsing pillars of carpet remnants, limp ruins on an antique site.

Found myself in Chapeltown. Rather beautiful. On a hill. Fine view. Some grand Victorian houses. Smart suburb once, I believe. Friendly petrol station. Three Indians look at me as if I was looking for something. I may be. Broken-down houses now, narrow alleys and deserted passages. Half the population at least must be coloured. One of the best-known red-light districts. One of the districts where . . . Lots of exotic shops. Few thriving: flaky paint, missing letters. One shop quite fascinated me. It had WAR--W STORES written on it. Short for War on Want perhaps? Till it flashed, what a fool I was, must have been WARSAW STORES.

The blind eyes of the missing letters. I thought about Jacqueline Hill again. Thought about her mother. Then stopped myself, because I was literally seeing *red*. Black-red. That's how you become part of a lynch-mob.

But I saw it clearly somehow. Saw it in the missing letters? Saw that there was a will to destroy women. To prevent them from being *seeing* subjects. Talking subjects. And I understood what I was doing, losing myself that way, wandering about, looking for signs that I could interpret. I must have felt that if only I could go through the broken sign, supply the missing letters, as I had done for Warsaw Stores, I must arrive at some answer. I thought about George Eliot's review of *The Grammar of Ornament*, which a student had just shown me. She thinks that the hideousness of the urban environment acts like a disease upon the mind:

> Think of certain hideous manufacturing towns . . . The dingy surface of wall pierced by the ugliest windows, staring shop-fronts, . . . and advertising placards have an effect akin to that of malaria; it is easy to understand that with such surroundings there is more belief in cruelty than in beneficence . . . if an evil state of blood and lymph usually goes along with an evil state of mind, who shall say that the ugliness of our streets . . . have not something to do with those bad tempers that breed false conclusions?[2]

Perhaps when you're surrounded by dereliction you feel like

inflicting it too? At least that way you're an agent, one who controls, enforces, instead of just having to take it.

As I was making my way out of Leeds, I saw, not far from a sign saying 'Harehills', something that summed it all up. An unfinished block of flats, entirely wrapped in huge sheets of polythene. They had been there so long in rain and smog and snow that they were no longer transparent, just grey with grease and dust. They were snapping in the wind, some of them half torn away, others dangling by a corner like creased triangles. They looked like spiders' webs left so long in a cellar that they'd become clammy with dust.

'Yesterday's country', they say in Canada, when a piece of clearing has been abandoned by a discouraged settler.

Yesterday's country. Land of dead expectations.

Looking back at the abyss

What those landscapes spoke of, I had to fight.

One of the worst things about the panic that had set in was that, instead of feeling self-righteous, as you should have done, if the high tone of indignation of the papers was anything to go by, you felt . . . guilty. Apologetic. About going out in the dark. About wearing attractive clothes. Being out in the streets. Almost, about being a woman. Being a woman meant that you were murderable, and it was wrong of you so to be. In order to make up for it, you had to be specially good. Stay indoors. Not wander away from the protective side of a man: your man. For no other was safe and perhaps even he?

A year after Sutcliffe's trial, around Malton where I live, the police mounted a huge manhunt for a man called Barry Prudhom. This man, disappointed in his ambition to become an SAS agent, and in the wake of the Falklands campaign, started shooting policemen. He killed two, wounded one: had also killed a householder later still, a postmaster. His targets were male: figures of authority, order. As the manhunt proceeded, a vigilante spirit overtook the male population of the district. The travelling greengrocer, a sweet old soul, told me he'd get his rifle out and would shoot anyone who came to his door that night. A gentle neighbour who lives on an isolated farm patrolled the grounds with his shotgun, protecting the wife and kids. A courteous solicitor kept his loaded army pistol in the top drawer of his desk. Not to mention the police, complete with helicopters, dogs and experts in survival in the wilderness. They ended up shooting their prey full of holes: Barry Prudhom died of more than twenty bullet wounds. The police were cleared in the enquiry that followed, as would have been any male householder, if he'd shot Prudhom. Every form of support, every sense of legitimacy that society could produce was with them. But the Leeds women who walked with a can of spray paint in their handbags were accused of carrying offensive weapons . . . can you *imagine* a well organized group of prostitutes trapping and shooting the Ripper in self-defence? Can you imagine the kind of support people would give to a vigilante squad of prostitutes? While the Ripper operated, twelve Leeds women were arrested for picketing the entrance to a cinema that was showing *Violation of the Bitch*[3].

Why is it that when men in a position of social or domestic authority became targets, they turned into the righteous defenders of order; when women were targets, they became guilty victims?

When the trial was on, I began to have nightmares.

I dreamt he was dead and buried at the bottom of my garden, in a shed, or one of those outdoors country loos where you sit on a board with a hole in it, and there is a big space between you and the pit. More precisely, he had not been buried, he was in a pit that hadn't been covered up, like Dracula. I was not afraid of his coming back to life, he was dead alright. What horrified me was that he was in *my* garden. Exposed to the air. I had to go and bury him. Perhaps he stank already. The thought of the shovelfuls of earth to lift sickened me: even to touch him through the intermediaries, a shovel, earth, was unbearable. Hence perhaps the pain that writing about him gives me: I'm forcing my *ink* to touch him.

A few nights later I saw him again. He was with a group of people I was quite happily going to join. He could not move, that is, he could not leave them. As soon as I saw he was there I tried to retrace my steps, creep out unnoticed, but before I was far enough, he turned his eyes and looked at me. His glance was terrifyingly blue. I woke up bathed in sweat.

I could not stop him (stop the abyss, as Pat Barker says[4]), from looking at me. So I had better face up to it.

It was dangerous to counterattack. I felt that. For there was protection in anonymity. As long as you were part of the crowd, your chances of being spotted were very small. I knew, because I had experienced the guilt there was in being a woman. Somehow, it seemed the Ripper was on the side of society. What would happen if I put myself forward to be seen, joined the side of prostitution? This was where my foreignness was useful. It would exactly reflect my position: still a foreigner in England, observing landscapes and social phenomena from a de-centered position. I had no 'inside' knowledge of any of it; no English childhood, none of the instincts that act as a form of understanding. I did not belong, either, to the 'classes' from which the Ripper had sprung. I did not even inhabit his landscapes. Lived east of them. My door of death was to the setting sun. West Yorkshire, west of me.

Yet it was also clear that, because I loved those landscapes, because I had 'chosen' to live in Yorkshire, because I had so internalized the case, and because I was a woman, I was also in it, of it. It was in me.

Where I was, then, was where I should be: half in, half out. Half foreign, half English.

It became clear as the trial proceeded, and as I started studying the case, that a major element of Sutcliffe's life had been his peculiar relation to language — his speech difficulties, his misreadings — and to foreignness. He had, after all, married an immigrant. A Polish-Czech.

And that was a place where identification occurred for me. I could recall moments in which my English had broken down — misreadings and mis-hearings of my own, provoked by the clash between my Frenchness and my Englishness, the several insights which are bound up with this dichotomy. They were not unlike Sutcliffe's hallucinations in Bingley cemetery. Coming back from London on the north-bound train after a stay in France and perceiving the talk around me as *French*: I only understood bits. Were I to find this too tiresome — were my resistance to being back in England, hearing English, more acute — wouldn't I start 'interpreting' what I hear *as* French, a French that would make more sense, would be exciting because it was in code (a message?). *Election* is *the* solution for mongrel beings, half-breeds, half-castes, the illegitimate, the sinners who want to be just and cannot stop themselves either from sinning or from wanting to justify themselves. I could understand this. I was once horrified at seeing there was a 'Ripper' recipe in the *Guardian's* Women's Page, until a closer inspection revealed it to be an innocent Kipper *pate* . . .

Indeterminacy, indifferentiation — the mind abhors it. I cope by moving fast from one world to the next, as you move your eyes up and down when you're wearing bi-focal glasses, avoiding the blur and sickness of the in-between line. Unlike those who enjoy translating, I avoid it: a caustic bath of infinite possibilities lies for me between languages. But if you are *doomed* somehow to the state of suspension — what do you do? Draw a phantom line, the line that goes through women? Isn't it either that or producing a complete theology like Freud's President Schreber? Psychosis, or neurosis.

What I could see was that it had to do with intermediary states. It belonged to a no-man's land, like the pieces of waste ground. No one seemed to have seen that. I began to detect a conspiracy that agreed with the murderer that waste ground was the place where dead women's bodies belonged. He had needed to believe that. And had been condoned in that belief.

But I knew something about no-man's land. I knew I was in it, and I wasn't dead. And I was damned if I was going to let myself be killed.

Right, you'll say. You're French, at least partly an alien —

alienated, though of England for more than twenty years. But the case concerns England. This is where it occurred. Not just the killings: *serial* killings, the type that Anglo-Saxon countries seem somehow prone to produce. And a scandalous series of misinterpretations.

A word about method

To write was to free myself from what had been the shared nightmare of women in the north of England. Also, to make sense of it. I believe in the redemptive power of the imagination. Otherwise I would not write. The reality of the material haunted me. I had seen, clearly, the body of each victim, imagined how the man must have struck. But I had also been fighting. I thought I had won. I was wrong. From the moment I started writing the book, I found myself going through the nightmare again, but in a different way.

New material has surfaced since Beattie, Cross and Yallop published their accounts in 1981. Gordon Burn had gathered quite a lot of evidence in his 1984 study of the Sutcliffe family, *Somebody's Husband, Somebody's Son*. There had to be more recognition of the work done by feminists (and others) on the structures I myself wished to put on trial. I also had to take into account the fact that Anglo-Saxon culture responds differently from the French to linguistic or literary speculation. Still, the main reason for writing was to put the 'case' into the context of a valid psychological, literary and linguistic structure.

I was foreign when I wrote in French, a resident tourist. Gulliver in Brobdingnag. I could look at things at one remove, made bold by my alienness, a kind of innocence, the distance which my native language put between me, and it. But in England, I was in it. I was using the language in which it had happened. Instead of looking for a thread to go through the labyrinth, I found I was part of the web I was hoping to disentangle, producing as I went the spidery substance of which tangles are made. I had no choice but to travel over it all.

And so it evolved, not thematically, but as subject, text, context, all part of each other.

I used every device my training placed at my disposal: psychoanalysis, socio-economic discourse, whether Marxist or not, linguistic analysis, myths, diary, fiction . . . with *relevance* as my only rule. If any recognizable method can be said to have applied, I suppose it's Roland Barthes'. Not just because he thought it was fair play to use the findings of any discipline under the sun, but because he had been led to see that the subject must be re-integrated into the discourse. Above all else, I was writing in a *woman*'s voice. Science, criticism (of society, as of literature) have driven a wedge between the object under study, and the subject of the observer. That seemed to be part of the process of *alienation* which the Sutcliffe case typified. The man was possessed by an *alien* voice. He had denied women a voice, and he had been denied his own voice at the trial. I was trying to retrieve that voice, to step out from under the shadow of possession: the blight of crows upon Van Gogh's field. The French Surrealist poet Artaud alleged that Society had made Van Gogh conspire in his own death. Perhaps Society had also conspired in the murder of women, the murder of the subject. As I retrieved my woman's voice I hoped to create the space in which the murdered protagonists would and could speak for themselves.

Two

Ripper: 13; Women: 0

God the football champ

He was called Peter William Sutcliffe. A nice Yorkshire name. It even figures in the house of the Brontës, the name of a place, engraved in stone above a doorway.

He became known as the Yorkshire Ripper.

Between July 1975 and January 1981, he killed thirteen, and maimed seven others: was arrested when about to do his twenty-first 'job'.

A hoaxer who called himself 'Jack' sent a tape to the police. The police had it played on the loudspeakers of Leeds football stadium, hoping it would jolt somebody's memory, but the Leeds fans drowned out the voice with chants of 'Eleven-Nil'. Eleven was the number of the known victims. Nil was the police score.

At his trial, Sutcliffe claimed he had heard the 'voice of God' speak to him from a grave in Bingley cemetery. Later, again and again, the voice had bid him kill. God had also sheltered him from detection, so that he could go on with his mission. God, obviously, was a high scorer.

The trouble is that Sutcliffe's 'mad' logic is supported by events. If it was God who made the fans identify themselves with the supposed killer, drown out his voice in their chants, then it was also God who prevented the police from finding the actual killer, even when they were holding him: nine times they questioned Sutcliffe, nine times they let him go. 9–0.

The police, when they realized that they'd finally got the right man, in January 1981, turned the scene into 'the victor's dressing-room in the minutes following the FA Cup Final at Wembley'[1]. The police had scored one hit only, but the winning one, despite the losing score of the previous years. God had changed team. As Sutcliffe saw it, He didn't want the mission to continue.

What does this make of women? Balls, in a game played by men. Targets. Numbers. A proof to be administered. A file of identity photographs, faces sad or smiling, made anonymous, virtually indistinguisable, items in a catalogue; Don Juan's list.

Women=Nil. 'We're not interested in you', the policeman told Ava Reivers who'd been arrested with Sutcliffe in Sheffield as he was about to murder her. 'We're interested in *him*'. Nowhere in the whole Ripper case do women figure as people. They figure as bodies, on which violence has left an 'obscene' inscription, which is in turn deciphered by the police and the media. They figure as evidence made to speak, like a ventriloquist's dummy, by the Attorney General. Repulsive *objects*, which the mind cannot deal with, shrinks from, as if they were inhuman. Discreditable or dispensible witnesses: the survivors' accurate description of their murderer was disbelieved; they were never called upon to testify. The female relations of the murderer were implicitly accused of being the real perpetrators of the deeds: Sonia, the wife, the butt of surreptitious or overt accusations. One of the sisters was persuaded to pose for one of the tabloids, and was made to look like Myra Hindley, the Moors Murderess of twenty years ago.

And God?

A will to *kill* women? When the fans identify with the hoaxer, do they mean to boast of his exploits, to vent their own hatred of women — or are they simply challenging the police, the fatherly authorities who've got them ringed in the stadium and want the public to gang up as one against the criminal? The question matters, it matters very much. But either answer leaves women in a similar position: as the non-human which has to be destroyed or denied. Pawns, broken pots, in a confrontation between Fathers and Sons, in which, instead of levelling blows at each other, the two parties strike *through* women. Laius and Oedipus go on endlessly meeting at the crossroads. But they kill women instead of each other.

Bad or mad?

You are incredibly biased, people will say. England — Yorkshire — is full of happy, well-adjusted couples. Society has evolved, equal rights for women have been recognized in all sorts of laws. Women's status has radically improved. They have access to power, to full citizenship, to all ways of making money. Look at our Prime Minister! You're taking an extreme case and twisting it out of all proportion.

Maybe. Of course, it isn't the whole story.

But tell me. Why was it that Sutcliffe could believe that God was ordering him to *clean* the streets by *killing* women? It's no good saying 'he was mad.' That explains nothing. He could have been mad and compulsively collecting butterflies, or had celestial visions, or believed he was Puss-in-Boots: his wife did, after all, believe at one point that she was Cinderella. You have to understand the specific form madness takes, before the word 'mad' means anything.

How is it that so many men, not just the fans, but the thousands of hoaxers who phoned the West Yorkshire police hotline to play practical jokes, those who wrote to the papers pleading, 'leave the Ripper alone, he's doing a good job' — could believe that killing was a job — or a joke? If the Yorkshire Ripper case is just a freak occurrence, how is it that any provincial city paper (*The Yorkshire Post*, for instance) records every week the killing or maiming, rape or battering of a woman? The incident generally does not make it to the front page, let alone become national news. It's not sensational enough, repeated often enough: no collective panic has set in. But the regularity of such incidents is chillingly telling. Did Sutcliffe's murders alter the crime statistics much for the region? Given the mistaken leads described by Cross[2] or Yallop's list of unsolved murders which could have been attributed to Sutcliffe in the period, not all that much.

And how come the reverse is not true? Why is it that no women go about murdering 'punters', convinced they're on a God-given mission to rid the city of its litter? It's not just that the case is never reversed: we can't even imagine it being reversed.

The Yorkshire Ripper: an extreme case, yes. But a disturbingly significant one, not least on account of the lies and silences which have been established around it.

Could you say, then, that Sutcliffe was evil? A 'man possessed' (by the devil) as Piers Paul Read called him in one of his *Observer* articles. A 'personification of Evil' from whom we must pray to be delivered?[3]

Evil, when he thought he was good?

Ah, but maybe he *pretended* to think he was good. That was part of his evil. Indeed, that is precisely what the trial established, when the jury at the Old Bailey found Sutcliffe guilty of murder. His case rested upon the Bingley cemetery episode, his having heard the voice of God which later had sent him on his mission. The medical belief that the defendant suffered from paranoid schizophrenia had been so unanimous that the Attorney General was prepared to accept the plea of manslaughter on the grounds of diminished responsibility. The judge's refusal to entertain this forced him to turn coat. He cleverly went on to expose Sutcliffe as a liar who was hoping to get 10 years in the loony bin instead of life for murder — in the process, he had to expose the psychiatrists as gullible. And yet, he must have known that in doing so, he was betraying his own conclusions about the case — was bringing about a miscarriage of justice.

What has been written since has, implicity or explicitly, endorsed this verdict of guilty ('bad'). The books that appeared straight after the trial, by Cross, Beattie and Yallop,[4] simply mention and proceed to ignore or express disbelief in Sutcliffe's testimony. Gordon Burn's solidly researched biography,[5] leaves the episode out of the chronological reconstitution of Sutcliffe's life, thus casting doubt on it. Sutcliffe's father and brothers are abundantly quoted, but the man as the subject of his own story is absent. It is odd that a family that produced such a liar should itself be trusted so completely. As for Sonia, the Sutcliffe family say she was always 'twisting'.

And so, the voice of God remains heard by Sutcliffe alone, and the psychiatrists who turned out to be prepared to believe him. Sutcliffe is silenced as a speaking subject; so is the 'subjective' science of psychiatry. Factual evidence is made into the only criterion of truth.[6]

It is as if, hearing the voice of God, Sutcliffe had heard the secret voice of Society: I say 'Society' for want of a better word. For Society supported him: it did not stop him. Perhaps it could not? Barry Prudhom, a killer of policemen, was caught by the police in seventeen days; he was a clever man, an expert in survival. Would it have taken five and a half years if he had been a killer of prostitutes? I do not doubt the good will of the police in the Sutcliffe case: I simply ask what the fact of his non-arrest means. He saw the failure to arrest him as the sign that God wanted him to go on. He saw everything that happened as having happened by design. When he met Yvonne Pearson, the one time he was not seeking a woman to kill, she said something about their encounter being 'fate', and he thought it was his 'signal'. It was meant to be. Yes, that was the madness; construing 'could not' into 'would not'. But why then did the media draw such profits from the case? Why was so much money flying about, all the cheque-book journalism, at the time of the arrest and trial? Why did the extraordinary inefficiency of the police, the reactions of much of the public, give him such support? Was it Society that was mad? Is it still mad, since it won't look at such questions?

It is as if Society in all its Might and Authority could not (would not?) during the trial, acknowledge the existence of the voice of God. It had to establish that Sutcliffe was a liar, and that the psychiatrists were fools.

I believe that this refusal, this inability, is as significant as Sutcliffe's actions.

It was pretty obvious even at the time of the trial that Sutcliffe was exactly what the psychiatrists said; their unanimity gives weight to the diagnosis. They had examined Sutcliffe separately. Some had been called by the Crown, others by the defence. It was also obvious that Sutcliffe was speaking what truth he could. And that the sentence was wrong. This has become absolutely clear now that he has been transferred from his maximum security prison on the Isle of Wight to a mainland psychiatric hospital. His condition had deteriorated so much that he had become a danger to the other inmates.

The trial attempted to make good come out of evil: to arrive at a wrongful verdict, denying diminished responsibility, for virtuous reasons. An editorial in *The Times* argued that public wrath was such that only a guilty verdict, and a life sentence, would appease it. So, that elusive entity, the public, was made to demand an eye for an eye. Judge Boreham, in demanding a trial by jury, achieved one positive thing: everything otherwise (including the failings of the West Yorkshire police) would have been swept under the carpet. The trial brought a great deal into the daylight, and for this we must congratulate the judge. It remains true, nonetheless, that the result of the trial was to bring about a *miscarriage* of justice — as the police had miscarried in their enquiry. If we add to this the hoaxer's tape, the fake telephone calls, etc, it looks as if all along Society had *chosen* to see the wrong thing, or managed not to see the right one. Misinterpretation ran like a black warp through the entire case. What was it they so wanted to avoid seeing? Their own complicity? Something that could not be seen? The stare of the Medusa?

What is certain is that, from Sutcliffe's own misreading of the words on the tomb in Bingley cemetery, right to the

Attorney General's wrongful indictment of psychiatry, the whole case poses the question of falsehood. Truth, throughout, had scored nil.

I want to claim women's right to citizenship in terms of a law better and higher than the law of taboos and violence that rules the city. I want to assert that there have been no women in this case. The case concerns men, consciously or unconsciously trying to establish, not just that women have no right to freely walk the streets, but that they should be denied as feeling and speaking subjects.

I am neither being flippant nor insensitive when I say that there have been no women in this case. Women who loved, were loved, have been murdered or maimed for life. The families, the friends, the survivors, have to go on living with all that irreparable damage: children have been orphaned in the most appalling, the most scarring, circumstances. One little boy lost the power of speech after the death of his mother. Only time perhaps, and faith, and love, and courage, will help now. But it seems to me that there should be a little comfort in the thought that these women died, not because of what they were, but because accident (and here I mean just *accident*) put them in Sutcliffe's way. They have died very much as if a lorry had run them over. Or if a bomb exploded as they were passing by. They were casualties, the victims of terrorism.

I am not going to disturb them yet again by recounting their deaths. This book seeks to understand what Sutcliffe did, and how Society was implicated in what he did; I do not want to dredge up the muck. I will name names for precise reference only. I offer neither thrills, nor lists.

I want to remove obscenity from the bodies of the victims and place it back where it belongs, in the acts of the murderer. I want to cleanse the bodies and demystify the construct of murder to show that the ghostliness is in the psycho-sexual, the social structures, the hovering myths, that possessed the killer.

Faced with a web of misinterpretations and untruths, I choose to start from what has been denied.

A murderous notion of 'objectivity' has ruled. All the social forces which have been involved so far as agents of order or meaning have failed to know what they are doing. I shall listen to the testimony of the subjective. As a woman, I want to speak as a subject: I shall let Sutcliffe speak as a subject.

Part Two

He Was The Bitch

'When we have reached the (female) wish for a penis, and the masculine protest (the male fear of passivity) we have . . . reached 'bedrock' . . . The repudiation of femininity must surely be a biological fact, part of the great riddle of sex.'

Freud, *Collected Papers*, Vol V, the Hogarth Press, 'Analysis Terminable and Interminable', 1937.

'Activity/Passivity . . .

Man
_____
Woman

'Always the same metaphor: we follow it, it transports us, in all of its forms, wherever a discourse is organized . . . Theory of culture, theory of society, the ensemble of symbolic systems . . . everything elaborates the same systems. And the movement by which each opposition is set up to produce meaning is the movement by which the couple is destroyed. A universal battlefield. Each time a war breaks out. Death is always at work . . .
. . . And we perceive that the 'victory' always amounts to the same thing: it is hierarchized. The hierarchization subjects the entire conceptual organization to man. A male privilege, which can be seen in the opposition by which it sustains itself, between *activity* and *passivity*.'

Hélène Cixous, 'Sorties', transl: in Marks and de Courtivron, *New French Feminisms*, Harvester Press, 1981, pp. 90–91.

' "Did you say *pig* or *fig*?" said the Cat. "I said *pig*", replied Alice".'

Quoted in R. Jakobson, in *Fundamentals of Language*, Mouton & Co., 1956, p. 72.

Three

The Shadow of Oedipus

I'll start with a story. A well-known story.

Chapter one. A man is travelling on a road. He's in a bad temper. He's just left his father and mother. He's worried about them, and about himself. An oracle (preposterous bitch) has just told him that he would kill his father and marry his mother. This of course is unthinkable, but he's been so upset he's decided to leave his beloved homeland, Corinth, and his beloved parents. He's seething with anger: anger at what's been suggested about himself, anger at having been forced to leave home. He reaches the crossroads.

An arrogant traveller, in a chariot, attended by three men, wants to push him out of the road as he drives past. Our man won't move. He's already conceded so much ground, he'd be damned if he's going to let a perfect stranger, another pushy, interfering fool, muscle him out of the way. The servants are insolent. Who do they think they're dealing with? Don't they know he's Oedipus, the son of the King of Corinth? They may not know, but he's going to show them. A brawl ensues. The exasperated traveller hits him with his whip. Blinded with rage, Oedipus kills him, and his servants too. Apart from one poor fellow, whom he allows to escape. When he's calmed down he feels sorry for what he's done. He feels the better for it too.

His rage is gone. Then as time passes he forgets all about it.

Chapter two. Same man. He's become a wanderer, he rather likes it. Would like to settle down too. He has discovered — the scene at the crossroads helped, though he never thinks about it now — how strong he is. How clever. But still, he is a wanderer. He needs confirmation of his status. He's burning to prove himself. He's decided to accomplish a feat. To deliver the city of Thebes from a monster that is plaguing it. A sphinx, they call it. Stands at the crossroads. You can't get into the city without walking past it. The cunning bitch, you think you've just escaped her, but however silently or fast you approach, there she is, barring your way, yapping her horrible sing-song. You have to listen. 'Solve my riddle', she barks at you, 'and you rid the city of me. Fail to solve it, and I'll devour you.'

The crossroads. The man does not try to escape. He listens for the song of the bitch. There she is. She's stopped, she's strangely quiet, almost hieratic. The man listens to her riddle. The man makes sense of her riddle. He gives her the answer. The answer is 'Man.'

Exit the sphinx. Does she die? Is it known what happens to her? And so Oedipus rids the city of its plague. The city gives him its queen to marry, as a reward. He becomes King of Thebes. Till another plague, and another riddle, and a third chapter. And Oedipus, the man, says, 'I'll destroy the man whom the riddle means.' And the riddle means himself. And his wife kills herself, and he blinds himself and goes into exile. He again rids the city of its plague: himself.

Freud made this story the archetypal story, the one at the root of the development of all human beings, and men most graphically. Each little boy desires to take his father's place, kill his father and marry his mother. But thereupon, in normal circumstances, the 'castration complex' intervenes. Like Chronos, the Old Titan, the Devouring Father, the real father threatens to 'eat' his child, to 'cut it off' unless the child renounces his desire for his mother. Caught between the fear of losing 'it' and renunciation of the object of his desire, the child generally chooses renunciation. I say, 'generally', because he can find a lot of other ways round, and they are often the ways of neuroses.

Even such a bare outline shows that, however complex Freud's formulations and uses of the Oedipus story are, they make it stop somehow at the first crossroads: as if Oedipus knew what he was on about, and Laius somehow too, and as if Laius' raised whip had been enough to stop his son on his way to Thebes. Thus major dimensions of the myth are missing.[1]

And what would have happened if Oedipus had been a girl?[2]

The question would get its most provocative answer if one thought of Cathy's fate in *Wuthering Heights* in terms of the Oedipus story — especially if Heathcliff is seen as Cathy's half, her 'whip' — and his vengeance as a 'return of the repressed': the unleashing of a plague (the sphinx's plague?) upon the two halves of the city in the form of the Heights and the Grange. Cathy after all, when bitten by the dogs at the Grange, briefly gets a swollen foot — which is of course what Oedipus's name means, his ankles having been damaged by the thongs which bound him to the mountain when his parents tried to have him destroyed as a baby. But that is another story . . . Or is it?

But to return.

Hélène Cixous has brilliantly underlined some elements of the Oedipus story which neither Freud nor classical interpretation take into account.[3] She stresses that the sphinx is *female*, and that she is represented as *monstrous*, half-woman, half-*beast* (a bitch with woman's breasts). She does not speak, she *sings*: her language is primeval, half-inchoate, not speech. She is *before* the city, she bars the road to the city, its male order, its laws. And, ironically, the answer to her riddle is, the man . . . 'Man'. Oedipus answers her riddle to gain access to the city of Men and deliver the city from this plague — and the answer to the riddle is pure tautology. The answer is, himself. Yet, saying 'Man', Oedipus does not know that he is talking about himself.

He does not know that the answer concerns him personally. The three ways of walking employed by the animal whose identity has to be guessed, who goes on four legs in the morning, two at noon and three in the evening correspond to the three crucial stages of his own life: as a baby exposed on a mountain, as a grown man who becomes King of Thebes, and as the blind old sage at Colonus leaning on his stick.

Cixous' point is two-fold: that this interpretation of the myth asserts that only 'Man' is ever going to be allowed to exist, to have full cultural and human stature — and also, ironically, how dangerous that is; not just tautological but ultimately self-destructive. Interpretations of the story similarly fail to see that manhood, the order of the city, has to be erected on the ruins of a dangerous, primordial femininity. The 'beast-woman' has to be eliminated before Oedipus can become King. The irony is that what he thinks he's got rid of makes a complete comeback: the death of the sphinx leaves the road to incest open to Oedipus, open to monstrosity according to city laws. He's about to become his mother's husband and to father his own brothers and sisters. He's about to become the sphinx — the plague, not at the gates of the city, but *inside* the city.

Meanwhile, you could add, femininity is only allowed to exist as a fatefully split entity: as a singing bitch, predatory, outside the walls; as a loving Queen, Jocasta, obedient to city laws, ready to be wed to whatever stranger the city sages see fit to reward with her: inside, a docile gift, clay in the hands of modelling Fate. Harlot or bride, and on both counts, monstrous.

Perhaps, indeed, tragedy exists so that people can be spared the devastating cost of the road to self-knowledge. 'Representation' gives them access to it without their having to be broken by it.

Likewise, we may have to watch the scenario of Sutcliffe's own encounters with plagues and sphinxes, his own murderously mistaken deciphering of riddles on his way to manhood, to be spared the inevitability of what they entail: fear and hatred of femininity.

Four

The Riddle On the Grave

'Initially and medially Z occurs largely in words of Greek or Oriental origin . . . in other classes of words . . . the difficulty of writing the character rapidly and intelligibly has told against an extensive use of it instead of (s) to represent the sound (z). Z is normally employed to denote (z), the blade 'open' voice consonant, the voiced analogue of (s).'

The Letter Z, *Concise Oxford Dictionary*

'When and under what conditions does an idea become so powerful that it is able to behave like a suggestion and turn into a reality without more ado?'

Freud, 'The Psychoanalytic View of Psychogenic Disturbance of Vision'

On 11 May 1981, Sutcliffe was called upon by his counsel, Mr. James Chadwin, to take the stand in his own defence.

It seemed far and away the most dramatic thing that had occurred . . . His voice, as he took the oath, came out as a piping treble . . . And his face, even when discussing the most sordid aspects of his crimes, seemed constantly to flirt with the idea of a smile.

In profile, he had looked stooped and stale and bovine. Now, head-on and liberated from the dock, he could have been merely a relation of that other self. His eyes . . . flashed inquisitively about the room . . . face transformed by its own liveliness into something pleasant, unalarming, almost personable.[1]

Read: the man's got a split personality. We're listening to a schizophrenic.

At this point Sutcliffe's face had about it an almost evangelical expression . . . And this is the man whom, not once in five and a half years, the police would publicly acknowledge as clever. His voice, that oddly high pitched voice had virtually throughout his counsel's questions a pathetic quality.[2]

Read: here is a clever liar.

Twenty strides and the lean, bearded figure, with his sallow complexion and alert eyes, was in the witness box . . . cool and articulate . . . the care he took in his choice of words was quite immaculate . . . Occasionally his eyes, unafraid and clear, raked the court, almost challengingly, a glimpse perhaps of the demons that lay beneath the unruffled exterior.[3]

For that read: a cool, calculating devil.

In a way Sonia was in the dock, too. For soon her enigmatic facade had been stripped away, revealing her as a domineering woman who henpecked her husband.

She, too, heard voices. She, too, was schizophrenic.
. . . Dr Milne told the court that Sutcliffe's version of his wife's behaviour 'accounts for his aggressive behaviour towards many women.'[4]

Here read what Beattie himself writes: 'So suddenly Sonia, not God, was to blame'. Spell it out: Sonia, not Sutcliffe, was to blame.

John Sutcliffe, the father, articulated: 'She controlled him. Controlled his mind. She'd twisted him.'[5]

Can we stop our ears as we step through this echo-chamber of interpreting voices, and listen to what the man said? I'll follow the *verbatim* report in *The Times*, May 12, 1981, alternately quoting and narrating in the third person.

It was while he was working at Bingley cemetery that Sutcliffe heard what he believed to have been God's voice. The date was 1967. He had already met Sonia.

He was digging a grave 'in the Catholic section at the top of the cemetery'.

> 'I was digging and I just paused for a minute. It was very hard ground. I just heard something — it sounded like a voice similar to a human voice — like an echo. I looked round to see if there was anyone there, but there was no one in sight. I was in the grave with my feet about five feet below the surface.'
>
> Swallowing repeatedly and licking his lips occasionally, Sutcliffe went on: 'There was no one in sight when I looked round from where I was. Then I got out of the grave. The voice was not very clear. I got out and walked — the ground rose up. It was quite a steep slope. I walked to the top, but there was no one there at all.
>
> 'I heard again the same sound. It was like a voice saying something, but the words were all imposed on top of each other. I could not make them out, it was like echoes.' Mr Sutcliffe did not face the judge as he gave his evidence, but spoke directly at his counsel, Mr Chadwin, swivelling occasionally and staring at the packed court. He said the voices 'were coming directly in front of me from the top of the gravestone, which was Polish. I remember the name on the grave to this day. It was a man called Zipolski.'

Mr Sutcliffe was shown a photograph and pointed out the grave of a man called Stanislaw Zipolski from which he said the 'voice' was coming. 'It is the one with the statue of Christ on the top.'

It was the first time he had heard the voice. He had looked at Zapolski's grave,

'because that is where the sound was coming from. That is what made me walk closer to it'.

Mr Chadwin asked: 'What did you see on that grave when you looked at it?' Mr Sutcliffe replied: 'I remember getting a message from the grave. I looked at several graves. I was looking around to determine where the sound came from. After looking at the grave, I walked back. I was kind of transfixed because of the voice. I just stepped back and I didn't know what to think at first.'

Having read the word 'jejo' in Polish on the grave and taken it to mean Jesus, a sense of meaning came, and Sutcliffe stepped back to the path immediately in front of the grave:

'I saw what I took to be a definite message about the echoing voice. I always thought it was on the same grave . . . I recall as Jesus was speaking to me'.

Mr Sutcliffe said he remembered the phrase: 'We be the echo'. Mr Chadwin asked: 'What is your recollection, not of what you heard, but of what you saw, that conveyed a message to you?' Mr Sutcliffe said he had read the words 'Wehvy' and 'Echo' in Polish. 'Echo' was spelt 'Ecko'.

He had taken this to be a direct message, telling him it was Jesus' voice that was speaking to him. Being shown a photograph of the gravestone, however, he agreed that the words which he described did not appear. Yet he remembered seeing them. That had not been the only grave he had seen. He had looked at several other graves in the vicinity of that one. He went on:

'It had a terrific impact on me. It was starting to rain. I remember going to the top of a slope overlooking the valley and I felt as though I had just experienced something fantastic. I looked across the valley and all around and thought of heaven and earth and how insignificant we all were. But I felt so important at that moment . . . I told no one because I thought that if it was meant for everyone to hear they would hear. I felt I had been selected.'

He did not know why he had been selected, particularly in view of the fact that he had ceased to be a practising Catholic and to be interested in religion over two years previously.

Climbing to the top?

There is no denying that Sutcliffe's prose is superior to that of the various accounts of him quoted above. It is simpler, has more care for accuracy. Reading it, it is as though we were being restored to something nobler, more human. And then, the recoil — as we remember what this was the beginning of . . .

One of *The Times'* subtitles to the report, a quotation from Sutcliffe, turns out to be pretty ironic. It is, 'God didn't make mistakes: the papers did'. One can picture the righteous glee of the editor choosing to give prominence to this particular piece of madness. But it turns against itself, because in this report, under our very nose, not just the paper, but the Court, are making mistakes. It's not just that the name on the grave is Zapolski, not Zipolski, and Bronislaw, not Stanislaw, as can be seen from the photograph of that grave pasted in the middle of that bit of testimony. It is also that the photograph is incomplete — truncated. No words in Polish figure on it. Which all goes to show, doesn't it, that Sutcliffe must have hallucinated the Polish words he saw — or, as he explains, when pressed on the topic, plucked them from gravestones in the vicinity and imagined that they figured on that particular tomb — he was suffering from a delusion, wasn't he? Give or take a little . . . Only, if you produce a complete photograph, taken at the right angle, as *The Sunday Times* did to illustrate extracts of Burn's biography in its Colour Supplement, then it is quite clear that the words Sutcliffe read are there indeed. They're hard to decipher now, being covered in green mould. But then, in 1967, only 1½ years old, they must have been perfectly clear. There is 'jego' or 'jejo'; there is 'ouczy' or 'ouszy' (wevvy).

The *Times* photograph was procured through the *Bradford Telegraph*. Convenient. Understandable. You can't check in a hurry. You ought to be able to trust the guys, it's their territory for Christ's sake, a few miles up the road. But what about the Court? We must assume, failing other evidence, that either they had the same photograph at their disposal as *The Times*, or they had a similarly truncated photograph. The significant thing is that no one bothered to check, because everyone must have been so persuaded it was either a fabricated or an insignificant story, it didn't make any difference either way. The offshoot of this is, that in its one intervention to substantiate the veracity of the witness, the Court presented him with falsified evidence, and made him agree to an untruth. Conversely, you could argue that if Sutcliffe had forged his story rather than remembered the composite elements of an experience, then he would have looked at the grave recently; would have known the Polish words were on it; would have quoted them right; and when doubted, would have insisted that they did indeed figure on it.

I shall assume he was speaking the truth, the truth of genuine delusion.

That is frightening: the experience is so easy to identify with, yet think of its consequences.

You've been digging for some time. You're in a sweat, out of breath. Annoyed, too, because the ground is so hard. Must have been freezing last night, or else you've hit stone. Your spade rings as it strikes the earth. You've got that ringing in your ears, and so, when you stop for a breather, you're a bit stunned, head in a whirl, you see black wires dancing. Your ears are buzzing. In my garden, when I've stopped digging, sometimes I've had the impression somebody was calling my name. I turned around: no one. Perhaps it was the telephone inside the house, muffled by the walls. No. As you've stopped, listened, suddenly you can hear the silence. You're aware of space, of the sounds in the garden, the things around you. You feel happy. Oh yes, it is easy to identify with the onset of Sutcliffe's hallucination. How could such a sweet thread weave such a deadly web?

Where was he for a start? In a graveyard. Digging a grave. Knowing what it was for, in a daily relation to corpses. Building for the dead. Those to be laid low.

He was *inside* a grave. In the grave. Laid low himself, as it were. Non-existent in the world of men. 'With my feet about five feet *below* the surface.' He could have said, 'my head at ground level', but no, he chooses a phrase that stresses 'below'. In the earth, where corpses are put. Like women are supposed to be. Lying down. Sleeping Beauty.[6]

And Prince Charming calls. Christ calls. 'Lazarus, rise!', and the dead man arose from the grave. Rather, the voice that calls is like an echo. The ringing of the spade on the hard earth, echoed by the narrow walls of the hole the man is digging? An echo-chamber. But the voice is not there. You have to climb out of the grave to find it. To hear it again. Climb to the top of the hill.

You raise your head. You get out. You stand erect. Climb up a steep slope. The word 'top' echoes again and again throughout Sutcliffe's testimony, the voice of his desire. He was in the Catholic part of the cemetery, which is at the top. He climbs to the top of the hill. The words he hears again cannot be made out, because 'they were all imposed on top of each other'. A visual focus for the voice at last is found. It is coming from a particular grave, 'the one with the statue of Christ on top'.

Later, when the voice has been identified, there is yet a further climb 'to the top of the slope overlooking the valley'.

And the rain falls, beneficent, fertile. The top is sheer bliss. You're the master of the world. You've discovered your own importance, you 'look across the valley' and think 'of heaven and earth and how insignificant we all are'.

A less lapsed Catholic might have thought that the moment curiously resembled a certain temptation in the desert, and that the God who required worship in exchange for all the kingdoms of the earth had cloven feet instead. But what is *evident* is the erection-like character of this experience. It is a dream-like analogue of a sexual 'climb' (further and yet further, then the release, the rain, bliss).

One should add, also, a social climb. Let us not forget that Bingley is John Braine's birthplace; that his Jo Lampton, in *Room at the Top*, which overlooks this same Aire Valley, longs for, and reaches, very concrete heights. He seduces the daughter of the wealthy local manufacturer (who could be the owner of the same textile factory where Peter's father works) — and having got her pregnant, marries into affluence.

And let us remember in passing that this social ascent is effected over the bodies of two women: Jo's French mistress, who commits suicide, and his English bride, who is made big with child by a man who does not love her, who uses her as a passport to fortune.

Two of Sutcliffe's Leeds victims were murdered close to a night club called 'Room at the Top'. One had spent the evening there.

Wuthering Heights may be dead, and all the nobility it entailed. Dreams of taking the top by storm stay around. The methods get worse.

Misreadings

That is precisely the point. Sutcliffe here describes himself as *making* it to the top, not by means of a sexual encounter (making love), not through a series of social acts (making his fortune), but by means of a delusion — a mystical experience that rests upon a series of misinterpretations — yet does for him exactly what he wishes. It relieves this much-troubled man who suffers from depressions, works as a grave digger, is the son of a textile worker, lives in an overcrowded council house with his parents and 5 brothers and sisters, has always had trouble adjusting at school and in earlier jobs, and who, shy as he is, has just met his first girl-friend.

Suddenly he stands above it all: 'I felt I had been selected'. He's one of the elect. The mystical experience is a shortcut to success, the solution to all the problems, the fulfilment of all wishes.

Perhaps those wishes are so great and so frustrated in the ordinary course of things that they have become irresistible. At any rate, something makes Sutcliffe construe all the signs he hears and sees at that moment into elements of the desired identification. The echo he's heard he thinks of as a voice, as intention, meant for him. As having a source outside himself. He looks for the concrete location of that voice by *climbing* to the top of the cemetery. And — this is where something really bizarre occurs — he locates it, not in an object that makes a noise (think of the leafy trees from which Joan of Arc's 'voices' come, the wind and the spring in the cave at Lourdes), but in something to which popular wisdom attributes supreme dumbness (silent as the grave) — a gravestone — but which has words written on it. That is, he finds the source of an aural hallucination in something visual, to do with reading.

Perhaps the link is in the topography of the whole episode: the fact that Sutcliffe is undergoing a displaced erection and orgasm. For one thing, he fancies that the grave where he finally locates the voice has 'a statue of Christ on the top'. The white tombstone does not have a statue on top: it is cross-shaped, and has a small black crucifix glued or screwed on it. Black on white: itself rather like a piece of writing. For another he says he can't make out what the voice is saying because 'the words were all imposed on top of each other . . . it was like echoes'. But echoes, if you think about it, have no visual dimension; if they did, that would be horizontal: words booming against walls, against rock-face, receding into the distance. Except in a well, perhaps, down a pot-hole? But they would be echoing downwards. It's quite difficult to imagine mounting vertical echoes, sounds imposed on top of each other: succession as ascent.

Unless . . . you've already somehow *seen* a piece of vertical writing. You don't see vertical writing in books. Or rather, the columns of script in a Western language may be vertical on the page, but you read *downwards*, resting the book on an object laid *low, laid flat*. But there is vertical writing on posters, on signs, in some poems and on tombstones. A glance at the grave of a man called Zapolski is enough to show that the wording there is not just vertical, as on all standing tombstones, it is three-tiered. There is writing on the three steps which support the cross. Indeed, there are five climbing levels: the slab, the three steps, the cross.

Even without Freud's interpretation of dreams of climbing stairs as orgasmic, all these ascents speak for themselves. What may well have happened is that the echoes — of his own desires, his own wish for sense, for achievement, for release — were pulling Sutcliffe irresistibly upwards, 'piling on top of each other' — and that they came home to roost on an object the shape of which corresponded to what was happening to him. He found a *visual* confirmation for an aural, but also a kinetic, experience. It is said that when we read (with our eyes) there is a sound in our head. Sutcliffe reversed the process: an external sound found a correlative in a written text. The grave might have seemed silent, yet it was a talking one: it had writing on it. Sutcliffe could read the writing. But you read English downwards, the words make sense downwards — but Sutcliffe's climb to his own strange epiphany must have had such a dynamic in it that the three-tiered inscription appeared to make sense upwards, culminating in its phallic Christ.

Linguistics, and the disciplines that surround it, might help clarify some of the more bizarre aspects of Sutcliffe's hallucination. Indeed, when a particular disorder has so much to do with misinterpretation, Jakobson must be followed in his claim that

> to study adequately any breakdown in communications we must first understand the nature and structure of the particular mode of communication that has ceased to function . . . (Some) psychopathologists (do) assign a high importance to the linguistic problems involved in the study of language disturbances.[7]

Since language disturbance is at the centre of the Bingley episode, it is worth asking whether, for instance, the linguistic notion of the sign may not shed some light on what happened.

What is called sign is a combination of a signifier and a signified. In language, the signifier is the sound of the word: 'grave'. The signified is the mental concept, what is meant by 'grave'. The two work together in an apparently undissociated whole to produce the overall sign, the meaning 'grave' which comes to mind when I hear the sound 'grave'.

There are also semiological signs, which are not language but indicate what happens to an object, an event, when combination, association, etc. make it signify one or several things: as in fashion, advertisements, etc., and it could be said that within what we call 'culture', practically every social object is a sign. Such signs, especially if they have symbolic or religious connotations, can range from the simple to the highly complex.

A short piece of wood or stone placed across a longer one signifies the cross on which Christ was crucified, and also by extension the crucifixion of Christ, or Christ himself, or protection against evil, or the Christian's resolution to die for the world as Christ died for it. A stone slab, prone or erect, signifies 'here lieth the body of one who is dead'. But it can also have multiple additional meanings. Indeed, in most cultures, tombs are full of complex messages, which could be coded as follows:

SOCIAL: the greater or lesser splendour of the tomb means that the dead person was important, rich, etc. or that their family spared no expense to manifest their grief and love.

DURATION: Hard stone — granite, marble etc. — is used to signify that the person, though dead, will last eternally (in God or in the memory of men).

RELIGION: especially when used in combination with another sign, like a cross or an angel, the tomb manifests faith in another life, or in Resurrection. The dead person sleeps in God.

On top of this, a multiplicity of other meanings can emerge from the decoration of, and inscription on, the grave. It can become a representation or memento of a person, (as in an effigy, a statue). It can express the grief of the family and friends, the tragic or happy character of the death, belief in the hereafter, etc, etc. The composite sign is meant to express the relation of the living to the dead person. It strikes the onlooker with its many messages. You could say that at one extreme are the pyramids, kingly chapels or Victorian statuary; at another the mound of stones in a western, with a makeshift cross planted on it.

The actual tomb of Zapolski bears several of the messages loosely listed above. The cross signifies the Catholic faith, the tiers a certain degree of social splendour: you climb stairs up to a throne, or to the entrance of a church, or to the altar. Perhaps they suggest the pilgrimage up to Calvary with — or like — the Saviour, and Resurrection is thereby promised. The words make the dead man sound loved and important: TREA-SURED MEMORIES OF A DEAR HUSBAND. They also testify to his foreignness: because of his name, and because of the Polish words at the bottom.

This is spelling out the obvious. But it becomes interesting to dissociate the object from the codes under which it signifies, and the messages that are thus sent out. For Sutcliffe, though he perceived the complete object (the grave and its cross and writing on it) and gathered the codes that were at work (social importance, religion, foreignness), completely misread the messages. Where there was a modest expression of the man's value and importance, socially and emotionally, he read a promise of his own human exaltation. Where there was a suggestion of Calvary and a hope of Resurrection through Christ, he saw that he had been chosen by God. Where there was hard, tiered stone, he read erection, a particular resurrection of his own flesh that had been deep in a dug grave when he first heard the voice, and that was now transformed into a vertical, lasting monument. Where there was a sign for a man called Zapolski, he saw a sign for a man called Sutcliffe.

This elaborate dissociation of signifier and signified occurred, it seems to me, because the name Zapolski was similar enough to his own name Sutcliffe, and also, an acceptable or even agreeable version of it.

Surnames or 'proper names' (names of places, etc.) are the words in which there is, as it were, most signifier and least signified. A form almost without content. What is Zapolski — except for the fact that to an English ear it is foreign? What you could say (especially given that an identification was taking place for Sutcliffe, that he was looking at that grave as if at a mirror in which he was seeing himself, elect, the son of promise) is that Zapolski looks and sounds a little like Sutcliffe. Hold this page to a mirror, and 's' becomes 'z'. To linguists, 'z' is a hard 's', 'k' a hard 'c'. If you connect this hardening to the other 'hard' elements of the sign, the stone, the climb, you could say that in that name, as in the monument, Sutcliffe was seeing a hardened, virile version of himself.

There are literary accounts of such wrongful readings of signs, such bizarre mutations of the letters of one name to another. One of the most startling aspects of this case is that in some ways it lays bare the connections there are between madness, crime and literature.

One such example is a short story by Balzac called *Sarrasine*,

... alyzed in great detail by Roland Barthes in a ... think it illuminates Sutcliffe's revelation.

... protagonist who gives the Balzac story its title, ... th century French sculptor who goes to Venice to ... d while there, falls in love with a beautiful soprano called ... binella. He hears her at the opera, is enchanted by the splendour of her voice, and she becomes his ideal of womanhood. It is the first time he has ever loved. He makes a statue of her imagined, perfect body. He attempts to make love to her. She is strangely evasive. Yet she is not virtuous, she is known to be kept by a wealthy lover, a Cardinal. Finally the secret is out. Sarrasine discovers that Zambinella is not a woman, that 'she' is a castrato, one of those young boys who were 'processed' and trained to produce lovely female singing voices.

The story of Sarrasine's abortive love for Zambinella is told, sixty odd years later, by a young and beautiful woman to the narrator of the tale. The narrator, who had met her at a grand Paris ball and had had his curiosity whetted as to Zambinella's identity, had hoped to seduce the young woman: his expectations are disappointed. Rather like Sarrasine's love for Zambinella had been disappointed.

At the heart of the tale lies a meditation upon the nature and origins — or lack of visible origins — of wealth in Parisian society under the July Monarchy. Zambinella had made a great fortune as both singer and prized courtesan. The family, at whose brilliant ball the story begins to be told, are his descendants. Zambinella is the source of their wealth. A wizened popinjay of an old man, he now haunts their 'salons' like a ghost.

What concerns me about this is the way Barthes shows how *Sarrasine* revolves around castration.

There are incipiently 'feminine' elements in Sarrasine the sculptor. He's been his mother's darling, shy, a loner, has been over-protected. When he falls in love with Zambinella, he is suffused, 'penetrated' by her voice: much like Endymion by Diana's moonlight in the picture that now hangs in the house of

Zambinella's wealthy heirs, and for which Zambinella posed as a nude model. The discovery that his feminine ideal is a man, and a castrated man at that, symbolically castrates Sarrasine. He will never be able to love a woman again. He has, in fact, never loved a woman: Zambinella was his first love. The revelation actually kills him: ruffians in the pay of Zambinella's lover, the Cardinal, murder him soon after he's found out the truth. It is as if — Barthes maintains — the castration which had been inflicted upon Zambinella passed on to Sarrasine as a contagious disease. Even the lettering of the names expresses this. Zambinella had the 'a' ending of Italian feminine nouns, but the harsh 'z' sound, the sound of the whip (what the COD calls 'the *blade* open consonant') marks him: both as male/hard, and as castrated/castrator. The name Sarrasine too is full of ambiguities. The word does not exist in French. There is 'Sarrazin', masculine, with a 'z', which means a cereal, and a Saracen. The 'z' of 'sarrazin' has been replaced by an 's': it is the sign of Sarrasine's secretly feminine nature, as is the 'ine' ending of his name. It is also a sign of the castration to come. Indeed, it is as if the 'z' had mutated to the name of Zambinella; as if the name 'Zambinella' lashed at 'Sarrasine', inflicted a feminine 's', an inversion, a soft, mirror-image of z, upon it.

Of course, though 's' is soft and 'z' hard, the letters in themselves are not significant. They become so through the whole complex of signs and mutations of gender inside the story. It is as if masculine and feminine signs, endings of nouns, letters, were caught in a process of travelling and displacement:* the marks of a world in which sexual identity has been

---

* Displacement' is a concept originally devised by Freud in relation to dreams. It suggests how, under the pressure of censorship, distortions occur in images, words, etc., so that what is *meant* appears in a modified form: omissions, regrouping of material, alteration in arrangement. A latent element is replaced, not by a part of itself, but by something more remote, something of the nature of an allusion. And there may be a shift in emphasis, what is important appearing as unimportant, and vice versa. See *Introductory Lectures on Psychoanalysis*, and *The Interpretation of Dreams*.

profoundly disturbed. Where indeterminacy, lethal mistakes about gender, prevail. Above all, it is a world in which 'woman' turns out to be a male suffering from lack — a castrated male. Where, as a result, the male in love with the woman suffers lack — castration — in his turn. It is also a story in which there is no woman.

Might it not be the case that the displacement of letters, the false interpretation of signs in Sutcliffe's revelation, were also symptomatic of a crisis of sexual identity? For it shows the mutation of the same letters as in the Balzac story, but in the reverse order. It is not 'z' which becomes 's', (Sarrazin, Sarrasine), but 's' which becomes 'z'. The soft, feminine signs become hard, masculine. Sutcliffe becomes Zapolski. Wasn't this because he thought that his alter ego, his secretly hard self, was speaking to him from that tomb? Wasn't this welcome because he feared he was soft, he felt threatened by femininity as lack, as castration? Now a father figure, God, was granting him the triumphant self he so desired. I say, 'father', not just because God suggests father, but because Zapolski was 49, old enough to be Sutcliffe's father. The patronym remains the same whether you are dealing with father or with son.

Yet there is something bizarrely feminine, and also bizarrely subversive, about the revelation. In the wake of theories of the sign, a great deal has been suggested in psychoanalysis as in semiotics about what establishes identity in language. What is relevant here is that Lacan, among and with others, not only describes the Father as the law-giver, the source of the symbolic, but maintains that it is 'the name of the Father' that guarantees the identity of words in language. If this is so, isn't it, to say the least, odd, that in the episode we are trying to understand, the name 'Zapolski', from which proceeds the voice of God, evokes both the name of the Father *and* acts as a disrupter of identity? For if I am right, and it is the vague resemblance to his own name that permits the identification for Sutcliffe, Zapolski is a scrambling of his own name. And even if I am wrong, and making too much of this, Sutcliffe still proceeds to misread the Polish words at the base of the grave (Jego, Ecko, etc.), disrupting the identity of words. You could say that he gets reassured as to his identity through the process of subverting identity in language.

Julia Kristeva has written at length about what she has in places called a 'revolution in poetic language' and at a later stage, the 'language of the maternal body'. In both cases, the identity which is connected with the name of the Father, and which gets defined as stable, orderly, rational, is destroyed: a 'bodily' language is born, or returned to. In some of the experiments of modernist poets like Mallarmé, she sees, besides a disruption of normal syntax and verse, a calculated reversal to the bodily sounds that precede organized language, sounds like 'k', which is the sound for pushing, defecating. . . . You could add, sounds like 'z', which is the sound for aggression. . . . The sounds babies make. The sounds humans make when they are still in a close bond with the mother's body. The sounds the jumbled Polish words make. . . . It is as if the moment which gave Sutcliffe his identity contained the elements for the dissolution of that identity, the threat of total regression.

Zip/Zap. 'Zip': 1. A light sharp sound as of a bullet in flight or of the tearing of canvas or the like. . . . 2. Energy, impetus, 'go'. 3. . . . a lightning fastener (COD). 'Zap': you zap a fly; a spaceship zaps another ship. Fast. Annihilate. Instant disappearance.

Jego. 'Mr Sutcliffe said he read the Polish word "jego" on the grave and took that to mean "Jesus".' 'I saw what I took to be a definite message about the echoing voice. . . . I recall as Jesus was speaking to me.'

'Mr Sutcliffe said he remembered the phrase "We be the echo". Mr Chadwin asked "what is your recollection, *not of what you heard, but of what you saw*, that conveyed a message to you?" Mr Sutcliffe said he had read the words "Wehvy" and "Echo" in Polish. "Echo" was spelt "Ecko".'

I am Jesus, speaking to you. Aren't you yourself called 'Jesus' by your fellow gravediggers? They think it's a joke, they call you so on account of your beard, your shyness, your modesty, your Catholic upbringing — your deep eyes? We be the echo, the echo of your desire to be what Society requires of you. To be Male. Climb further on and on. Grow hard. Stand upon others: the dead, who lie at your feet. Be pitiless. You can do it. Stand erect above the dead. Thus when 'they' have brought you low — when the wicked, the castrating bitches, bring you low, my son, stand erect upon death. You are at the top. You deserve to be. Prostrate yourself at my feet, my son, and worship. I am death. 'Paranoid schizophrenia', the psychiatrists said, but how is the term to be understood?

Mr Chadwin's distinction, 'not what you heard, but what you saw', goes to the heart of what appears to me the deeply schizophrenic character of this moment. For the gap between what is heard and what is seen is, in effect, unbridgeable. How can an inscription which cannot be understood until it has been deciphered be *heard* from a distance? And how can an actual echo be corroborated by the letters 'Ecko'? Only the reading activity, the reading aloud inside the head or actually with the mouth and throat, can transform written signs into sound. It must have been the division inside Sutcliffe, the lack of a coherent, interpretative centre, that made him construe his own perception (the voice, the echo) and his own interpretative activity (reading the words, taking them to mean the voice) into something — somebody — outside himself.

And that is the paranoia element: eliciting meaning (a meaning that fulfils the expectation), building it up into something cogent, continuous, in total disregard of the way in which perception and language function. In a dance of slipping and mutating letters, foreign writing that vaguely resembles the words that have taken shape in your head to define what you're hearing gets treated as a *secret code*, meant for your eyes and ears alone: the very proof of your election. Sutcliffe, the weak, becomes Zapolski, the strong. How could Sutcliffe have told his family, his friends, of his 'experience'? Its esoteric, private nature was absolute. It was proof of its authenticity. In any case, nobody would have believed him because nobody was meant to. 'If it was meant for everyone to hear they would hear'. Sutcliffe alone was on a direct line to God. At best, his supporters, those who will unconsciously concur with him, the police who let him go, the hoaxer, the fans, will be on an indirect line to God. But if a woman speaks words that fit the pattern, 'you could call it fate', those words immediately fall into place. 'I thought it was my signal'.

Freud's Schreber too believed his fate to be 'predestined', prescribed by the 'Order of Things'.

It is of tremendous significance to the whole episode that Sutcliffe should have recently met Sonia. Not just because (as will be seen in the following chapters) it was such a revolution in his life to get a steady girl-friend, and that it called on his virility, but because she was foreign.

Sonia's father, although he had emigrated from Czechoslovakia to England in 1947, was Polish by birth — which might have made Sutcliffe particularly aware of that Polish section of the cemetery. Sonia's parents spoke Czech at home: Sutcliffe might have gone there, heard a foreign language spoken, echoing sounds which could be construed into surprising meanings. He would at least, one imagines, have heard Sonia speak her native Czech. At any rate, being closely confronted with actual foreignness was a novel experience for Sutcliffe. As well as this, Sonia's surname was Szurma. Z doubling s. S hardened by z. She had been christened Oksana. To help her adapt to England, and to sound more ordinary, it had been changed to Sonia. The hard Oksana had mutated into the soft Sonia. She was a woman after all, womanliness is supposed to be soft.

In identifying with the name of a man called Zapolski, Sutcliffe effected the *reverse* mutation: a 'z', a 'k' became substituted for the 's', the 'c', of his own name. He fitted himself into the 'male' role, as Sonia had been fitted into a female one. (Perhaps they were both misfits. Perhaps Sonia was too masculine and he was too feminine. They both had to make some exchange of parts). Also Sonia's forbidding and ambitious father, who was an educated man, felt he was above his fallen semi-working-class station in Bradford, and would only be interested in a successful and ambitious son-in-law. He was called *B*odan *Sz*urma. Bronislaw Zapolski. Was that the secret name of the Father, consecrating the symbolical election of a son?

BRONIS/LAW ZAP/OLSKI   LAW ZAP

God's Law is to Zap. . . .

Flash-like

The Thunderer.

A beloved Father. TREASURED MEMORIES. *MEMOR-IES. WEHVY. OUCZY. YEARS.* DIED 19th June. Sutcliffe was born in June. A.dear husband. Husband to be. Just met a girl. That husband, unlike John Sutcliffe, had been a dear husband. A good husband. A foreigner. A man from other parts. A man constructed with signs other than those which are normally recognized. Treasured. The tomb becomes a treasure chest. The quest up the hill had led to a treasure trove. The treasure is a code: a secret.

The Father speaks emphatically, in capital letters. But with apparently inchoate sounds, movable letters. Julia Kristeva would say that the Father's speech here is also 'pre-Oedipal'. He speaks the 'semiotic' language of the Mother. The language of the Dark Continent. Of the Repressed.

Does he sing the song of the Bitch?

Has Sutcliffe met with a sphinx in the shape of a cross?

Five

A Man Possessed

Many people have had revelations, heard voices, felt heat; a sense of bliss, timelessness. Everything is suddenly boundless, significant. They are sure that there is another reality, that it is higher than 'this'. Call them mystical, psychic, or plain deranged, there is no doubt that experiences, such as the one Sutcliffe described, do occur.

The major question they pose is that of their meaning. That, it seems to me, can only be gauged by their consequences. Without getting into the thorny case of Joan of Arc, you cannot deny that the French poet Claudel's conversion in Notre Dame led to — at least, did not impede — the writing of great verse; that Pascal's night of 'joy' drew from him some extraordinary prose, and much virtuous living. On the other hand, in Hogg's novel, the revelation to the 'Justified Sinner' that he is one of the elect, nudges him on the way to fratricide.

Is it only time that tells, then? Or is there something in the character of the revelation itself that makes it good or bad? In Sutcliffe's case, was it the association with death, or the mishearings and misreadings, that made it bad? Yet it was positive at the start. 'The first two years were the best', Sutcliffe said while being cross-examined by Sir Michael Havers. 'There were no signs of the purpose or why I had been chosen to be here. . . .' What was said was 'that I should have faith and that I should believe and that there was no need to be depressed'.

Then why the murders that followed?

Isn't it the overall context of Sutcliffe's personality and background — his peculiar 'femininity' in the midst of an aggressively male society — that gave the graveyard episode such ominous dimensions?[1]

His father is called John Sutcliffe. A baker by trade, he had served in the Merchant Navy as a cook in the Mediterranean during the war, then gone back to his home town of Bingley, where in March 1945 he had married Kathleen Coonan, a girl of Irish descent. A big, tough, good-looking working class man's man. A real lad, hard-drinking, philandering, in love with a fight, he cut quite a figure in the community. He was 'well-known locally for his achievements on the cricket and football fields', a member and sometimes soloist of the town's male choir. Brought up in the country in a fairly tough area in Gilstead by a hard mother, his talents seem to have been of the extrovert kind. Besides being a natural at all sports, he also had a talent for acting. He is a clever man, too, with a good memory, one gathers from the precision, articulacy and speculative slant of his reported speech. Also shifty.

Peter William Sutcliffe, the eldest child, came into the world on 2 June 1946. A puny baby, he was at 5lbs a mere scrap of life who had to be kept in an incubator for ten days. Unlike the children to come, his first sister Anne, his brother Mick — 4 years younger and at adolescence also a good 5 inches taller — he remained throughout childhood weak, weedy, and over-sensitive. He still couldn't walk when he was 18 months old, when his father got him a pair of lace-up leather boots, specially reinforced, 'which seemed to do the trick'. A good talker though, but a mummy's boy, always 'holding onto her skirts', 'clutching onto her clothes' 'his face half-buried in the folds'.[2] He grew to be a quiet, retiring boy, unwilling to go out and play with other children — chronically shy. He never joined in the ordinary rough and tumble nor in games. When sent out to play, his skinny legs proved 'an irresistible target for the mockers'. His father's efforts to cure him of his aversion to sport all floundered. The child couldn't overcome his 'embarrass-ment about anything to do with his body'.[3] He was fond of reading though — always down at the library with his sisters. He remained passive and retiring, but never complained at the Roman Catholic Primary School, St Joseph, where his Irish mother had sent him: and among children, some of whom were of Eastern European or Italian descent, the offspring of refugees, he was the one who was taken for 'the foreigner'.

Peter failed his 11-plus, much to his father's indignation, and went to Cottingley Manor, a Secondary Modern, a much rougher place than the relatively sheltered Primary. Among bigger and tougher boys, the teasing turned into persecution. He could no longer evade it, retire into invisibility, into corners, as had been his wont. When he could no longer take it, he started playing truant. He would pretend to be off to school, slam the door loudly from the inside, then hoist himself into the loft. It was his 'burrow', as Burn calls it. There he'd sleep, listen to the noises of the house, or read comics by torchlight.[4] The parents only found out when the headmaster asked them why the child hadn't been to school for a fortnight. The father went storming up to the headmaster — or had a 'satisfactory' talk with him, according to who's telling the story. It worked: Peter never played truant again, never complained again — though whether that meant that the persecutions had altogether stopped is not known.

The family had moved, in that period, to a rougher area, Ferncliffe Estate, up the hill the other side of the valley. They liked to regard themselves as being at the hard working, 'res-pectable' end of the social spectrum.[5] The father boasts that the children were well-dressed and never had free school dinners. Yet the overall sense of a social fall must have been clear, not just on account of the rougher neighbourhood, but because the father's pattern of being 'mostly either out or asleep'[6] increased. When back home he was more often than not drunk, bullying, leaving no one in doubt as to who was master, sometimes violent. There were six children. The mother was overtaxed, friends would pour in and out of the house. Peter, unlike his father, was always in: quiet, invisible, tidy, even meticulous about his own appearance. He would lock himself in the bathroom for hours: he could stand rooted for half an hour or more in front of the mirror, lost to the world.

He continued to be shy, over-sensitive. Would blush and avert his face if he caught anyone looking at him, but would watch people surreptitiously. His ambition at school — apart from a period in which he played the clown — seems to have been to 'disappear into the woodwork'. The teachers would say later that they barely noticed him. He was always the last to speak. Yet he was not a bad pupil. He was even gifted at Art. A doctor at court would say that he had an IQ of between 108 and 110, several points above average. Yet he left school without a single certificate. He didn't even *sit* his exams. From that social test too he shrank.

Pro/stitute: one who exhibits herself, stands forward. The reverse of Sutcliffe.

You can call a girl a 'tomboy'. There is no equivalent term for a boy who has the tastes and temperament of a girl. That is because, as feminist writers like Ann Oakley and Lee Comer argue, while a girl may, for a while, 'emulate acceptable masculine behaviour', no such toleration is extended to the boy. 'The traffic is only one way . . . a boy may not join ranks with his inferiors'.[7]

This may be even more the case in a working-class milieu, perhaps because awareness of subservience to machines, or to management at work, makes the man's need to be superior to somebody, and preferably females, all the more acute. What is striking is that Sutcliffe seems to have failed to evince all the normative traits that, according to most observers, mark out the construction of masculinity. Tolson, for instance, stressing that for the growing boy 'manhood is a perpetual future', describes his consciousness as shaped, partly by the father's paternal presence in domestic arguments and neighbourhood violence, and partly at play, among his peers. The working-class boy (by contrast with the lower middle-class boy, for whom respectability is at a higher premium),

> expresses himself, not so much in an inner, competitive struggle for achievement, as through a collective toughness, a masculine 'performance', recognized and approved by his 'mates'. . . . In effect, working-class masculinity becomes a kind of 'performance'.

Many studies have shown that there is 'an explicit system of taboos and recognitions of status . . . (in) the testing of masculine prowess — in fights, arguments, explorations of the local neighbourhood', in the learning of 'a masculine language, which prescribes certain topics (sports, machines, competitions) and certain ways of speaking (jokes, banter and bravado)'. 'In all this, there is little room for deviation. . . . In its defensive conformity working-class masculinity is itself an imposition'.[8]

In the light of this, Sutcliffe as a child seems to have exhibited all the wrong features, the features which are called 'feminine', which mark him out for others perhaps as inferior, outlandish, threatening — maybe *foreign*: his smallness, his weaknesses, his shyness. There is early evidence of linguistic ability, his taste for reading, for staying at home, for the mother's company and pursuits. The retarded mobility, the dislike of games and sports, of all the father's pursuits, all the normal, the boisterous occupations. The preoccupation with his own mirror image, female narcissism. His reluctance to fight, the withdrawal, like a Jane Eyre, into invisibility. Being 'deep' is regarded as a virtue in Jane. There is no doubt that when Peter is described as 'deep' by his peers, it is with a certain amount of unease. The burrowing inside in terms of space (the mother's skirts, the loft, the bedroom or bathroom in which the youngster locks himself, the corner of the schoolyard, the back of the class room), the unwillingness to get out are regarded as near sinister.[9] Presumably because that is what girls are supposed to do.

The lack of masculinity extends to girls. Peter is repeatedly reported to have been shy of them, hesitant to make advances, blushing whenever sexual matters were being broached. It extends to jobs. He had eleven different jobs between leaving school just before sixteen and his marriage. He often loses jobs through bad time-keeping. 'The industrial environment certainly didn't suit him', Burn remarks.[10] Women are the ones who are supposed to be bad time-keepers — whose fluid, capricious and 'organic' natures are supposed to make them unfit for rigid rules, the reign of machines. At Fibre Products where Sutcliffe has his first job, 'he would be remembered as a "queer bugger" with the look of a "frightened animal" '.[11]

It is between the period of his leaving school and the approach of his eighteenth birthday, when he keeps his only long-lasting job as a gravedigger in Bingley cemetery, that Sutcliffe shows signs of adapting to the hard male world of which he's suddenly decided, it seems, to have become a part.

He buys a motorbike as soon as he leaves school. He becomes an expert but reckless driver. A stint as a mechanic develops in him a taste for motors. Hereafter, he'll always be fiddling with one engine or another — motorbike engines, then car engines.

And he starts body-building.

He puts himself on a course of one of the 'bulk-builders' foods advertised in the body-building periodicals. He buys a bullworker at which he practises every night in private for years and years. The results soon become apparent. He eventually becomes so strong that he surprises his friends on several occasions with the power of his grip, his fitness. He's even reported to have ended up defeating his bully of a little brother, Mick, at arm-wrestling.

Body-building ads swarm over the pages of boys' comics. 'Don't be half a man', Charles Atlas advises (Atlas: a pseudonym? If so, what a destiny is there cut out!). 'One day, I discovered a secret that changed me from a timid, frightened 97 pound weakling into "The Worlds Most Perfectly Developed

Man" — a "magic" method that can help turn you into . . . a real HE-MAN from head to toe . . . a man who STANDS OUT in any crowd'.

The secret? DYNAMIC TENSION. You 'simply take the sleeping muscles already present inside your own body — build them up. . . . You end up covered with rock hard SOLID MUSCLE!'

The comic-strip which accompanies the ad is quite informative too. 'The insult that made a Man out of Mac'. For his lack of physical strength Mac is insulted by a beach bully in front of his girl-friend. He is doubly humiliated. He's fed up: he mails the coupon to Charles Atlas. Next picture: he is rolling his new-found muscles in front of the mirror. When the beach bully reappears, Mac flattens him before the dazzled adoring eyes of his reconquered girl-friend. Mac has become a Man, a real he-man.

Let us note in passing the 'slip' that transforms Ma*c* into Ma*n* (as *s* into *z*). Let us also note that Mac proves his manhood, not by conquering a mountain, surviving an ordeal or making love well to his girl-friend,[12] but by felling his adversary in front of her. (Could it be that, among the many motivations, Sutcliffe also felled adversaries for the sake of the woman he loved? To prove something to her?)

What marks out body-building — by contrast with traditional games — is that it is a solitary, a narcissistic pursuit. It entails no relation to others. You note your progress, your success, in front of a mirror. Manhood is an essence to be reached. A proof to be administered.

Above all, it is artificial. Sutcliffe's late access to manhood seems to have been borrowed by, in some ways, magic means. Motorbikes. Speed. The man who shrinks from a fight with another man has a cool nerve when he's in the saddle or at the wheel. He is reported to have performed all sorts of daring feats, such as riding the motorbike straight into his house and up the stairs. Later, with his friend Keith Sugden, he giggled as he rammed the kerb with his car. There is even a story of his overtaking while a car was coming straight at him the other way: it was the other car which was forced off the road, with a great screaming of brakes. It is as if the borrowed power of the engine was transformed into his own, enabling him to do, in the semi-unreal world of speed, what he could not do in the world of everyday physical encounters. You can put on that power and remove it at will. It is detachable. Sutcliffe is supposed to have kept the engine of his favourite motorbike under his bed. Similarly, he will keep his 'male instruments' — a hammer and a screwdriver — hidden under the seat of his car, wrapped up inside his coat: the industrial tools or engines stand as a substitute for powerful manhood.

Indeed, there is little doubt as to the phallic nature of motors in Sutcliffe's life. At Clarke's, an engineering firm where he kept a good job as a long-distance lorry driver for most of the years of the killings, he nicknamed his big truck 'Wee Willy'. The irony is that the name actually boasts the phallic relation to the lorry while pretending to hide it (like the engine under the bed). The joke is of a piece with the casually reassuring, yet horribly truthful 'you can trust nobody these days', to Josephine Whitaker whom he'd accosted in a park and was about to murder. The best way to conceal a thing is to display it, but with a show of ordinariness, of witty understatement. Everyone can see that a lorry is big. Call it 'Wee Willy' and nobody will go further than the joke, nobody will take seriously the implications of phallic super-power that it contains. Nobody therefore will attach any importance to the note *stood up* against the window of the cab, written in *capitals*, which warns, 'In this truck lies a man whose latent genius if unleashed would rock the nation, whose dynamic energy would overpower those around him. . . .' Nobody will dream for a minute that the lad at Clarke's whom everyone jokingly calls 'The Ripper' because the police have questioned him several times, and because he fits one of their photokits, could possibly be him.

Fiddling with engines, his hands always full of motor grease, and driving, were quite obviously a form of sexual displacement for Sutcliffe. His attacks on women will all be conducted from, or into, one of his motorcars. As if he needed their power (his tools under the seat), or was possessed by it. His description in Court of the one time he managed not to kill makes him sound as if he were wrestling with a tempting devil, and that devil in some way was the car:

> 'Did you ever try to resist what you had been told to do?' Mr Chadwin asked. Mr Sutcliffe said he had tried. 'There was one time. . . . I was on my way to the Leeds red-light area. I got half-way there and I was still in a turmoil. . . . I was arguing, getting answers. . . . I finally stopped the car and turned it round. I was shouting in the car. I set off back and was changing *up and down the gear-box*. Eventually I got back home, locked the car and went to bed. I felt a great sense of achievement at that stage'.[13]

Like driving, body-building is a thing you do alone, which has an end in itself. Sutcliffe never competed in races, nor at wrestling, nor boxing — unlike his brother Mick, who could have been, Burn says, a professional boxer. The aim is to change a frightened weakling into not just somebody strong but somebody Supreme. If you can't do it you've got to overdo it, become 'The World's Most Perfectly Developed Man'. The message in the truck (here lieth Superman under the guise of an innocuous lorry-driver) is the direct offspring of Charles Atlas's promise. Body-building also entails getting a phallic tool. Not 'Wee Willy'. Like the murder instruments, like the motorbike engine, the bullworker can be put on and removed at will. Sutcliffe hides it in yet another burrow: in his wardrobe. He only takes it out when he is alone, to do his exercises. 'In the privacy of his room', as the ad says. Thus his secret magically makes a real 'HE-MAN' of him. He gets the brand-new (the term for a car, an industrial object), 'rock-hard SOLID MUSCLE' he desires. The supreme — the lasting — erection: hard as a standing gravestone that will deliver the conclusive proof that he is not half a man (=woman). Hulk-like (for the Hulk and his peers spread all over the pages of the comics where the Charles Atlas advertisements try to appeal to youngsters), his chest and shoulder muscles will 'swell so big they almost split' his coat seams. It is well-known which piece of his clothing gentle Bruce Banner never splits as he turns into the green giant — which part of his anatomy all that growing and hardening makes more potent. Meanwhile, the ad goes on to promise that your fists get turned 'into sledge-hammers'. . . .

Yvonne Pearson was battered to death by a sledge-hammer.

Can one fail to see the parallels between the artificial ways in which Peter Sutcliffe constructed his masculinity and the graveyard episode? There he was *inside* a grave, his feet about five feet *below* the ground when he first heard the voice: in a hiding-place, earth, mother's skirt, womb, in a frightened animal's burrow. The voice made him stand up, climb upright. The lettering on the grave, and the message it delivered, magically, secretly, made him rock-hard: chosen. The voice of God turns him into an 'essence', something as hard as stone. It delivered Sutcliffe once and for all, it seemed, from the persecutions and harassment and sense of inadequacy his family and environment had levelled at him. It revealed Power to him. Not the power of the Engine, this time, nor the power of built-up Muscle, but the power of Death: the Absolute.

And yet . . . and yet there remains this inborn, this inescapable femininity. The lack. The need to put it on. Secrecy. Concealment. Hiding the tools under his seat — in his own womb?

It is useful and healthy to think that there must have been, whatever the state of disturbance, repeated moments of choice. The episode in which he managed to turn the car around testifies to the survival somewhere of something like consciousness, something even like conscience.

Yet the pressures that came from his background upon a fragile psyche were such that one could almost think of Sutcliffe as a man possessed.[14]

Possessed by the desire to be 'a Real Man'.

Six

The Construction of Masculinity
I. Fathers and Sons

Whether you follow sociological, psychosexual or psychoanalytic models, two elements appear crucial in the formation of
masculinity.[1] The first is the ambivalent image of the father.
He is both friend and foe, the source of identification (the
image of what must be aspired to and imitated) but also the
rival for the mother's love. He is furthermore the law-giver.
He gives weight to taboos, is often absent from home,
threatens the child with lack — castration. He deals in
negation. The second is the constructed nature of masculinity.
It is a projection, something ahead, that is gradually built up
through a complex process of socialization, the early formative
years, the schooling, the peer-groups, etc. 'You will be a man,
my son'. That future tense, following all the 'ifs', is essential.
Tolson calls masculinity a bribe.[2] It is certainly something the
boy feels to be ahead. The need to be tested, not to be found
wanting, the importance of courage — a thing which plays a
much lesser role for girls — are all signs of this.

It is pretty obvious from what has already been said about
Sutcliffe's childhood and youth, that none of this seemed to
work in the right way. And yet the pressure never let up: the late
virility, developed through motors, through body-building,
through work at the churchyard, is proof of this. Somehow he

managed to produce the image, voice the codes. But the context in which this happened was so muddled that a psychically overcharged and virtually untenable situation resulted from this. One more trauma, and the house would tumble down.

Clashing Models

In many ways John Sutcliffe ought to have provided an ideal father figure, entirely recognizable and right in the working-class context in which the family grew up. A sturdy, physical extrovert, with communal tastes and accomplishments, even his faults (the occasional fighting, the bullying at home, the pub-drinking, the womanizing) fit a clear pattern. He comes across from various accounts as warm, attractive, likeable, tolerant — with a gift of the gab and a large-scale personality. He seems to have been genuinely bewildered and horrified when the identity of the Ripper was discovered. As far as his first-born was concerned, he was, he contends, very much taken aback by the lad's diminutive size and general failure to exhibit any expected male characteristics. By his own account he put a lot of effort into trying to get him to produce the right results — like buying him a beautiful football at Christmas when he was ten and trying to teach him how to play — and was much relieved when the body-building and motorbikes finally showed clear evidence of manhood. 'The first welcome signs of manliness in his son', Cross says.[3] It was 'gratifying' to the father, is Burn's remark. In other words, as far as identification with the father goes, John Sutcliffe seems to have produced the right image, and exerted the right pressure.

But it looks as if a quite different type of pressure was being exerted by the mother. Kathleen Coonan, a conscientious Catholic who would take her children to church in the early years of her marriage and register them at the Catholic Primary where she herself had gone, was of impoverished stock. She had suffered something of a social come-down in marrying John Sutcliffe. Her grandfather had come from Connemara to live in

Dawlish where he had built up a porcelain and ironmongery business. His daughters — one of them Kathleen's mother — would talk nostalgically about the fine house, and of going to church in a pony and trap. But the business had collapsed, and the grandfather with it. Having moved to Bingley, he drowned himself in the Leeds to Liverpool canal that ran close to his new home. Kathleen's mother had been scarred by these upheavals and traumas. She had married relatively late, at 30, an Irishman whose family ups and downs were comparable with hers. He was a devout Catholic and had made her a convert. But he had died after only seven years, leaving his prematurely orphaned widow with premature orphans. The son had been ill. It had been, for the second time round, a household of women, the mother and two daughters, keen on keeping up appearances, on presenting a quiet and refined front to the world.

Kathleen herself had been 27 when she married. Wistful for the better times her side of the family once had known, soon overworked and overwhelmed by a chaotic household, not much helped by an absentee husband, she tried hard to be a good mother. She was a virtuous mother: no philandering on her side, and in later years, though in rather poor health, she got a job cleaning offices to supplement her husband's wages which tended more and more to be spent at the pub. He 'brooked no contradiction'. She seemed 'content to live in her husband's shadow'. She must have been scrupulous in her religious observance: the Catholic ban on contraception must have had something to do with her giving birth seven times in ten years. She became more lax in later years, ceased going to church on Sundays as the many pregnancies and hard work took their toll. But she remained keen on respectability. She was shocked and indignant when her 16-year-old daughter Maureen got pregnant, and according to some reports, turned her back on her.

She was deeply attached to her first-born. Quiet, shy, gentle, thoroughly domesticated, always ready to run errands for her, tidy in his habits, Peter must have given her much of the emotional and material satisfaction she failed to get from her rowdy and unreliable husband — perhaps also from her quarrelsome and gregarious younger children (with the possible exception of Carl, the third son).* Perhaps he also gave her social hope: the boy might do well, he was decent, proper, considerate. He showed more signs of refinement than the rest of them put together.

Peter — someone called him the 'favourite daughter' — certainly seems to have felt deep love and sympathy for his oft-betrayed mother; to have adopted her values. He served as altar boy for several years, for instance. He also took her side, and he must have felt corresponding aggressiveness and resentment towards his ill-behaved father. The psychiatrists who questioned Sutcliffe and Sonia speak of the couple's positive 'hatred' for John Sutcliffe. It is plausible to think that Sutcliffe chose Sonia for a girl-friend at least partly because she fulfilled his mother's ambition for her son: she was educated, ambitious, respectable — a cut above the others.

It is also likely that he chose her because she was *like* his mother — and so like himself. A foreigner — wasn't his mother of Irish origins, a Catholic among Church of England protestants, effectively agnostic, people like his father? Hadn't he himself cut the figure of a foreigner at primary school? Wasn't she socially downcast? Her father, Bodan Szurma, had been a physical education teacher in Czechoslovakia and claimed descent from an aristocratic Ukrainian family. The job he'd found as an immigrant in Bradford was as a woolcomb box minder, 'one of the dreariest, poorest-paid jobs in the mill'.[5] He later became a yarn-tester, but his wife's job as a nursing auxiliary was the main source of income, and he spent a lot of time and energy trying to educate his daughters so they would

---

* 'In lots of ways she was an exceptional person, me mother. She were right patient and a right good mum. . . . She could feed us and clothe us and look after us materially, but she didn't seem to have enough discipline to cope. She just couldn't handle us six kids. She worked too hard and she'd too much to do at home. She had it all to do herself and she had no control. She'd do owt for a quiet life', is her daughter Maureen's account of things.[4]

get on in the world. He set very much store by their irreproachable conduct.

Kathleen's family had experienced a similar fall. Hadn't she herself been one of two impoverished daughters? And thus, the 'favourite daughter' — Peter — brings to his mother another favourite daughter, another mirror image of herself. On the day of the wedding, Maureen said, Kathleen never took her eyes away from the young couple, her face flushed with joy.

Virility, respectability. The one required by the father, the other by the mother. These are socially incompatible demands: the aggressive form of virility John Sutcliffe seeks for his son is essentially working-class. The respectability the mother desires is lower middle-class, veering on plain middle-class.[6] The clash is complete, and the cost paid by Sutcliffe when he nearly squares the circle and manages to satisfy both his father that he is sufficiently virile and his mother that he's doing the right thing with Sonia, is perhaps expressed by the first break, the first voice of God.

It is also, alarmingly, bound up with a new-found necrophilia, and a darker, smudgier side to the pattern, which must have something to do with Sutcliffe's schizophrenia, the accumulation of uncertainties so great that they created a charge of unbelievable violence. This has much to do with the image of the father.

A split personality

Far from being a model of working-class masculinity, John Sutcliffe was deeply flawed. The dream of social respectability was as active, if repressed, in him as in his wife. It riddled him with contradictions.

He had nurtured a myth according to which he was descended from great folk, and his own father had come a cropper. I say 'myth', because the story functions as a kind of archetype, is not corroborated by the rest of the family, and Sonia has accused him of boasting 'like Chanticleer', reminding him that pride comes before a fall. Be this as it may, he felt the need for the story, and fed it to his family and to biographer Burn.

He had, he says, a wealthy, successful grandfather, John 'Willie' Sutcliffe. (William, it should be remembered, is also Peter Sutcliffe's second name, 'Willy' is the name he gave to his big truck.) The grandfather had moved in the most prosperous and respectable circles of Bradford, had owned a grand house on the moors overlooking the valley. 'Up there, it was beautiful', is John Sutcliffe's reminiscence of such moorland views. It is remarkably similar to Peter's moment of exaltation at the top of Bingley cemetery. The resemblance goes further: John also remembers the grandfather's exalted position when, 'an imposing presence', head of the Accounts Department at Bradford Co-operative Society, he had dominated everybody:

> 'He must have had a staff of about twenty girls in his office. It seemed to stretch as far as the eye could see, and there were desks all the way down with girls scribbling away at them. And me grandfather's desk was at the top of the office, high up, facing them all'.[7]

And so perhaps it was his father, not his mother, Sutcliffe was trying to please when, at the top of Bingley cemetery, he felt there were 'thousands of men' under him.

But then, it had been all fall. John Sutcliffe's own father, Arthur, although he had had a grammar school education, had married below himself, and had held a series of menial or peripatetic jobs. His wife, Ivy Sutcliffe, the daughter of a foundry-man, 'as low as you can be in a town this size' (these are John Sutcliffe's words) had started work at twelve in the mills. She had loved work and the money she made. The family describe her as hard, unloving, totally dominating her husband, who was a dapper little man, fond of ball-room dancing. Arthur eventually deserted his family and ended up living in a caravan. The five children seem to have been neglected. The elder boy, John, had had to look after the younger ones, as well as (according to Beattie) ensuring the minimum degree of communication between his father and mother who for whole periods would not speak to each other, by ferrying messages from one to the other.

All these generations were employed by the Bradford Co-Operative Society: the grandfather is head of accounts, the father a door-to-door collector, the son a baker. At home they move from the big house on the moors to a cottage to a terraced semi-detached house to a council house. The grandfather had sat at the head of his table, served by his woman, in front of a mound of food. The father had been henpecked and had become a kind of gipsy. It is not difficult to imagine what a fund of insecurity there is in big John Sutcliffe's insistence upon his own seat at the head of the family table with a mound of food for his Sunday dinner — or in his aggressive patriarchal stance — and his marrying a gentle, respectable wife. Wasn't he thus avoiding his own father's fate? The compulsive philandering, to the point that no woman was safe from his advances, including his sons' girl-friends, was also proving something. And being out always, leaving the care of his children to his wife, spending much of his wages at the pub, wasn't that to make up for the way he'd been exploited as a child, made to take responsibility for his brothers and sisters, and even his parents? Wasn't there some deep insecurity at the bottom of it all? Deep, to the point of neurosis?

For while on the one hand he insisted on his patriarchal status, on the other he would do things that punctured that confident image. His son Mick, the second son to live, and the big one, spent four consecutive Christmasses in jail; he collected convictions for robbery, assault, bodily harm and grievous bodily harm. John Sutcliffe would adopt a moralizing stance to the lad, and yet, he himself pilfered from allotments at nights. He was arrested on Christmas Day 1961, when Peter was fifteen, for breaking and entering: he had climbed into a house, stuffed his pockets with raisins and sweets and left a trail of them as he tried to escape, chased by the youths who had been having a party at the house.[8] Yet Christmas was his big day in the year. The apparently 'aberrant lapses'[9] were repeated, generally when he was drunk. The pillar of the community, the choir soloist and cricket virtuoso knocks his own self-created image. His son Mick thinks he's forfeited the right to criticize anybody, but John Sutcliffe remains totally self-righteous:

> 'He turns round to me an' says, "You're going crackers, you; you're getting worse as you go on". An' two weeks later he gets fuckin' caught nickin' a load of silver hissen coming down Sherriff Lane, coming home from some cricket do in early hours of the mornin'. I can remember me mother shoutin' and bawlin' and playin' hell. He'd even tekken a kettle for some stupid reason. He were pissed up.'[10]

His neurosis is two-fold. First of all, having two personalities, a respectable one and a petty criminal one, with no realization that they are in a state of conflict. Further, John Sutcliffe used to upset his son Carl by being odious at home and pleasant abroad, a pattern which his son Peter will reverse. But also, there is something both compulsive and puerile in the pranks which the father indulges in, especially when he seems to enter into competition with his own son Mick. He'll go one better than the lad, he'll take the kettle. The virile son spends Christmas in jail; well, he too has destroyed the Christmas spirit. It's as if both father and son had to negate the traditional family occasion. The mother screams, not just because respectability has once again been shattered, but because domesticity is being violated.

At night, John Sutcliffe, drunk, burgles homes. His patriarchal self 'throws its weight around the house' and perpetuates cheer and jollity at the Christmas table. Thus, he is projecting a pattern which his eldest-born will imitate, but with hideous results. It will not be a matter of burglary, nor even of 'grievous bodily harm', but of murder. Peter will attack Teresa

Sykes on bonfire night; he will slaughter Jean Jordan immediately upon moving into his new home with his wife; he will return and butcher her body in Manchester at the end of the housewarming party, a few days later. He will sally forth, looking for a victim in a new spot, Sheffield, the day after the New Year, on January 2, 1981. . . . He battered Yvonne Pearson to death on a Saturday night after having helped his parents move house, and went back Sunday morning to help them finish up and take his mother a small present for her birthday.

The father had set up the pattern of duplicity.

John Sutcliffe had also shown how cunning, how vindictive, he could be when it had turned out that, for the first time in their married life, his wife was being unfaithful to him. He laid a trap for her, exposed her in front of her children, complained bitterly at home and, finally, took his revenge by going to live for three months with a dumb neighbour, Wendy Broughton, whom his wife had befriended.

And he had shown, repeatedly, a taste for what is *damaged*, as well as for the low: in an affair with a mute, when reputedly 'sharing' a crippled woman with his father Arthur Sutcliffe — but also throughout, in his assumption that all women somehow were fair game. It was as if he needed something — somebody, who, by outward tokens, was 'lower' than himself, so he could be reassured as to his own superiority — or was he, himself, crippled emotionally, and did disablement in a woman make him feel comfortable? Beattie reports that John's mother, Ivy, wouldn't speak to his father for years. Perhaps Wendy Broughton's dumbness reminded John of his mother?

Kronos: Devourer/Devoured

He also loved offal.

Now stop. Things are already getting pretty queasy when you start finding something odd about John Sutcliffe's love for disabled women. What if this were simply the sign of a large physicality, a simple, expansive recognition that flesh is flesh is flesh? And what about this bourgeois squeamishness about what is a cheap, tasty, and traditionally working-class, food. Not just working-class, not just English: 'pieds et paquets', trotters and tripe, is a great delicacy in France. My own parents love it. And when Burn quotes John Sutcliffe saying that tripe is a 'beautiful' food, that it tastes like water, that it's lovely with salt and vinegar on it, what grounds have I to draw yet another piece of life into this murderous net?

I'm not the one who is drawing the net. I'm just searching about carefully, fearing to choke, straggling from knot to knot so as not to remain trapped. If the above remark was all there was, I wouldn't make anything of this talk and taste of John Sutcliffe. But there is a *hell* of a lot more provided by Burn again, who is to be congratulated for getting the evidence, though he fails to say what *he* sees in it.

It starts with the grandfather. On page 6 of *Somebody's Husband, Somebody's Son* we have this reminiscence from John Sutcliffe:

> (My grandfather) 'was a great man for tripe and pigs' trotters and best beef sausages, chicklins . . . all stuff like that. . . . He absolutely loved offal. . . .'
>
> . . . . 'when I was a kid, I used to stand at the side of his chair when he was eating . . . all of a sudden he'd look down . . . and say, "Hello, would you like to try a bit of this?" And he'd chop me a lump off. It didn't matter what it was; it were me grandad's dinner; and it were beautiful.
>
> 'And it's stood me in good stead to this day that I can eat *anything* out of a butcher's, be it trotters or be it cow-heel or be it tripe or chicklins — anything at all in the offal line. I *love* it . . . man's food.'

Nothing strange about this: offal, 'man's food', is being associated with the Patriarch, 'big' John 'Willie' Sutcliffe, and the taste passed on through lineal descent, and through initiation, from the tall seated man to the little boy, whose strength will be founded on this. Instead of 'tall seated man' I

was going to say, 'ogre' ('working his way through huge
platefuls of offal' is the way the grandfather is described to us);
and it turns out that might have been the right word. For John
Sutcliffe describes how he tried to console himself, and console
his son for his diminutive size and being bullied. The father tells
the boy he has known a walking-matchstick-man who then
went into the army and turned into an all-in wrestler: 'I
could've eaten him for breakfast when I were at school. Later
on though, he would've made mincemeat out of me'. Again, I
know that this is ordinary talk; but we are confronted with a
case in which the metaphoric turned into the literal. We must
pay attention to what the words 'mean' literally, not
figuratively.

That Peter didn't have the right taste is clear. Neither he, nor
Kathleen, his mother, would eat offal: 'I know Peter were never
very fond. You couldn't sit him down to a plate of cow-heel or
chicklins or owt'. That lack of appreciation of man's food is one
of the many signs of his weakness. 'A right mother's boy from
the word go'.[11] No way could he make 'mincemeat' out of other
men.

The father's language is permeated with metaphors of
eating, or of being eaten. And the Sunday joint, for instance,
was procured from the pet-food horsemeat shop. In a tough
society, where it's 'dog eat dog', where you've only got money
for basic needs, it is normal that language should be 'basic'.
The Sutcliffe men talk of eating, defecating, fucking, drinking:
'I told him to piss off . . . I brayed shit out of him'.[12] Even Carl,
the third son, the other 'mummy's boy', chaster in his speech
than brother Mick, speaks like this to his father. John Sutcliffe's
appetites are more robust, more 'catholic' than most. But a few
episodes put this in quite a different light. It's as if the boundary
between the metaphoric and the figurative were so thin that it
frequently breaks.

Around the time of his setting up house with his wife after his
demob in April 1946, and the birth in June of his 'puny' son
Peter, John Sutcliffe's weight dropped from over fourteen stone
to just nine stone six. He had never been ill before, and none of

the doctors seemed to know what was wrong with him. Finally, round the time of the birth of his second son, Thomas Arthur Sutcliffe, a plump healthy-looking baby, he gave up his job at the bakery where he had worked with apparently no ill effects in the five years before the war (and he'd worked as a cook in the hot kitchens of the merchant navy during the war). That seemed to effect the cure. 'Just as his sickly self had seemed to find its echo in Peter . . . so his renewed sense of well-being seemed to be reflected back at him from Thomas Arthur'.[13] But Thomas Arthur started refusing food and had to be rushed to hospital where he died at three months old and was buried without ceremony in a common grave.

Freud explains how sometimes the child's fear of being 'castrated' by his father becomes displaced into another fear: that of being 'devoured' by the father. And he points out how much that is on the terrain of the old Greek myths: Kronos, the old Titan who had castrated his own father Uranus, devoured his own children to save himself from the self-same fate.

It is difficult, especially in the light of what Freud has shown us, not to read John Sutcliffe's wasting illness as psychosomatic. The man had never been ill before, and baking and cooking jobs had never bothered him. The possible reasons for the illness are numerous and contradictory: how is one to know for sure? But speculation there must be: this is the father, these are the early years of a man whom the media, as if somehow sensing that all this had to do with a 'beast of prey' tearing apart an edible victim, called 'the Ripper'.

It may be that John Sutcliffe found both domesticity and paternity unbearable. He had lived a free bachelor life in the male world of the navy. Now suddenly he was shackled. Perhaps things weren't working out too well with his wife. Perhaps the married state brought him back to his own early years, his parents' marriage, his henpecked and subdued father. To cap it all, his own misery and diminished substance were being reflected back by his first-born. The child's puny size threatened his own masculinity. His loss of weight was the expression of a loss of substance: he was being bled — drained away — devoured — by his son. Or he was imitating his son: we have seen that there was something compulsive, something possibly infantile, in this big man: he imitated his son Mick's stealing in later years; he shared his father's, wanted to share his sons', women. He felt ashamed of his first son's diminutive size, and unconsciously mimicked it.

Or again, perhaps he was jealous of his son, of the amount of notice his wife took of the boy. If he were to be ailing too, then perhaps she would look after him.

He goes on losing weight. His wife is pregnant again. His children are eating him up. That's not what he thinks, that's what his body says. Then he changes his job, turning himself into an unskilled labourer. Let the social tumble become complete, let's stop feeling that the grandfather was Head in a Co-Op where I'm just employed, let's go completely working-class, be relieved at least of the respectability pressure, of the whole family history and memories. Also, by ceasing to be a baker (or a cook), the man ceases to play a nurturing role. He ceases to be a producer of food. Bread, cakes: not the food of real men. Real men eat meat.

He starts feeling better. Domesticity, women's work, has been contained. The new baby is plump. He's alright, and consciously, the man must have been very pleased. And yet, wasn't it satisfying, somewhere, when the baby went and died? The father was in power again, he was the one who lived, who ceased to lose substance: it was the baby whom death took. He had eaten his son in a way and taken his revenge for what the first-born had done to him. The two grandfathers (his own subdued father, Arthur, his wife's dead but religious and respectable father Thomas) were both dead with it. They had been exorcized. And in the one who hung on and lived, Peter, did the second name William, the name of his own grandfather, big John 'Willie', stand him in good stead, see him through, like those scraps of food big John 'Willie' used to hold out to him when he worshipped at his knee by the dining-table?

It is striking that both parents let the baby, Thomas Arthur, be buried without ceremony in a common grave. The common grave one can understand: cheaper for the hard-up, the grief-stricken couple who don't want to have to deal with it all. But without ceremony, when Kathleen is so conscientiously religious? It is as if there was a will to be totally rid of the baby, as if he's made to pay the price for something.

But was Thomas Arthur the only one to pay a price? For Peter comes home from his grandmother's at that point. And still the boy, who is now about 18 months old, won't walk.

John Sutcliffe tells Burn that 'of course' he 'understood that it wasn't the lad's fault that he had been born that way'.[14] That he, the father, was very 'gentle' with the boy. Went and bought his son special boots that did the trick, got the lad on his feet. By this time Kathleen Sutcliffe was expecting her third child.

John Sutcliffe seems to me here to be indulging in his desire to project a respectable image, no doubt sensing that the smart London journalist will like the admirable toleration and capacity to cope that he claims to have evinced. But is there no gap in that story? Consider the evidence: John Sutcliffe, ill from a never explained wasting disease, still grieving for the dead baby (or so he thought), his wife probably worn out by all the sorrow and a third pregnancy, has his failure as a father doubly rubbed in. The healthy son dies; the other one won't walk. And the survivor goes on clinging to his mummy's skirts. Spoiled by his grandma too. Did he, John Sutcliffe, who at three found his own way to school over the moors, his mum hard, never there, did he ever have the chance to hang onto his mother's skirt? No, he fended for himself, he did. The man is, by all admissions, not gifted with the sweetest of tempers: Carl claims that they were all frightened of him:

> 'He were like a monster. He were never in the house, but when he was he ruled the roost. When he came in drunk we'd all sit there in fear; you didn't move. . . . Oh Christ he had a foul temper. I seen Maureen get a beating off him when she was almost fifteen, an' once he beat me black and blue when I was a kid. . . .'[15]

What I'm getting at is that far from having been gentle and understanding, John Sutcliffe may well have gone into a terrible rage. Consider what followed. With the help of the specially reinforced boots, the child learns to walk. But he goes on for years, as if for refuge, hiding in his mother's skirts. And he who was an early, a good talker, who perhaps had learned to talk while he was at the grandmother's, develops a grave speech defect. He begins to stammer. It'll take him years to conquer this speech defect. He'll have to articulate slowly, deliberately. Otherwise he trips over his words.

There is a precise model for the violent scene between father and baby son which I suggest happened in this case. That of Freud's Rat Man, as recounted in one of the case studies. During a violent scene between the 3 or 4 year old child and his father, the child, who is being beaten, hurls all the words of his meagre vocabulary at his father, as if they were insults: 'Table! Chair!' The child's violence is such that it not only scares the father, who stops beating him — but it scares him too. Hereafter he will always repress his own aggression, turn it inwards.

The grown-up behaviour of the Rat Man — his gentleness and shyness, his fear of women, his latent homosexuality, as well as his misinterpretations and misreadings, the way he trips over his own acts, bears a strong resemblance to Sutcliffe's. Also, his language suffered a shipwreck, as Sutcliffe's tongue had done. The great difference is that the Rat Man's aggression remains turned inwards. He becomes a neurotic. Freud would say that relations between the Ego and Id are disturbed in his case, whereas Sutcliffe is driven by psychosis. It is the relations between the self and the world, his very relation to reality that is shipwrecked. An initial trauma may have been made worse by the episodes already discussed — the persecutions at school, the demand that he be both virile and respectable. Is it credible that someone who had shown no capacity for aggression whatsoever in his first fourteen years would become capable of such horrendous violence later? Isn't it more likely that his considerable capacity for aggression was so paralyzed by some violent scene, a scene such as that I have suggested, that it ceased to function for years, that the child stored up the violence to which he was the victim until the recoil of the charge became boundless? How else does one explain the stuttering speech of one who started life as a 'good talker'?

In all respects, in terms of his own double personality, of the violence and puerility of his own need to assert his virility, of his repressive and subversive attitude to marriage and home, the father had been a disastrous model for, and influence upon, his son.

Peter Sutcliffe will only start killing after his own marriage, and after his wife has had a miscarriage. Domesticity and faltering paternity, which had been so problematic for the father, will trigger murderousness in the son. Is it in the absence of a son to devour that women in such situations become the victims?

Seven

The Construction of Masculinity
II.   'Peer Groups'

'Laddish Pranks'

'Women are for frying bacon and for screwin', a line which
Mick and his friend Jack would 'chuckle over while buying the
big sticks of pink seaside rock known as 'wife-beaters' to take
home.

Multiple anecdotes and descriptions, in the four books
written about the Ripper case, portray a society in which
contempt for women, and violence to women, are the norm.

It is as if John Sutcliffe's sons had taken on, and exaggerated,
opposite sides of his personality. Peter and Carl were the
secretive ones. Mick comes out of all accounts as a coarser,
rougher and franker version of his father. He had a taste for the
outdoors, the hills and moors where the father had spent
happily-remembered early years. He kept all kinds of dogs,
terriers especially; ferrets too, in the bedroom and even in the
bed he shared with Peter. Ready always to go out shooting and
poaching at dawn, but enjoying in the meantime the nasty
surprises he could spring on timorous Peter, who didn't like
animals. One can imagine the kind of harassment Peter must
have suffered at the hands of his ebullient little brother, the
main representative of laddish values in life. Mick had no
compunction about bullying his way past his elder. He boasts

to Burn that he 'felled' Peter one day as they were both racing to their dinner. He also had a precocious zest for all illegal activities. Besides theft and burglary he relished pilfering from the council tip. He loved all kinds of fights ('once you get him down, make sure he stays that way. Use your feet, use anything you've got to keep him there').[1] Boxing and, above all, laddish pranks.

Mick seems to have set up a kind of standard for his stripling of an eldest brother to emulate. He reinforced the macho image of the father, and Peter, once the bullworker had given him power, set out to imitate what his model did — with something like secret resentment perhaps. There is the story that he punched a man, who was taunting him on a racecourse, so hard that he sent him flying over the barrier, while Mick was there. It is as if Peter was having his revenge for all the years of harassment: he 'fells' somebody else. He also seems to have enjoyed a kind of delayed adolescence in the same period. The pally atmosphere that prevailed among the gravediggers at Bingley cemetery provided Peter with something like a peer group for the first time in his life. He learns to play pranks with them, and with Mick. Suddenly, it's an explosion of pranks. Peter becomes known for his acute sense of humour.

The boy who had been mocked at the Secondary Modern School now pursues screaming girls from the neighbouring Grammar School with bones he's dug up. He even goes further: he hits an old guy, Bishop, who had befriended him at first, but whom it turns out everyone is rather contemptuous of, with a mallet. He hangs starlings by their claws from the clothesline at home, where Mick at times pegs rabbits' skins to dry, cracking a joke about 'dead men's grip'.

He may be terrified the first time he comes up with a skull. He soon gets used to it. He impresses his pals, Laurie Ashton and Eric Robinson, by his cool nerve and wit. He jumps on to a coffin, which makes the corpse sit up, and plays the ventriloquist with it. Wipes his hands on a corpse before digging into his lunchtime sandwiches. He goes one better than Mick. Mick 'combs' the council rubbish tip: Peter takes rings

from the corpses and sells them. He even offers one to his sister
Maureen, about to become engaged. He earns extra money at
the morgue, dealing with the victims of nasty car crashes. He
pulls a big one on Mick, smuggles him one night into the
mortuary with his key, to stare at one of the bodies. Mick is the
first to lose his nerve and leave. Little Peter has indeed become
big brother. He's also learning how pranks can help you take
your revenge, again by displacement. He hurls a 10-year-old
girl, the sister of one of his sister's friends, down the top of the
stairs at home. When she looks up, totally surprised and with
fortunately nothing broken, she sees Peter on the landing, with
a sick grin on his face. The most direct revenge is exacted from
the body of a woman judge. Peter had developed a habit of
running his vehicles illegally (in what looks like an imitation of
the father's aberrant lapses, of Mick's systematic breaking of
the law): never licensing them, speeding, etc. He had been
convicted once by a woman magistrate. Now he gets hold of the
dead body of another woman magistrate, shaking it and boasting she would never sentence anyone else, 'bitch' that she was.[2]

These anecdotes come from various sources, and may not all
be true. Even supposing them to have been exaggerated, some
of them even invented by Peter's gravedigger friends to please
the journalists paying for them, they are still revealing of the
kind of things Peter did, as well as of what passes for humour in
that world — let us not be too contemptuous, their like will
probably bury us all. They also show how a pattern was
becoming established, whereby through the medium of
something called 'joke', an actual act of violence might be
performed. Hatred, rebellion against the social order, become
legitimate. The male code permits him to hurt and even wound
(old Bishop), provided it is disguised by play. 'We are less
ready to find fault with a thought, if it has made us laugh'.[3] The
same applies to deeds.

What the 'code' expresses is not just aggression between
males, it's the permissibility of aggression against females,
provided consensus (that they're somehow sub-human) or a
witty twist has first blanketed the fact that, being weaker, they

shouldn't be fair game in a contest for maleness. You can throw a little girl down the stairs because it's for a laugh and she's only a silly kid, anyway. You can threaten Grammar School girls because they're priviledged 'stuck up' bitches. You can desecrate the body of a woman because it's a bold prank and you need a bit of humour in this job otherwise you couldn't stand it — but also because a magistrate is a representative of that repressive order that Sutcliffe and his friends have (rightly or wrongly) a grouse against, and Sutcliffe is venting communally felt resentment when he taunts her. '. . . If we look at the joke, we observe that an impulse that is ordinarily controlled and, indeed, does not even seem to be particularly clamorous for discharge, is deliberately afforded release'.[4] Doesn't Society prefer to allow working-class youths to vent violence that way — a way that won't rock any boats — to their being subversive? Better laddish pranks than riots — or a strike?

Sutcliffe's integration into the male world by means of communally shared laughs makes pranks of particular importance to him: when he indulges in one of these, the 'boys' are *with* him. And that is a conviction he'll take into his killings. Twice he goes out armed with a sockful of gravel, or a brick in a sock for a weapon, to attack a woman, while his friend Trevor Birdsall is in the car. Trevor waits for him. Trevor doesn't think much of it. The lad's a bit bold, that's all. Another friend, Ronald Barker, says that Sutcliffe used to invite him (and his brother) to go and give it to 'one of the old bags' in Lumb Lane, one of Bradford's red-light districts. He finds this more or less normal: it's a prank. You kick instead of paying. Doesn't everybody laugh when you buy a piece of sea-rock, and call it 'the wife-beater'? The whole atmosphere is so permeated with an idea that violence to women is OK given some rules, of which a laugh is one, that none of Sutcliffe's gravedigger friends, who have such clear memories (however refreshed by money they may be) of their mate's old jokes, seems to have even envisaged the possibility that he might be the Ripper.

What Hamlet Sees

The play-acting in the joke conceals the literal violence of what is being done. It also permits it.

That violence is shared, either by the immediate audience, or by an 'ideal' one. Even when, in the family circle, Sutcliffe laughs more than anybody else at his own jokes, he is laughing with imagined listeners. The joke is 'the most social of all the mental functions that aim at a yield of pleasure'.[5]

For instance, there is a social and an anthropological history underlying John Sutcliffe's remarks about offal, his grandfather, and it's being 'man's food'. To him it represented man's power, both social — the desk at the top of the office — and domestic — the patriarch at the head of the dining table.

Meat-eating: classifications of the different cuts of the beast. Squeamish people like me like eating muscle, but not organs (kidneys, hearts, lungs, brains, liver, etc). Perhaps organs are uncomfortably recognizable, personalized — the same as the organs in our own bodies. We're reminded of cannibalism. Taboos. Bataille says that the eye is the 'cannibalistic titbit'. That if one eats it, one is breaking the supreme taboo. Writing this, I've suddenly remembered how a flamboyantly macho uncle of mine used to eat the eyes of fish, saying they were 'the best'.[7] Tripe, though an organ, seems to be a category apart. The revulsion must be on account of their being intestines: bags of shit. The link with defecation and decomposition, with images of maggots, is too powerful a reminder of death for most of us.

Mick, the macho one, used to hang his game till maggots bred on it. Chitterling is cheap, since there isn't much demand for it: that makes it a working-class food. There is, as I have said, a social as well as an anthropological history to all tastes for food.

John Sutcliffe's love of offal is meant to show that a real man will eat even what puts most people off. In a way he dared to eat death. He also dared to eat men: 'make mincemeat out of them'. And all the men around dare to 'eat' women. A girl is reported to have offered herself 'for breakfast' on Peter's and Keith's kitchen-table. 'Felling' a man, and 'fucking' a woman (no other word seems appropriate) are equivalent to eating them up. And not a morsel left. You'll even have an appetite for more, since you've only had them 'for breakfast'. The consumption is wholesale.

But the figurative (which is not as figurative as it sounds, given the violence) can slip, by means of jokes, into literalness. Thus Mick's friend Jack sent to a man, as a 'present' from a prostitute the man had rather fallen for, a . . . bag of animal guts.[8]

As 'language', an overt message, you could translate this as: 'if you can go with that one, you've got a strong stomach'; or, 'let her be; she's not worth your attention; she's only a bag of guts'. And everyone laughs because the man's 'base' taste has been exposed. If you're a real man, you're not going to fall for a tart. You may be promiscuous yourself, but promiscuity is not acceptable in a woman. But there are more savage, more literal meanings here as well. Guts are 'a bag of shit'; our prostitute is 'nothing but a bag of shit', totally despicable, the lowest of the low. The substitution of a parcel of guts for a 'present' from the woman shows her up for what she 'really' is: not human, just matter, the most 'mortal' piece of flesh, from a dead beast as well. Women are, in the language of that male world, continuously associated with shit. 'A right mummy's boy, as soft as shit', John Sutcliffe complains of his son Carl.[9] The parcel of guts further implies that the prostitute is not a person to be loved, from whom presents could count. It is also a way of denying that femininity exists, that there is such a thing as female genitalia. It is an *anal* joke (yet another displacement). For you don't go to a prostitute for her guts — unless you want buggery, in which case you're again denying or refusing female sexuality — but for her cunt, her womb. The parcel of guts is a way of denying that the prostitute is a woman.

That is also what Sutcliffe's attacks against prostitutes will mean: having a go at 'one of the bags' is simply like kicking a ball. A game. A prank.[10]

Jack's 'present' speaks without words: it is the package, and the whole context, that 'speak'. However, some of Sutcliffe's jokes at that period already speak without words: the starlings on the clothesline are a savage parody of domesticity. He turns the paraphernalia of laundering, of which Sutcliffe is so respectful normally (he does his own washing), into a mortuary: the birds upside down like shirts, their stiff claws made into pegs. Death and witty display show them up for what they 'really' are. The same will be done to prostitutes later by 'the streetcleaner'. The carefully packaged bodies will be meant to show Society how obscene these women 'really' are. That same society had provided the values, and the codes.

There is an aspect of laughter which is evil. At times you laugh because you have a sense of superiority over the object of your laughter. You laugh because you no longer perceive who you're laughing at as human; but you are (human); you relish your own immunity from the harm that is befalling these puppets. This — presumably — only applies to certain types of jokes[11], but it does apply to Sutcliffe's. When he tells Doreen Sugden about his new job in the graveyard, 'I've a real job. I've five thousand under me and not one of them complains', he's not just fulfilling his father's dream of the grandfather at his top desk with all these quiet girls under him. No, he, a weak man, until then the underdog, has at last found that he can be 'above' others, and is revelling in the thought.

His taste for dead and damaged bodies will extend later to the horror rooms in Morecambe's Wax Museum. One of these is an exhibition of Victorian gynaecological wax models of women's torsoes. The womb, and its month by month growing foetus, are shown open to represent the stages of pregnancy. Burn, who discovered this macabre taste of Sutcliffe's, makes much of it, calling the section that describes the murdering period Peter's 'Room', as if the man had been a Victorian collector of horrors — a replica of his namesake, Jack the Ripper, who is thought to have been a surgeon. I don't see this in the same terms. The 'room' certainly didn't constitute a primary motivation. Sutcliffe had already begun to kill when he found the museum. The gruesome models may have provided further visual fuel. They may have been a vindictive solace to Sonia's failure to have a baby ('it's so horrible anyway'). They did not *produce* the murderousness. The fascination strikes me as an extreme form of the father's love of offal. *Because* you're not frightened to stare death in the face — in the belly rather — of consuming it — *because* death and corruption are what people feel most repelled by, then you, who dare be intimate with it, who dare 'eat it' (as Hamlet's beggar eats the fish that ate the worm that ate the king), prove that you are a real man. Sutcliffe may be ashamed of his own body, embarrassed by the smell of his own feet. He may be modest, shy of girls. But he demonstrates that he's even more manly than other men, than his pals, than sturdy Mick: he'll spend more time than anyone else in the Chapel of Ease, in the horror rooms. In his relish at discovering his ability to cope with death, Sutcliffe begins to revel in mastery. Mastery over the great Taboo. He is Superman, the Transgressor. He can go further. He can 'play' with corpses, he dare humiliate the dead. Thus he defies Death. He also realizes that Society allows you to be a man by standing over someone who is dead. There are deviant, secret routes to masculinity. Exhilarating too, because they are such a release from a long nightmare of fear and persecutions and taunting and teasing at the hands of the strong. Thebes has been delivered from its plague. Sutcliffe at last can become King. The voice from the grave tells him he's been *chosen*.

He laughs his 'silly giggle'. Even when he chuckles, his own femininity gives him away.

A *scandalous* equation allows someone like Sutcliffe to substitute a *dead* person for a living adversary. Is it because we're so frightened of death? We banish our sick and our dead to hospitals and morgues, we leave them in the hands of our undertakers and gravediggers. We clean our cities of what scares us, thus opening the way for other forms of 'streetcleaning'.

The equation makes the dead as dangerous as a bully. Therefore it is not cowardly to attack them.

Similarly, some day, if it were revealed to you that prostitutes are neither human beings nor women — that they are litter, the dregs of the earth, a 'plague' upon the city — then it will not seem base to exterminate them. You knew this anyway: doesn't the joke with the parcel of guts show it? Everybody knows this. If people object, it's because they don't understand. This is what Peter Sutcliffe believes to this day.

This ultimate substitution has not, however, yet occurred. Sutcliffe has not killed. And there is no telling but that, had he grown up in a less violent and damaged family, or had he had other forms of release, he might have left it at that.

Homosexuality might have been such a release.

Eight

The Taboo of Homosexuality

> 'Paranoia is defined in Freudian psychoanalysis . . .
> as a defence against homosexuality'.
>
> Laplanche and Pontalis
> *The Language of Psychoanalysis*

There are clear indications of homosexual tendencies in Sutcliffe. I'm not just thinking of his lack of interest in girls and of his own girlish temperament. But his friendships with men often take on a passionate character; and he seemed to be most attracted to men who were similar to himself. His friend Trevor, for instance, self-effacing and shy, cissified, weak, and who, on account of a heart condition, had been rather fussed over by his mother.

Being to a greater or lesser extent 'mother's boys', in fact, is something that Keith Sugden would retrospectively identify as the characteristic linking most of Peter's friends, not excluding himself. 'Trevor Birdsall, Eric Robinson, Richard Varley, Patrick Slater, me and Pete — we were all more or less dominated by our mothers. It seems as if he were drawn to people with something missing in their make-up like that'.[1]

Peter spent a great deal of time around twenty with that same Keith Sugden, whom his mother liked as a gentler and more considerate friend than any of the others. So close were they, and so admiring was Peter's gaze when Keith played the guitar (which Trevor Birdsall also did) that Keith used to be asked how his 'boy-friend' was. Half-men both, they had similar tastes: they would drink a bottle of light ale when the standard manly order was for a pint; they liked the same type of music, were both shy with girls. Sutcliffe, by all accounts, was extremely upset when Keith got engaged to his future wife Doreen. He is reported to have done everything in his power to break up the engagement, including organizing a party with good-time girls to make Doreen jealous. 'There was a time when I used to think that Peter was in love with Keith', Doreen Sugden is reported to have said. Similar types of friendship later grew with Laurie Ashton and Eric Robinson — they formed an odd three-some — and later still Trevor Birdsall, who Sutcliffe would spend hours talking to in the car when he'd seen him home to his wife.

The friendships never grew into more than friendships, largely, it seems to me, because the taboo on homosexuality in this environment was so complete — and on anything that savoured of feminine ways. Any man who wore an earring could expect to have it ripped out and the lobe daubed in whisky for 'healing'.[2] The way John Sutcliffe assures Burn, his interviewer, that Peter had 'no affectations whatsoever' is so keen you get the impression the man had much rather have a multiple murderer than a 'puff' for a son:

> ... It never occurred to John Sutcliffe that Peter — or any son of his — could turn out to be any less than 100-per-cent 'normal' (or a 'puff', 'bum boy' or 'bender' as homosexuals are invariably called in Bingley).[2]

Sutcliffe's occasional bouts of aggression may give the measure of the intensity of his repressed desires. Steve Close, a friend he'd gone camping with, tells how viciously Sutcliffe attacked him after he had made a sexual joke. ' "I'm going to cut your dick off, you bastard!" . . . . It was only when he slashed my private parts that he calmed down'.[4]

That the taboo should be so great on feminine tendencies, so little on violence, gives a terrifying measure of the scale of values present. Femininity is bottom — and meant to stay bottom wherever it may be traced. That is what killed, more than anything else.

A question immediately arises here. Did Sutcliffe's feminine or homosexual tendencies then predispose him to murder? For Havelock Ellis, in his *Studies in The Psychology of Sex*, suggests that this is often the case. Discussing the feminine features he sees in the Marquis de Sade's personality, he claims that 'the most extreme and elaborate forms of sadism . . . are most apt to be allied with a somewhat feminine organization':

> I have noted some of the feminine traits in de Sade's temperament and appearance. The same may often be noted in sadists whose crimes were very much more serious and brutal than those of de Sade. A man who stabbed women in the streets of St Louis was a waiter with a high-pitched, effeminate voice and boyish appearance. Reidel, the sadistic murderer, was timid, modest and delicate; he was too shy to urinate in the presence of other people. A sadistic zoöphilist, described by A. Marie, who attempted to strangle a woman fellow-worker, had always been very timid, blushed with much facility, could not look even children in the eyes, or urinate in the presence of another person, or make sexual advances to women.
>
> Kiervan and Moyer are inclined to connect the modesty or timidity of sadists with a disgust for normal coitus[5].

Sutcliffe certainly evinced the same features as the sadists Ellis mentions: the shyness, the fastidiousness — and there might well have been the motive Kiernan and Moyer invoke. But we must beware of calling certain traits 'feminine, as if 'femininity' was a definable 'essence', and then connecting it with cruelty. For this would be simply repeating the pattern that made Sutcliffe kill: what if all these sadists were killing out of hatred for what they saw as the 'femininity' in themselves?

Homosexuality and Paranoia

All this sends us back to where masculinity and femininity become formed: to childhood.

Peter Sutcliffe seems to have refused identification with the father until puberty. Whether that was because of his inborn weakness or because he felt too deep an antagonism to this model of male behaviour, is open to question. I have suggested, with the Rat Man in mind, that violence on the part of the father may have triggered such antagonism. It may also have been that the child wanted to 'identify' with the person who loved and protected him: his mother. Rather than 'Oedipal' desire, he seems to have wanted not to have been 'out' (born?): to have tried to disappear within the camouflage of the mother's skirts. If I was to follow Freud, still remembering the Rat Man, but also thinking of President Schreber, I would have to account for Sutcliffe's homosexual tendencies by a secret desire to seduce the father — by a secret love for the father. Did Sutcliffe 'decide' to 'become a man' so he could at last conquer his father's love? There may be something in that. Something also in the fact that he tried so hard, in later years, to be a good son — and a good brother to his brothers. John Sutcliffe maudlinly complains to Burn that Peter, always considerate and the more so as time went by, ready to oblige, help with a removal, etc, would have been the one he could have relied upon to look after him in his old age.

We have seen what a mess the father was and what potentially schizophrenic elements there were in his make-up. The model of manhood he presented to his sons was split, and we have remarked on how they either took to one or the other side of his character. But the father's incipiently 'double' self was kept within the bounds of neurosis by the strength of his own sexual identity, and the clarity of his choice of class. Peter Sutcliffe, however, was almost pushed into psychosis on account of his inability to fulfil the roles which his world's definition of masculinity demanded of him. It's as if the schizophrenic motif were doubled: only the logic of paranoia could make the act of selfhood stick together.

From under Schreber's two imaginary persecutors — Flechsig and God — Freud's analysis exhumed the figure of the persecuting Oedipal father. Schreber is seen as having displaced the fear originally directed to the father on to the two substitute figures. In Sutcliffe's case, if it is indeed true that, as Freud contends, 'what lies at the core of the conflict in cases of paranoia among males is a homosexual wishful fantasy of loving a man', we would have to reverse what we have been assuming so far — that Sutcliffe 'loved' his mother and 'hated' his father, and suppose that he 'loved' his father instead. We would also have to understand how the 'love' for his father turned into hatred. And how a conscious, though intermittent, hatred for his father could turn into a hatred for prostitutes.

Freud does provide a model when he analyzes the way in which 'the familiar principal forms of paranoia can all be represented as contradictions of the single proposition "I (a man) love him (a man)" '.[6] These forms of paranoia include erotomania, delusions of jealousy, narcissism, regression, and megalomania. All elements which are or will be present in Sutcliffe: he will become obsessed with secretive sex, red-light districts, be jealous of Sonia and his mother. He spent hours as a youth in front of the bathroom mirror; the 'Zapolski' revelation makes him feel 'chosen'. But the most immediately relevant form of paranoia is 'delusions of persecution'. In such delusions, Freud argues, the 'love' for a man ('passive homosexuality') is loudly negated. The reverse is asserted: 'I do not love him — I hate him'. Projection then makes this proposition into yet another: 'He hates (persecutes) me, which will justify me hating him'. It may well be that such a structure applied to Sutcliffe at the time of the graveyard episode, and that later mishaps brought about a transfer of the 'delusion of persecution' from the father to 'prostitutes', perhaps a compound figure of the 'bad mother'. 'Persecuting' prostitutes takes the place of what, for Schreber, is represented by the two 'male' persecutors (Flechsig and God) — while obedience to 'the voice of God' enables Sutcliffe to achieve the homosexual 'desire' that is so impossible in fact.

The figure of the 'bad' mother

The relationship with the mother may well be as complicated as that with the father. Certainly, the youngster's identification with his mother must have added to the strains and contradictions in his life.

The boy sides with his neglected mother, who supports him. All the sons felt that support. 'She'd stick up for you, me mother, even though she might call you a bloody fool after',[7] Mick testifies. 'Me Mum had to buy everything we got', Carl claimed:

> 'She had had a bad heart, she couldn't even walk, but still had to go out cleaning while he (the father) went to pub wi' sixty quid in his pocket. He were always a skinny git with his money. She were always complaining that she never had enough. . . . She were knackered but he never used to give her any help. . . .'[7]

Peter the boy sides, like Carl, with his mother. By temperament he is like her: quiet, patient, self-effacing, stay-at-home, but by cultural necessity — being a boy — he must dissociate himself from a feminity that he sees as impotence, exploitability. Part of him wants to be like his mother and as unlike his father as possible (make a good husband, be respectful of nice girls, be a good citizen). But another part wants to do to her, and to all women, what the father does. The pressure to identify with the father, and the peers, is too strong. How else can you be a man? It's the same impulse that makes the son of a battered mother defend her and hate her for being battered, for being passive. As a male who needs to be potent, to be 'on top', he must dissociate himself from the threatening feminity his heart tells him to support, and his desire to be strong tells him to keep at bay. Just so, Sutcliffe must have wanted to deny the femaleness he found in himself, and deny the mother he loved. Because the femaleness made him the butt of persecution, a foreigner among men. It was *because* he was like his mother, on the side of his ill-treated mother, that he was ill-treated. Hatred against the persecutors — the bullies — turns into hatred against the object of persecution — the mother — who by association makes him like herself.

A complex light is again thrown on these contradictions by Freud's notion of bisexuality (the co-presence within the self of 'male' and 'female', 'active' and 'passive' characteristics).[9] In the case of Schreber, the female element was allowed under the complex disguise of his 'theological' theory. In the case of Sutcliffe, it looks as if the female element was being violently disallowed throughout, made into what has to be hated.

It would make sense to argue, in the face of Sutcliffe's violent assaults (armed with a knife, a screwdriver) on women's abdomens and bellies, also of his 'fetishistic' pushing up of the brassiere of several of his victims, that a deep hatred of the *mother's body* was venting itself (i.e. something in excess of the repressed homosexual tendency). I find Melanie Klein's description of the infant's 'Paranoid-Schizoid Position'[10] most suggestive about this. She stresses the importance of infancy in the fixation of *psychotic* disorders.[11] She argues that the first sources of anxiety are connected with breast-feeding; that breast-feeding initiates an 'object-relation' between the infant and its mother; that in periods of privation or tension, aggressive impulses are reinforced, and that greed (primarily of an *oral* nature) can become so intense as to produce strong destructiveness. This stems from there being 'in the uncon-scious a fear of annihilation of life', the working of the 'death-instinct', which is the source of anxiety.[12]

A child's sense that he is 'persecuted' would in that perspective be the projection of a child's own sadism. Melanie Klein quotes the case of a five-year-old boy who thought he was being threatened by wild animals with fangs, claws, etc. In effect, the child was expressing his 'sense of being threatened by his own destructiveness'. 'The fear of being devoured by the father derives from the projection of the infant's impulses to devour its object. In this way, first the mother's breast (and the mother) becomes in the infant's mind a devouring object'; (as in the case of a girl who thought her mother's shoe would eat her up, or a boy who thought he'd been bitten by his mother's breast); 'and these fears soon extend to the father's penis and to the father'. The child thus internalizes a 'good breast' (gratifying) and a 'bad breast' (frustrating). The splitting results in a severance of love and hate. Processes are formed that prepare the ground for the onset of the Oedipus complex.

The 'destructive impulse' (which is what concerns us in relation to Sutcliffe)

> is turned against the object and is first expressed in fantasized oral-sadistic attacks on the mother's breast, which soon develop into onslaughts on her body by all sadistic means. The persecutory fears arising from the infant's oral-sadistic impulses to rob the mother's body of its good contents, and from the anal-sadistic impulses to put his excrements into her (including the desire to enter her body in order to control her from within) are of great importance for the development of paranoia and schizophrenia.[13]

This could be read in relation to Sutcliffe not just in the terms posited by Melanie Klein (the infant stage) but in terms of Sutcliffe's later boyhood, youth — and manhood, in which indeed the infantile, regressive element is so strong (down to his having developed a taste for boyish pranks between eighteen and twenty, when most adolescent boys go through that stage so much earlier). There seems to me to be something regressive as well in the repetitiveness of the attacks.

'Frustration' and anxiety in relation to the breast, the mother's body, may well have existed in the puny child who started life separated from his mother by an incubator, remained a weakling (a poor eater), and whom the birth of a little brother, Thomas Arthur, banned to the grandmother's house temporarily. The reluctance to walk, the attempt to disappear into the mother's skirts, into corners, burrows, which I've tried to account for as a feminine, passive tendency or the desire not to have been born, could also be seen as what Melanie Klein calls the 'desire to enter (the mother's) body in order to control her from within'. Acute anxiety, fear perhaps of his own aggressiveness which I've already presented in terms of the Rat Man, may well explain the child's inability to confront the world, to get out. Conversely, the way in which that inability exposes him to persecutions at school, marks him out as a mummy's boy, may have led to a projection of the figure of the persecutor on to the mother. The 'bad breast', the 'bad womb', threaten him, want to castrate him, keep him in. He wants to stay in; he knows he can't. It would not be too far-fetched to interpret the inchoate, the 'semiotic' nature of Sutcliffe's hallucination in Bingley cemetery as also the voice of the mother — the 'good one', who will later point out to him the 'bad' ones, the ones to be lacerated, into whom to 'put his excrements'.

All of this may be right; or part of it. What is staggering is that you can make sense of Sutcliffe whether you follow the Freudian paranoiac model, or the Kleinian model. It is nearly as if things made too much sense, or made sense too easily. It may be because crime brings out basic psychic structures, being so extreme; or because crime has to do with excess of meaning.

What seems to be the case, at any rate, is that, by the time he is working as a gravedigger in Bingley, something in Sutcliffe fundamentally hates women; that hatred is self-hatred, hatred for his own weakness; and he does not know this.

At the same time, his love for his mother is the cornerstone of his fragile identity. His mother is good. His mother is an Angel. She is the centre of the house. He will get a girl like her, and his mother is pleased when he, at last, introduces a 'nice' girl into the family. 'This is Sonia'. On the solidity and lovability of these two women — the mother, the wife-to-be — he relies to see him through.

Nine

The Triple Catastrophe

I return to Sutcliffe's testimony on 11 May 1981.

Sutcliffe met Sonia on St Valentine's Day, 1967, when she was sixteen and attending Grange Grammar School, Bradford. They used to meet at weekends in Bradford, though not at her house. He did not go there for the first few months. He was not interested in prostitutes and had never gone to a red-light district. He and Sonia were happy. Then Sonia left school to go to Bradford Technical College to do A-levels, and this was where she became involved with another man. Sutcliffe was told about this by his brother: Mick, specifically. According to Burn, Mick very much enjoyed breaking to his brother the news that he had seen Sonia 'in a fuckin' sportscar with a feller'.[1]

'I was working on contract with the waterworks and had an assistant with me who did not understand very much about the workings of the job. I had arranged to leave early that day to catch Sonia coming out of the Tech.' The man concerned had taken advantage of the fact that he could not meet her during the week.

'I wanted to catch her before she got home and before she got into his company again. . . . I left early and unfortunately there was a disaster at the

waterworks which nearly drowned several men,
through the assistant. I was blamed for that,
although they said I could leave at the time
suggested. I caught Sonia going down the road. I
approached her but she walked the other way as if
shocked to see me, so I knew what I had heard was
true'.

They argued all the way home. When they parted, nothing had
been settled. At work, Sutcliffe had to go to the head office for a
meeting with the waterworks chief, and was demoted. A state of
depression ensued, which might also have had to do with the
sequel of a motorbike accident in '65 or '66. (Sutcliffe's
relations say they remember no such accident). It took six
months before the difficulty with Sonia was solved, and she
gave him her word that she was not going to see the other man
any more.

The depression during that period led to Sutcliffe's first
encounter with a prostitute. He could only see Sonia at
weekends. The other man (reportedly an Italian ice-cream
vendor) was meeting her two or three times a week. Sutcliffe
'didn't know where (he) stood at all'. He was blaming Sonia all
the time, suspecting that 'the relationship with the other man
. . . was not just platonic'. 'He didn't want to blame her', and
thought his only way out was to do it himself. By that time he
knew there were prostitutes operating in Manningham Lane,
Bradford. He'd seen them 'blatantly along the road'. So he
decided to approach one:

'We were on the way to her place and were talking
and I realized what a coarse and vulgar person she
was. By this time we were practically there and I
realized I didn't want anything to do with her.

'Before getting out of the car I was trying to wriggle
out of the situation, but I felt stupid as well. We went
into the house and when she got into the bedroom,
she started taking her clothes off. She had told me it
was £5 and when we were in the car I gave her a £10

note. She had told me that when we got to her place
she was going to change it. (So I asked her) if she was
going to change it. She said "No" without looking at
me. I said to her: "We'll call it off then", because I
was only too glad to call it off. She said she didn't want
to call it off and said we could get the note changed at
the garage where I picked her up.

'We went back to the garage by car and she went
inside and there were two chaps in there. I don't
know whether she did this regularly, but she
wouldn't come back out. One of the men came
banging on the car roof when I refused to go away
and the other one escorted her away. There wasn't
much I could do about it, but I was a bit annoyed
and drove off.'

It was not because he was 'out of pocket' and 'nothing to show
for it' that Sutcliffe felt annoyed, but because he had wanted to
'resolve the situation with Sonia and hadn't done it'. That, and
having been 'involved with someone like that' had made him
feel worse than ever. Up to that point, he had never had any
desire to harm prostitutes, but the incident changed his
attitude towards them. He started receiving messages that gave
him reassurance, brought him round from his deep state of
depression. There were hundreds of messages. They kept
saying that Sutcliffe 'had got to go on with a mission', and the
purpose of it was 'to remove the prostitutes. To get rid of them'.
The depression had had to do with Sonia's involvement with
the Italian and the incident with the prostitute. Now 'the voice
of God' was saying 'it was prostitutes who were responsible for
all these problems'.

Two or three weeks later, Sutcliffe saw the same prostitute in
a Bradford public house. She was with another woman, also a
prostitute. They were talking to men. Sutcliffe approached the
one he'd been with and told her that he hadn't forgotten, but
she 'could put things right so that there would be no hard
feelings':

'She thought this was a huge joke and, as luck would have it, she knew everyone else in the place and went round telling them all about the incident. Before I knew what was happening, most of the people were having a good laugh.

'I was giving her the opportunity to put things right and give back the payment I had made to her.'

The 'voice' started again later, when Sutcliffe was thinking 'all kinds of things about Sonia, perhaps not reasonable things to think about an innocent person': he was thinking that Sonia was a prostitute as well, but he had 'reassurances that she wasn't and that she was a good girl'. The voices were telling him that 'prostitutes were responsible for all the trouble'. The two were connected: the need for reassurances about Sonia's innocence meant it was the fault of the prostitutes.

Some time between one and four weeks after the visit to the pub, Sutcliffe attacked a prostitute in Manningham Lane with a sock filled with gravel. He was with his friend Trevor Birdsall. He wanted to kill the woman because he had been told that prostitutes 'were the scum of the earth and had to be got rid of'. He had known the woman was a prostitute because 'she was walking slowly along the kerb, looking at cars across the road'. The force of the impact tore the toe off the sock and its contents had spilled out. The police had spoken to him about the incident but no charges had been brought. He had also been convicted in October 1969 after he had been found equipped for theft. He had a hammer in his car and had assaulted a prostitute. The fact that the woman who had been attacked by Sutcliffe had not pressed charges had been perceived by him as a sign of his divine mission: 'I felt I was not meant to be caught or punished.'

Giving evidence, Sutcliffe claimed he had taken no interest in the activities of prostitutes during the period 1969 to 1975. It was at the end of this period that he married Sonia. In the meantime, he had gone on suffering from depression. He had moved to London for a year, while Sonia was at the Macmillan

Teacher's Training College in Deptford, then they both returned to Bradford. Sonia had had a nervous breakdown, and had been hospitalized, suffering at least one relapse. 'She just looked grey. She looked terrible. She was taking tablets and started to put on a great deal of weight. . . . She had lost her personality altogether'. That was over when they got married in 1974.

They were living at Sonia's parents' home and that had been difficult. He wanted to move, but Sonia's mother had insisted they stay to save money so they could buy their own house. That was when he had renewed his attacks. Again he was out with Trevor Birdsall. He had seen Olive Smelt in a pub in Halifax, had told Trevor she was a prostitute (she was not), had got out, followed her down the street, and hit her. 'She fell down. I was going to kill her. I had the knife with me at the time. I was going to kill her but I did not get the chance'. Earlier that night he had had strong feelings that he must kill a prostitute. 'Consequently I did it with Trevor still in the car. I knew that was my mission.'

He had been unable to stop himself each time, for 'it was God who was controlling me':

> 'Before doing it I had to go through a terrible stage each time. I was in absolute turmoil, I was doing everything I could to fight it off, and asked why it should be me, until I eventually reached the stage when it was as if I was primed to do it'.

Dr. Hugo Milne, the psychiatrist who had spent the longest time examining Sutcliffe while he was in Armley Jail, was on the stand for three days as a defence witness. He explained in detail what symptoms had led him to establish his diagnosis that Sutcliffe was 'suffering from schizophrenia of the paranoid type'. The great difficulty, he admitted, was that 'what the individual says is very often the symptom, is in fact the sign of the schizophrenic disorder'.[2] It was this — the fact that the only real evidence was what Sutcliffe *said* about himself — that he had successfully concealed his mental disease from his family

THE TRIPLE CATASTROPHE   115

for 15 years — that gave the Crown their opening, enabling them to argue that the whole defence case rested on subjectivity — on the telling of lies.

The 'symptoms', however, were numerous, according to Dr. Milne,[3] 'suspicion, an uncontrollable impulse and paranoia concerning prostitutes'; 'preoccupation with prostitutes to the extent of delusion' (phrases like their being 'the scum of the earth' and their being 'responsible for all sorts of problems'); ideas 'of grandeur with special powers'; 'hallucinosis'; 'feelings of depression'; 'misinterpretation of that which is either written, spoken or demonstrated'; 'misidentification' (eg thinking that women who were not prostitutes were prostitutes — like Olive Smelt); 'over-controlled behaviour' (remaining calm in the most stressful circumstances); 'psychotic detachment' (splitting himself from the enormity of what he had done); 'lack of insight'; 'thought argument' (arguing in his head with the voice); 'religious delusions'. Having a 'primary schizophrenic experience' (presumably the first message from 'God') was 'the most crucial symptom in the diagnosis of schizophrenia.'

Dr. Milne's diagnosis was corroborated by other psychiatrists. Dr. MacCulloch said that Sutcliffe had four of the eight first-rank signs that indicated paranoid schizophrenia: bodily hallucinations; influence of thought; delusional perception; passivity (thinking he was controlled by someone else). He also thought he could read the thoughts of his victims. Dr MacCulloch told the court: 'I have considered the alternative diagnosis of personality disorder involving sexual abnormality and sadism, but there appears to be no evidence of this'.[4]

Well, the doctors had it right, didn't they? Everything they said at the trial is recognizable in terms of what we have seen about Sutcliffe's 'primary' experience, of what he said in Court about prostitutes, and of the complex damage the man had suffered at the hands of his social environment and family. But listing it all as classified symptoms (four out of eight) may make it possible to slot Sutcliffe into a known category of 'sick irresponsible' criminals.[5] It further erases the connection there may be between Sutcliffe and the rest of us. It disposes of the whole question, thus simply reinforcing the type of mechanism that *produces* the likes of Sutcliffe. Shove the mad aside, into the 'loony bin', as you shove aside the sick and the dead. Thus you revive the terror of death, of disease, of 'abnormality'; and the man who proves to be above those terrors will think Society is *with* him when he cleanses the streets.

So there is no alternative to trying to see what happened to Sutcliffe, and what that meant, in lay terms— but terms that posit that there is a sense there somewhere — that a subject, somewhere, speaks.

Since the whole case revolved around how much Sutcliffe lied, it is worth noting when he obviously did. The Attorney General made Sutcliffe confess that after the first prostitute had laughed at him with her friends at the pub, he was a lot more than 'annoyed':

> Sir Michael: After you began to hate prostitutes. . .
> S: No, I do not hate prostitutes.
> Sir Michael: But you were pretty cross, especially after she taunted you — you came out frustrated and tormented?
> S: — Yes.
> Sir Michael: Humiliated, outraged and embarrassed?
> S: That is what I said.[6]

It is easy to imagine the pitch of rage in which Sutcliffe must have been, remembering the attack on Steve Close, the felling of the man on the race course, and other anecdotes like the one in which Sutcliffe crashed his beer mug on to a pub table, sending liquid and glass splinters all over the room.

Another major lie: Sutcliffe claims that between 1969 and 1975 he did not go to prostitutes any more. But there are overwhelming testimonies from his brothers, brothers-in-law, friends and work mates, that he did and that in fact he was obsessed by them.[7] How indeed would he otherwise have

known so intimately the geography of the red-light districts, of
Leeds and Bradford especially? How much he actually 'went'
with prostitutes is not known; perhaps not very much at all.
Still, there are stories, in Burn and Cross and Beattie, that he at
least once, perhaps twice, caught 'something' that made him
have to go to hospital for treatment. If that is so, it adds a
further motivation for the zealous hatred expressed by the
'streetcleaner', for this meticulous man's sense that prostitutes
are responsible for all evil. A motivation that would have found
further sources of support in the grisly illustrations of venereal
diseases among the wax figures of Morecambe's second
Victorian horror room. The 'Museum of Anatomy' illustrates,
as a sign says, 'the awful results of men leading immoral lives...
Male sexual organs in varying degrees of rottenness. . . .'[8] and
female organs or statues likewise. 'Off one of 'em mucky
bitches' is what Peter is reported to have told Keith Sugden
who was asking him where he'd caught 'it':[9] disgust at his own
'uncleanness' being projected onto the whole prostitute
population.

The lies fall into a pattern. Sutcliffe wants to project onto the
Court the image of the conscious, socially well-meaning self
he systematically cultivated: that of a nice young man, polite,
considerate. The gap between his language and that of his
father and brothers by itself testifies to the good persona he was
aspiring to — the 'good person' aspect was certainly trying very
hard to come into prominence. He is not denying that he did
commit the murders, not denying the violence of his attacks —
but he claims he was only 'annoyed' (a proper word), and that
he didn't normally have anything to do with 'coarse and vulgar
persons'. But the events he narrates are in my opinion too
congruent, too significant, not to be true.

Given all that we have seen so far, it is easy to imagine how
appalling Sonia's reported infidelity must have been to him. At
last he had found something like sexual identity. At last he had
a girl-friend, and she was 'good' — like his own mother. She
was the living proof that he belonged to a better world than
Mick, who would, in Carl's words, 'fuck a pig in knickers . . .

(fuck) anything that moves'. And that same Mick gloatingly tells him that his oh so superior girl-friend is having a good time with a fellow in a sports car. An Italian.

So suddenly everything threatens to slip from his grip again. The other man is not just foreign, he's flamboyant, he's rich perhaps, and he's got plenty of time to court Sonia: he's not tied to an industrial job. By contrast, and on all these counts, Sutcliffe is the underdog. He has to make a complicated and tense arrangement at work to catch up with Sonia. When he does, her shock at seeing him proves her infidelity to him. Instead of catching up with her, he loses her even more: he knows the worst, and they quarrel. When he goes back to work it is to discover that a parallel catastrophe has occurred. Owing to the incompetence of the assistant who was standing in for him, there is a landslip, several men are almost drowned. Sutcliffe is severely reprimanded and demoted. As a male with his female, he's been found wanting too, and in the worst possible way. W.T. Clark, Sutcliffe's engineering boss for several years (at the time of the crimes) says that Sutcliffe could not bear to be told off (which was occasionally brought about by his bad time-keeping): it upset him so much it brought tears to his eyes. Here, bad time-keeping (the difficulty of seeing Sonia who went home straight after college, earlier than work finished for Sutcliffe, the bungled arrangement with the assistant, the mistake of the assistant) provokes a disaster. And a disaster at the waterworks. Everything we've seen about the language of the Sutcliffe family ('he were pissed,' 'I brayed shit out of him', etc;) suggests that 'waterworks' must also have had symbolic connotations. Disaster at the waterworks was the social equivalent to a near landslide of 'manhood'.

And the next event spells this out. There is the other quarrel with Sonia, at the close of which, Dr. Milne says in his report, Sutcliffe tells Sonia to 'go' with her Italian, offering her a Durex. That same day he decides to go to a prostitute. The encounter with the prostitute leads to the fiasco described in the testimony.

Here too he may be twisting what happened. Perhaps this

can be rectified by imagining the scene. He's forced himself to go. He's chosen a bold, seasoned woman, it'll be easier that way. As they are going to her place he discovers with terror that he doesn't desire this woman. He rationalizes this: she's coarse, vulgar. He is afraid of losing face, but he goes. One can sense this through all that isn't said. She's begun to undress, his testimony moves on to haggling about money. Several of the survivors, Marcella Claxton, Olivia Reivers, said that Sutcliffe failed to have an erection. Sutcliffe's misery can be imagined. He's thought the supreme remedy was going to work, that once he'd 'been' with a prostitute everything was going to be 'alright', all he had to do was dare: and nothing that he had expected happens. The likelihood of his being abnormal, 'impotent', grows, and anguish with it. He thought everything that was wrong between Sonia and himself was going to be solved, and everything's been made worse. Prostitutes are supposed to deliver the proof that a man is a man. The reverse has occurred. All the patient efforts put into becoming a man, the body-building, the bikes, the cars, the gravediggers' pranks, the girl-friend — all for nothing. Not for nothing. At least he won't be robbed. He doggedly asks for his change. For this thrifty, careful man, holding on to his money, what is his due, would at least keep some of his act together.

However, not only will the woman not give his five pounds back, she deceives him, then mocks him with the men at the garage. Then, just as doggedly and heedless of the context, he demands his change in the pub where she denies him and mocks him further. The whole pub ends up laughing at him. As they used to do at school. . . .

The five pounds that the prostitute retains become the symbol of Sutcliffe's 'lack': he's been 'feminized', 'castrated' (that is, found impotent sexually and 'had' financially). The five-pound note will remain as potential nemesis thereafter: the one lead that will bring the police at all close to Sutcliffe will be the new five-pound note given by Sutcliffe to Jean Jordan in Manchester, and retained by the poor woman: in the struggle, her bag fell and remained far from her body. Despite his search a week later, Sutcliffe couldn't find it, and the serial number, traceable to a limited number of firms, the payees, will lead to his being questioned several times — and let go.

He's been 'feminized' another way too. Strangely, he's offered Sonia a Durex prior to his going to look for a prostitute. It is as though he were mounting a scenario in which Sonia and he are two virgins desperately deciding to jump in at the deep end, but with separate partners. Was he trying to hold on to her symbolically at least — by offering the Durex he was both allowing the 'act' and protecting Sonia from insemination — like a thoughtful mother or elder sister? But he was also participating in the act. It was he who, shod with *his* Durex, would have been 'penetrating' Sonia by means of his rival, or, it was he who would have been 'put on' by Sonia's lover. There is no discounting the ambiguity of the gesture, its homosexual dimension. *But* by going to a prostitute in the meantime, he was, symbolically again, ensuring his control over women. He was protecting his woman; he was performing the act with one who was universally licensed. His failure to perform the act sends the whole structure tumbling down.

And he gets mocked — taunted — 'had' — in *public*. He who has learned to have the laughs with him is now again being laughed at.

In all respects — in his social life (the waterworks, the pub), his love and domestic life (with Sonia), his sexual identity — he's been found *wanting*. There's more than something missing, as Keith Sugden says of the mother's boys. It's everything missing.

No wonder he is, as he says, in a state of 'turmoil', deeply depressed. Near suicidal.

He's placed Sonia and the prostitute in a *parallel* situation. And now the thought occurs: what if Sonia were a prostitute? She's being unfaithful. She may have 'gone' with the other man (she didn't, according to what she said to Dr. Milne; but obviously Sutcliffe feared otherwise). Isn't a woman *either* totally virtuous, like his mother, *or* a prostitute? And Sonia, by going out with the Italian, has made him laughable in the eyes of Mick, as the prostitute has made him laughable in the eyes of the whole pub.

In psychosis, Freud tells us, the ego 'in the service of the id, withdraws from a piece of reality.' A loss of reality is necessarily present: 'psychosis disavows it and tries to replace it.' The transformation is carried out upon 'the memory-traces, ideas and judgments' previously derived from reality. However, these are continuously being altered by new perceptions: 'Thus the psychosis is also faced with the task of procuring for itself perceptions of a kind which shall correspond to the new reality; and this is most radically effected by means of hallucination[10].'

In other words, Sutcliffe cannot bear the 'impotency' with which the triple catastrophe he's suffered afflicts him. The crisis of sexual identity he'd suffered from before had been solved by a prior hallucination, the 'voice of God' speaking from the grave, which reassured him as to his own power. Now the 'voice of God' starts again from inside a state of turmoil. Freud does tell us that, in many forms of psychosis, the delusions and hallucinations are 'of a most distressing character . . . a sign that the whole process of remodelling (reality) is carried through against forces which oppose it violently.' And so the voice of God comes up with a message: it is prostitutes, the 'scum of the earth', who are 'responsible for everything'. The topography of the grave, the process that 'made a man out of Mac' come to remind him that you can regain the lost power by laying your enemy low. To the original image of the Father as persecutor (or Mick, the arch-male), for which other figures could be substituted, in the place of whom other people could be 'felled' (the man on the race-course, the little girl down the flight of stairs), he now substitutes another female figure: the prostitute.

If prostitutes can be seen as guilty, as evil, as low in essense, 'felling' them will turn into a deed of goodness. In his social environment, we have seen that all women are low, but prostitutes are the lowest. 'Old bags', 'parcel of guts', 'the mucky ones'. You can mark them as low, show them up for what they are. The parcel of guts, for instance, showed Jack's gullible mate the 'real' obscenity of the woman he liked. The paranoiac delusion enables Sutcliffe to believe that he does not hate prostitutes, but that it is his mission to punish them, to exterminate them. It is a miraculous solution. It expels onto a thousand-headed emissary goat all the misery that his own inferiority causes him. Instead of hating himself for being 'low', he can hate them with fury. His hatred is excessive as he hates with the zeal of a Superman.

The evil-doers are legion: as many as the occasions on which Sutcliffe has failed to prove his virility. It is, magically, the fault of the prostitutes that he's been traumatized by his father, persecuted both at school and home. It is the fault of prostitutes that he's lost Sonia to another man, that there has been a disaster at the waterworks, that he's been robbed, taunted in public. It is enough that *one* prostitute should have been the agent of *one* of the disasters. Psychosis turns her into the magic cause of it all.

However, it can only do so because it has been aided and abetted by the pressures and ideology of Society[11]. That is, he has been forced to become aggressively male, to deny his possible tendency to homosexuality, to fear and hate the femininity inside him. In a way, it is out of a deep hatred against himself that Sutcliffe turns against women. You could even say, remembering the strangely inchoate character of his first hallucination, and relating it to Oedipus's encounter with the Sphinx, the singing she-dog, that at that cross-roads Sutcliffe had met not only with the 'Name of the Father', but with the voice of the bitch — the bitch inside him — the bitch that the city will not allow to come within its walls — that has to be hounded as evil. It is out of hatred for the bitch inside him, and because he is the bitch, and because that is taboo, that Sutcliffe decides to kill.

He *decides*. Whatever mitigation can be found in the awesome pressure of environment, temperament and accumulation of misfortune, however absolute or incurable psychosis may be, I do believe that moments of choice, involving at least a minimal play of freedom, do occur in all lives. It may be idealistic optimism, but it's better to live with than socio-sexual determinism. Somewhere Sutcliffe *knew* he was committing crimes. Why otherwise would there have been the terrible turmoil before each crime, till he reached the pitch when he was 'primed' to it? Why the one time he wrestled with his car and managed not to kill did he feel 'a great sense of achievement'? I also believe that the only kind of reparation that could occur would be for him to be cured enough to realize at least to some extent what he has done. There was evidently no chance of a total cure: the extent to which the whole personality was damaged is too painfully evident when you study his family history, and the psychiatrist who ventured an opinion on the matter, Dr. MacCullough, did say that although there might be some improvement, he would always remain a dangerous man. What is tragic is that the decision to condemn him as guilty led to his spending two or more years in prison, his state worsening all the time, and any chance perhaps of that improvement coming to pass was forfeited.

He decides. He goes out equipped with a sock full of gravel, then with a hammer and screwdriver. The first woman he attacks, and who survives, chooses not to press charges. The second time he is caught by a clever policeman. It is thought he only went out equipped for theft. But he gets a conviction, and *that stops him*, in the same way as the woman's reluctance to prosecute was a sign that he was 'meant' to go on.

This is 1969. The conviction stops him. He will not try to kill again until 1975.

Ten

The Fall of the Virgin Mother

Discussing a case of paranoia, Freud makes the following observations:

> This patient's homosexual position was easily surveyed. . . The whole of his youth was governed by a strong attachment to his mother. Of all her many sons he was her declared favourite, and he developed marked jealousy of the normal type in regard to her. When later he made his choice of a wife . . . his longing for a virgin mother expressed itself in obsessive doubts about his fiancée's virginity. . . .[1]

All that is said here is applicable to Sutcliffe. Either jealousy, or a fear of his own loss of power in relation to Sonia, precipitated the first delusions about prostitutes, the first attack. It is the collapse of the image of the mother, compounded by multiple cracks in the image of the virgin wife, that will precipitate Sutcliffe into relentless murder.

The mother's bag

1970. Kathleen Sutcliffe has learned to make life easier for herself. Her husband is always out, working late, sometimes holding night jobs, constantly boozing or philandering. She's started a job cleaning offices and during the day she looks after her daughter Maureen's baby. On top of all the work in the house.

One day, John Sutcliffe unexpectedly phones home. It is unexpected because he has never done so before. She doesn't recognize his voice and she says, 'Is it Albert?'

John Sutcliffe finds himself 'bloody trembling'. He pretends to be Albert. Three times he phones his wife, still pretending, and arranges an assignation. At home he behaves as if nothing is wrong. 'Typical', Maureen will say. At heart he was 'right deep, secretive, like all the lads.'

On the third night of impersonating Albert, he's told Kathleen to meet him for the weekend at the Bankfield Hotel, bringing 'something nice to wear in bed'. On the Saturday afternoon he rummages among his wife's clothes and finds a brand new Marks and Spencer nightgown.

He's told Maureen, Peter and Sonia to meet him at the Bankfield at 7.30 pm, but he won't tell them why. When they're all there, they suddenly look at the entrance and see their mother 'pacing up and down nervously outside'. The next thing they know is that their father is 'tapping her on the shoulder and leading her triumphantly in the direction' of their table. Then he gets hold of his wife's handbag, opens it, and produces the nightie. The mother does not protest. She looks numb. Stunned.

Peter had only just got his own relationship re-established with Sonia. She's broken off with the Italian.

He says, 'I know how it feels, dad,' but the father says dismissively, 'You can't. You're not married.'

Awful scenes follow. John Sutcliffe keeps persecuting his wife to get the name of the man out of her. It turns out he's a policeman, a nice, quiet younger man, a friend of Mick's, a 'decent bloke' who lives two streets away. John Sutcliffe goes for Albert, threatens to tell *his* wife, to report him to his superiors. 'We are members of the public who are supposed to be protected *by* people like you. And it comes to a pretty pass when we need protecting *from* people like you.' The ladies' man's self-righteous indignation is only slightly less obscene than his exposure of his wife to her children and future daughter-in-law. John Sutcliffe spies on his wife, sees her at the pub talking to another man. He waits at home for her and hits her 'with the back of his hand across the face', breaking the face of his watch at the same time against the frame of the door[2]. He goes on brooding, being suspicious, trying to involve his children in the spying. Finally, in 1972, he takes up with a dumb woman his wife had befriended, Wendy Broughton, carries on the affair under his wife's nose, and in '74 moves in with her. She only lives a quarter of a mile away. Kathleen is, by Carl's account, miserable. So is Peter, who says he feels it is 'too near his own doorstep' (Mick's account). He tries to remonstrate with his father, who claims he is only 'getting (his) own back'. 'He'd taken a bloody long time about it — four years to be precise', is Jane's, another daughter's, comment[3]. The Sutcliffe family are in a financial mess — presumably John Sutcliffe gives his wife the minimum amount of money, if any. Deciding his wife had been 'taught her lesson' John Sutcliffe finally moves back home. 'I knew that she would *never* do it again'. Yes, Kathleen had been suitably broken. 'Thinking back to the Saturday at the Bankfield Hotel', Burn comments, 'Peter would say he believed he could see his mother start to die from that very day.[4]'

Peter and Sonia get married soon after the father's return, on 10 August 1974.

The facts speak for themselves. Kathleen Sutcliffe has always been the 'Angel'. The 'virgin mother', faithful to her husband, her sons, supportive of them, even against the police, though she sided with order, the police, in telling them off afterwards. Wifely virtue as against the husband's promiscuity had been the rule, the cornerstone, in that family. It goes with the mother's respectability, a middle-class value that Peter believes in that has guided him in his choice of girl-friend.

Suddenly, *publicly* (in a pub, the very place where the prostitute had humiliated him the year before), the mother is shown up by the father to be but a 'prostitute', too. Her bag is open, 'her' contents spilled on the pub table. She may be just a parcel of guts, there's the sign of her sinfulness, the brand new nightdress. For the first time, initially at least, Peter sympathizes with his father: 'I know how it feels'. The father refuses the sympathy, but rubs in the code: 'You can't. You're not married'. It is marriage, proprietorship, that gives the husband the grievance. Not a question of feeling, it is a question of right. A man has to show that his wife is under his thumb. He has to assert his superior power. Break her by means of every trick in the book. The son of Ivy Sutcliffe, a woman who, in Maureen's words, had been 'born sour', must have been deeply damaged and insecure: why else would he have gone to such lengths to take his revenge, to humiliate his wife so completely, why should it have taken him so long to work the thing out of his system (four years), so that in the short term nothing but breaking her spirit would satisfy him — nothing but *killing* her in the long term? The children, and Peter in particular who was closest to his mother, must have been deeply affected. The example John Sutcliffe set was poison. Full of unflagging, plaintive vindictiveness, the man who enjoys burgling houses and stealing other men's women (pilfering the contents of the good breast) is now acting the virtuous citizen, indignant that the police, who should 'protect' him, should instead have laid hands on his own piece of property. The man who enjoys breaking the law now invokes the law as his champion. Up to the eve of his own marriage, Peter is confronted by yet another split model of behaviour. Terrifyingly, the father of the man who has already tried twice to 'knock' women, shows his son that mastery over the dumb (Wendy Broughton) is the means of asserting control over the threateningly independent wife at home.

The Marriage Hearse

> But most thro' midnight streets I hear
> How the youthful Harlot's curse
> Blasts the new born Infant's tear,
> And blights with plagues the Marriage Hearse.
>
> Blake, 'London'.

Sutcliffe and Sonia got back together round 1970. Sutcliffe's testimony mentions that she then went to London to study painting (later on pottery); and that a nervous breakdown ensued.

It is very difficult to write about Sonia. To her credit, unlike various members of Sutcliffe's family and his friends, she has not sold her story to anyone. So nobody knows it. Virtually all testimony about her is from hostile witnesses. She's made that clear, and recently dissociated herself from Burn's book, having first 'been granted a disclaimer by the High Court which dissociated (her) entirely from' the contents of *Somebody's Husband, Somebody's Son.*

> Mr. Burn gives about as much insight into the sort of husband I had as he would be capable of giving the characteristics of my own grandfather. . . . The person who could have shed some light on Peter Sutcliffe the son was his mother. But she, rest her soul, is dead. (*The Guardian*, May 19 1984).

Sonia did talk to Dr. Milne. The rest must be surmised — even possibly wrongly. And the risk is to give offence, to hurt a sensitive and fragile person.

I shall be as discreet and tentative as I can, but the public character of the crimes and the case itself prevents me from sparing her as much as I would like to. I think she was, she *is*, very much a victim of the whole ugly turmoil. But she is part of it.

The 'facts' seem to be as follows.

From the start, Sonia stood out against the kind of women

the Sutcliffe sons were seeing. She did not have a 'beehive' hairstyle, but long hair; she did not wear mini-skirts, but long, 'hippy' or 'arty' clothes. She was not promiscuous and untidy in her habits, unlike the daughters of the chaotic Sutcliffe household. Brought up severely by a stern father, who was adamant his daughters should get on, her outings were strictly controlled, as was the style of her parents' home. She had to be back home twenty minutes after school. Her friends were probably vetted, and for a long time the Szurma family seems to have thought that Peter wasn't good enough for her.

Then came the episode with the Italian. What she, what the Italian, what her parents felt about it all — how much she took in of Sutcliffe's depression and his further slide into psychosis — is not known.

What is known is that after several months she did get back together with Sutcliffe. The Sutcliffe family report a marked change of behaviour in her after that date. Of course, she's older — 18 or so — more confident, and they either dislike or hate her, so what they say must be taken with some reservations. There seems to be some truth to it though. Up to then, on her long Sunday visits, she's tried to vanish into the background, like Peter. She retreats into corners of the house to make herself invisible. The lack of manners shown by everybody concerned must have quite bewildered her, given the highly controlled situation at home. Mick narrates with indignation how she once asked Mrs. Sutcliffe to make her a cup of tea, with one sugar please. Presumably in that house you didn't ask, you just helped yourself, no one was treated as host or hostess. It is easy to imagine how hard Sonia found it to adapt. Why she spent so much time in a place she had so little liking for can also be figured out: she and Peter couldn't go to her parents, who, unlike the Sutcliffes, didn't keep open house. And they probably didn't allow her to go out with the young man, only go to his people.

When she re-appears in the Sutcliffe household, she seems to have decided to fight them for possession of Peter. She is no longer the 'mute', but she communicates with Peter as if the rest of the family weren't there. She 'quietly upbraids him' if she thinks his funny stories are dragging on too much. She corrects his manners. She controls him when he gets over-excited by just saying 'Peter!' 'Like a schoolteacher, telling a naughty boy how to behave,' is John Sutcliffe's description of it. She attempts to re-educate him in his tastes for clothes and music, weaning him from 'taproom rock 'n' roll' onto 'light classics'. She takes him to hear her sister Marianne give platform recitals at the piano; to occasional opera and ballet performances. Then she goes on to Deptford to embark on a three-year course with painting, then pottery, as her main subject. She lives in a hall of residence operating a strict curfew on male visitors. So when Peter, the only person she has social contact with apart from her sister, comes visiting at weekends, he has to sleep in the car. He attempts to move into the area by renting a bedsit. That only lasts a few weeks and he moves back home.

In the middle of her second year, Sonia's emotional and physical isolation in London has 'started to manifest itself in progressively confused and erratic behaviour'. Detached and uncommunicative in public, she has outbursts of rage in private. Sutcliffe once has to keep her arms pinned to her sides to prevent her from lashing at him. She is losing a terrible amount of weight, a stone in a short period, and she looks ashen. Eventually she breaks down. She is transferred to a psychiatric hospital in Bradford. Schizophrenia has been diagnosed. She is convinced 'that all the machinery (is) stopping and the world (is) coming to an end'. When she sees Peter she thinks he is an aeroplane. She also, 'thinks' she is the second Christ, that you can see stigmata on her hands. She is restless and insistent that she wants 'a bigger teddy-bear'. She is now on drugs that make her put on an unhealthy amount of weight. She looks bloated, 'terrible' as Peter said in court. She becomes lethargic. Once, when she is out visiting the Sutcliffe's, she tells Jane, the youngest daughter, that she thinks she is Cinderella. She is wearing a little summer dress and silver sandals[5].

During all that time, Peter faithfully visits her and helps to pull her through. He thus wins the hearts of Sonia's parents who are touched by his dedication to their daughter.

But during these years 1970–1974 — what with Sonia being in London, then in and out of hospital — he's been left very much to his own devices. This is the period in which he develops his knowledge of red-light districts. Also the period in which he contracts VD.

The effect of all this upon Sutcliffe, plus the domestic existence that followed, must have been highly complex. But it had its positive side too. He had got Sonia back. His jealousy could be appeased: all the more so as her strict isolation in London, and even her breakdown, put her very much at his mercy. She loses weight just as John Sutcliffe had lost weight at the time of Peter's own birth. She is the weakling, the one who is being devoured — the underdog. He has the opportunity to show off, to demonstrate his loyalty, his tenderness: he convinces her parents that he really is an unselfish and steady young man. They adopt him: Bodan Szurma teaches him to play chess. Sonia, taking him in hand, fighting his family for him, educating him, must have been fulfilling some of his ambition, or made him feel at least that he was fulfilling his mother's.

And this is buoyed up — made possible perhaps — by the fact that at the same time he haunts red-lights districts. We have seen in what kinds of ways he behaves there, 'having a go at one of the bags', insulting the women, at least as much as 'going with' a prostitute or two. But this satisfies his cultural need to prove his malehood and it vents his viciousness for the time. Two quite separate levels of life have become established. Dr. Jekyll-like, his 'good' self tends to Sonia, pleases and courts her family, goes for nice healthy walks on the moors. His Mr. Hyde self, meantime, is kept within the bounds of particularly aggressive, yet codified, pranks. Like his own father, he has two selves, but his good self is the domestic one, his bad self the outside one.

But there is a darker side to this, which must all the time have brought new dimensions to the psychosis. First of all, the relationship that has developed between him and Sonia is one in which Sonia has the upper hand. She tells him what to do; shouts at him sometimes, according to the members of the Sutcliffe household. She nags him. His wife shouted at him to such an extent that he was embarrassed because he thought the neighbours must have heard her, Dr. Milne reported that Sutcliffe had told him — she even 'screams' at him[6]. You could say that she is the one who is wearing the trousers.

This stops during the time when she is sick (her violence or upbraiding can be attributed to her being 'defective' on account of the illness). But it starts again the moment the newly-married young couple move in with the Szurmas. Sonia has been reluctant to settle in socially inferior Bingley. Her parents are encouraging her in her desire to save, so that Sutcliffe and she can buy a house of their own. But given the strictness of the Szurma household, given the inevitable sexual anxieties in a newly-wed man living with in-laws, given the precedent of John Sutcliffe's own illness shortly after marriage, i.e. the neurotic inheritance of allergy to domestic life in the Sutcliffe make-up (Mick has got divorced almost straight after getting married; Carl never marries; even Maureen's marriage breaks down pretty quickly) — the pressures that married life brought to bear on Sutcliffe must have been intolerable. And they were none of them pressures he could even acknowledge. For the part of him that must have hated being 'controlled', told what to do, upbraided, domesticated by Sonia — the part that had formed through identification with male models around him, psychosis made him suppress.

His brothers are full of stories of how Sonia henpecked him, stopped him from accompanying them to the pub on Sunday lunchtimes. There always was a 'job' for him to do. In that tug-of-war, it seems that Sutcliffe wanted to please both sides and live up to both of them. Without any realization of the kind of 'splitting' he was resorting to in order to accommodate them both.

One thing, however, he must have been acutely aware of,

though he has not mentioned it to the doctors: in the first year of the marriage, Sonia had at least one miscarriage. Perhaps she went on to have more — again, difficult to know, as the sources differ[7]. It was said in the end that she would never have children. She claimed that did not bother her very much. Sutcliffe on the other hand is reported to have been much affected by this. He liked children. In the late seventies, he went on to court a Glasgow girl whom he had met on one of his trips as a long-distance lorry driver. The girl was called Tessa, and one of the reasons Sutcliffe liked her was that she had a large family, sisters with little children who Sutcliffe played with during his visits[8]. Perhaps that large and fertile family reminded him of home.

His liking for children seems genuine and he even spoke at one point of adopting some Vietnamese orphans. His disappointed fatherhood must have been acute, not just because he wanted and expected children, but because it was a further exposure of his failure to be a 'man'. His own father had had seven children and he couldn't even produce one.

Did he repress his disappointment, as he was repressing his resentment at Sonia's domestic sway? Did that disappointment turn into further hatred of women? The fascination for the Morecambe 'horror rooms' suggests this. Wombs were obscene, ugly. Wombs were nothing but wounds and should be 'shown up' as such. Women, after all, *were* nothing but a 'parcel of guts'. There was no life for him there. He would make damn sure there would be no life there for anybody. His killings made 23 orphans. And he wanted to adopt some . . .

'The outcome of all such situations will undoubtedly depend on economic considerations — on the relative magnitude of the trends which are struggling with one another[9].' The magnitude of the trends, in Sutcliffe's case, is such that one can really speak of over-determination. The head spins as one uncovers yet another source of strain and splitting.

A further 'dark' side to Sonia's breakdown is that her 'image', shaken already by the episode with the Italian, which had led to the first attempts at murder, becomes further damaged. From 1970 to 1974, the mother's infidelity has been rubbed like salt into a wound by John Sutcliffe's vindictiveness. The mother's image has been distorted, mangled. Now Sonia falls to pieces. She becomes thin, then fat; violent, then lethargic. She loses her beauty. She loses her modesty too: several times she wanders out and strips naked. She *thinks* she's wounded. She's got stigmata. She thinks she is Christ. Sutcliffe has been called 'Jesus' by his fellow gravediggers. There is a sense in which, we have seen, Sonia is also Sutcliffe's double: a foreigner, quiet, a loner like him. Now she exhibits her wounds, the sense of persecution he himself has suffered from all his life without ever being able to represent it to himself. Instead of being a source of strength and pride she's become a source of weakness.

This, as has been said, has its positive side and calls out the best, the most loyal and tender, in Sutcliffe. But it also calls forth a furious need to protect — furious in that the plight is so desperate, the weakness of those who have to be protected (Sonia/himself) so great. Sonia is only given a clean bill of health in 1976, only then is she allowed to resume her teacher's training, two years after marriage. Sonia can be frenetic, she behaves irrationally at home as well as in public[10]. His mother, too, has been stripped in public, at the hotel and in the pub.

Perhaps all women are evil, all women are prostitutes.

Come the honeymoon in Paris, 1974. A prostitute comes up to them as they are walking hand in hand. Sutcliffe shows no response to this. Later, on another occasion, when they are coming out of a station Sonia 'is dragged away by a man who (thinks) she (is) a prostitute.'

> 'I must have thought that the man thought Sonia was a prostitute rather than Sonia saying anything to him. From that time we stayed glued together'.[11]

They get back, live with the Szurmas. The cramped conditions. The fear of making noises when you are making love. Having to be on your best behaviour. Sonia's outbursts. The miscarriage.

'He was told by workmates that there was "a plague of prostitutes in Keighley" and on that basis went there to look for them. It was in this way he became involved with Rogulskyj' (Doctor Milne's report)[12].

His mother is an adultress. Sonia may be a prostitute: even in the most respectable circumstances, during the honeymoon, when everything about them should proclaim that they belong to the good camp, the camp of decency — now that, being 'married', as his father would say, he can understand what it is like for a man to be threatened by his wife's potential for 'evil' sex — even when they are walking hand in hand, prostitution threatens to come between the bride and the bridegroom. It threatens to stain the bride, claim her for its own. She must be protected at all costs. His mother must be protected at all costs . . .

The solution, already hit upon, surfaces again. Prostitutes must be responsible for it all. They are the evil ones. If only Sutcliffe can find them outside the home, destroy them outside the domestic circle, then his wife, his mother, 'his' women will be safe, cleansed.

In 1969, when he feared that Sonia was a prostitute, the 'voice' had comforted him, told him that prostitutes were the guilty ones. The honeymoon incidents, almost *parallel* to the earlier 'catastrophe' (a prostitute approaches him; a man approaches Sonia as if she were a prostitute), have revived all of Sutcliffe's fears: lack of virility; failure in his relationship with Sonia; the crumbling and collapse of the respectable world for which he opted when he sided with his mother as a child and chose Sonia for a bride. The only way to prove that Sonia and his mother are *not* prostitutes is to *define* other women (you can identify them by 'magic' signs, the way they adjust a skirt, walk, or are simply out in the streets at night, alone) *by killing them*. It is indeed the mechanism of the 'emissary goat' that is here being activated. The fact that women should be selected at random for killing is enough for them to be burdened with all the 'evil' in the city — the evil in Sutcliffe's life. Death, that spoke from the gravestone of a man called Zapolski, will put Sutcliffe *above* the threateningly 'sexed' and unruly women in his life, and will 'cleanse' them of the evil that might otherwise afflict them. Welcome are the 'voices' that point to the 'evil ones', the 'plague' that has descended upon the city. The complaint of a workmate, a letter from a priest indignant at the 'immorality' in certain districts, are all signs. God's word is his command.

It is as if the Id (Peter's violence, his repressed homosexuality) has combined with the Superego (the male code)[13] to produce the voice of God. It enables him to vent his resentment against the women (his mother and his wife) who, through their nagging or their having become associated with prostitutes, have replaced the father as the persecutor. Because he uses substitute victims, because he kills outside, he can remain good at home. In effect, he kills women who are versions of Sonia and his mother, so that he can continue to love and respect them, can allow himself to be controlled by Sonia's domesticity.

After Sutcliffe and Sonia have moved into their own home in Heaton, a well-to-do district of Bradford that overlooks the Aire valley, Sonia becomes, by all accounts, a meticulous housewife. Despotic too. She keeps the place spotless, insists that her husband remove his shoes when he comes in, that they put a towel on the sheets when they make love. She decorates the whole house, hardly ever entertains, and there isn't a weed in the garden. The policeman who came to tell her about Peter's arrest claimed the house was frigid in its orderliness. Even the dishcloth, he said, was folded into a neat square on the sink. Peter, we've seen, has always been meticulous. He does his own washing, and keeps his laundry in a black dustbin bag (which is why Sonia never sees the stained clothes after the murders). So in a way Sonia's tidiness *satisfies* a need in him. Yet his own 'streetcleaning' seems a savage parody of the cleanliness she imposes upon him. Rather like the starlings on his mother's clothesline. His 'controlling' God is the wicked counterpart of the one who is wearing the breeches at home.

I have said that Sutcliffe goes out to kill outdoors versions of Sonia and his mother. I do not mean that, as one policeman told Sonia, 'it was you he wanted to kill.' Her brave and pathetic reply, 'if that was so, once would have been enough', puts paid to that particular piece of cruelty, which implies that 'it was all *her* fault really', 'other women were paying for what *you* did to him.' Which in turn implies 'wives, be submissive to your husbands or else . . .'

What I mean is this: Sutcliffe has been taught to hate and repress his own weakness *as* femininity. He's learned to fear and hate all behaviour in his women that will show him up as weak. Yet he loves his mother and his wife, and he wants to be good to them, so his fear and hate will be vented upon substitute images of them.

The first two women he attacks (Mrs. Rogulskyj and Mrs. Smelt) are roughly his mother's age. Neither of them is a prostitute. Mrs. Smelt even has a job cleaning offices, like his own mother.

A high number of the later victims will either be attractive young women (from sixteen to late twenties), many of them dark (like Sonia), or older women (Vera Millward, Mrs. Jackson, Margo Walls). Two of his victims are students, as Sonia was.

The 'doublings' are eerie.

In '75 Sutcliffe meets in a Bradford pub a young girl he's known all his youth. He chivalrously drives her home to Keighley. He's never made advances to her and doesn't then either. A few months or weeks later, he drives the *same* way and batters Anna Rogulskyj.

He drives home, for her protection, the secretary from Clark's where he works. In the same period, he kills Josephine Whitaker, a bank clerk, and Margo Walls, a secretary.

He kills Josephine Whitaker on 4 April 1979. It is in that same month of April that he meets Tessa Douglas in Glasgow and charmingly courts her. He meets her in a pub, as 12 years earlier he'd met Sonia. Even the names, Tessa, Sonia . . . : Tessa, Sonia, Josephine, all pretty, dark-haired young women . . . The 'mistress' and the 'wife', or the dream double of the wife, and the wife whom he loved over the body of the victim, laid low out there in a dark place in Halifax. Some of the victims fall as substitutes for the mother or the wife. Others have weird affinities with him: Helen Rytka is a loving twin. Sutcliffe kills her at a time when he himself is involved in an elaborate 'twinning' process with his friend Trevor Birdsall: They cultivate their likeness to each other, grow identical beards. Peter calls himself 'Dave' when he introduces himself to a prospective victim, also sometimes says 'call me Trevor'.

But above all, Sutcliffe seems to be involved in a process of 'splitting' of the 'Dr. Jekyll and Mr. Hyde' type. The extreme goodness of Dr. Jekyll has its necessary counterpart in Mr. Hyde's viciousness, Peter's progress is paid for by the crimes of 'Dave'.

Spring '77, February: 'Dave' kills Irene Richardson; April: he kills Tina Atkinson. Yet it is the best time ever for the young Sutcliffe couple: Sonia is at last about to get her Teacher's Diploma, which she receives in June. She discovers the house in Heaton; heaven for the town girl, the immigrant's daughter. Number 6 Garden Lane. She tells the owner, a Pakistani barrister, Mr. Rahman, that she is Czech, and a concert pianist. She shows Peter the house.

That same night, he goes out drinking in Chapeltown. Jayne MacDonald forfeits her life.

Two Saturdays later, when they're in the process of buying the house, Sutcliffe goes to Lumb Lane, Bradford. Maureen Long is attacked, survives multiple skull fractures, wounds in the chest, abdomen and back.

18th August. Sonia proudly signs 'Sonia Szurma Sutcliffe' next to her husband's signature. Early September. She begins teaching in Holmsfield Primary School. They move in on 26 September. On a Monday, the same day, Sutcliffe buys a new car, a red second-hand Ford Corsair. The following Saturday,

1st October, he drives to Manchester. Everything is new: car, house, wife's job. He's even got brand-new banknotes in his pocket. He's never had it so good. He picks up Jean Jordan. And kills her.

A week later, Sutcliffe and Sonia have a house-warming party. Considerate as ever, Peter drives some guests home. He drives on across the Pennines to Manchester, finds Jean Jordan's body — but not the bag containing the compromising new note. In his rage, he stabs and tears at the body. Tries to cut the head off.

14 December: he attacks Marylin Moore in Leeds.

21 January '78: he batters Yvonne Pearson to death.

31 January: he murders Helen Rytka in Huddersfield.

May '78: It's Vera Millward's turn, in Manchester.

During that time, the Sutcliffes have had their new house pebbledashed, then painted pink, so it matches the others in the street[14].

Seven murders or attempted murders in 11 months, the period corresponding to the purchase of the 'dream house'. Nine in just over a year, the best year they've ever had in terms of their careers, prospects and social ascent.

Kathleen Sutcliffe, the mother, dies in November 1978. The period of her death corresponds to a slowing down of the murders.

Is it because success fills him with a sense of panic that Sutcliffe kills? Because secretly he hates success, the pressures of domesticity? Or because he's become so accustomed to feeling that his success as a man depends on the destruction of women (a kind of tit for tat, Hyde-for-Jekyll process) that, every time something good happens to him on the domestic front, he has to go and kill out there on the streets?

The steps of his ascent are the bodies of women. His 'house at the top' is 'paid for' by the blood of eleven victims. No wonder some of them, or their relations, are suing for compensation. Are they suing in the right quarter? Everything we've seen about the social conditions in which Sutcliffe grew up and lived, the violence, the aggression to women, everything we've come to understand about the amount of damage the man suffered at the hands of his own damaged family, the whole appalling *overdetermination* and the repetitive pattern of the murders, all this cries out that it was not just *one* man killing. That man was indeed 'possessed'. When Sutcliffe says that he killed when he finally felt 'primed' to do it, you can almost hear the awful cogs clicking and whirring into action, so 'logical' does the madness appear when you try to understand what precipitated it.

Part Three

Contexts: A Custodian of Order?

Man for the field and Woman for the hearth:
Man for the sword and for the needle She:
Man with the hand and Woman with the heart:
Man to command and Woman to obey;
All else confusion.

> Tennyson (quoted E. Zaretzsky, *Capitalism, The
> Family and Personal Life*, Pluto Press, 1976)

Therefore, O Aholibah, thus saith the Lord God . . .
Behold, I will deliver thee into the hand of them
whom thou hatest . . .

And they shall deal with thee hatefully . . . and
shall leave thee naked and bare: and the nakedness
of thy whoredoms shall be discovered, both thy
lewdness and thy whoredoms.
I will do these things unto thee, because thou hast
gone awhoring after the heathen, and because thou
art polluted with their idols.

> *Ezekiel, 23*, 22-30

Sir Michael asked when had it first crossed Mr.
Sutcliffe's mind that the God he was in touch with
was very evil, quite contrary to the sort of miracles
he had been told about as a Roman Catholic. Mr.
Sutcliffe said it seemed similar to the contradiction
between the Old Testament and the New.

> *The Times*, Wednesday May 13, 1981

Eleven

'The System'

Aren't there so many determinations to be discovered — such an accumulation of unfortunate accidents — that it has become rather like the Nuremberg trials: who then is responsible?

If Sutcliffe hadn't married and had become a homosexual instead — *if* he had had children — *if* he hadn't become so accustomed to the sight and presence of death by working as a gravedigger — *if* his family had been less violent — *if* he hadn't been born 'weak' . . . You can go back to great-grandfather Sutcliffe or grandmother Sutcliffe and say that if she had been a kinder woman her son John would have been a less flawed father etc. etc. The thing can become — it *is* in a way — so diffuse that in the end nobody is responsible. Or everybody is, which comes to the same thing. Inevitable. Accidental. Human nature, or the human condition being what it is, these things will occur.

It is time to come out and point an accusing finger.

Sutcliffe was responsible. He 'knew' what he was doing. Whatever the pressures upon him, whatever the degree of psychosis — he did what he did.

By the same token, his father is, I think, more than anyone else, after Sutcliffe, also responsible. Again, however much of a victim of background and circumstances he may have been, whatever capacity for love he may have shown in some quarters, he was a very bad husband, and a dreadful father to his sons: one — Mick — is a violent alcoholic; Carl had to go to borstal when he was 15; the third is Peter.

And the whole aura of aggressive macho values is also responsible: the friends, for instance who regarded prostitute-bashing as a joke.

It must not be forgotten, however, when one talks of background in this way that there are working-class families with very different attitudes to the Sutcliffe 'peer-group'. To get a balanced picture, the story of his victims should also be told. The story of the loving home of Jayne MacDonald, whose father died of grief. The story of Emily Jackson, who went in for prostitution because she *liked* it — no doubt the money was handy too; it also took her mind off the acute pain caused by the death of one of her children. But the easy-going tolerance of her husband, and her own love for her children — like the love of Wilma McCann and Jean Jordan and others for theirs — should be celebrated. As should the heroism of Olive Smelt, who took a job in an old men's home to try and cure herself of the aversion to men her bludgeoning left her scarred with. There is perhaps more *real* courage in such deeds than in the heady storming of enemy positions: Victoria Crosses don't go to the right quarters.

Fiction is probably the only way in which such a celebration could occur. The victims have been hurt too badly not to be spared the limelight of any further discussion. Pat Barker's remarkable novel, *Blow Your House Down,* is the fictional answer. It gives life and humanity back to the working-class women — prostitutes or not — and some working-class men too, whom the 'Ripper case' had taken it away from.

Indeed when one thinks along those lines, it becomes clear that one of the things the 'Ripper' (as a construct rather than an individual) did was inflict damage upon the working-classes. The case evinces an imitative pattern of exploitation.

Yes, it is true that the ideology of aggressive maleness that surrounded Sutcliffe made his murders possible: but how come such attitudes exist? If they don't exist so conspicuously or so viciously among the middle or privileged classes, is it because they don't need them? Are these attitudes the offshoot of exploitation? The net must be thrown much further for anything accurate to be said about who *is* responsible.

The Need for Domestic Supremacy

A social phenomenon such as the 'Yorkshire Ripper' case could only be fully understood through a historical analysis that would give it its full context. It is certain that 'seeking the causes and sources of violence and crime through an emphasis on pathological individuals or deviant relationships' can only be done by 'those who would ignore the simple fact that violence is endemic to modern Western societies'[1]. The Yorkshire Ripper was made into a sensational scarecrow *because* his pathological dimension enabled the system thus to mask the normal level of violence that his acts expressed and maintained. Yallop, describing the murder by strangulation of Margo Walls, then the attack on Dr. Bandara, (also using a rope) adds that women didn't have to be worried about those[2], since they were not the doing of the Yorkshire Ripper. Only when it was thought that *he* was the author was there any reason to fear: wasn't the fact that those two women were killed or nearly killed in the space of a month reason enough for the Leeds women to be frightened to go out at night?

It would take a historian and a sociologist to unravel what is meant exactly by, 'the system', as I have used the term: what structures, what forces made up the 'voice of God'? However, a large body of work exists already from which some elements that seem particularly applicable can be extracted. They should provide something like the outline of an answer.

It is feminists (Kate Millet, then Shulamith Firestone, then Juliet Mitchell followed by others) who have brought the family into the arena of political discussion[3]. Eli Zaretsky[4] gives their arguments an emphasis which makes them particularly relevant. An historical shift was brought about in the family as a productive unit before the advent of capitalism, he contends. With the rise of industry, material production was 'split' between its socialized forms (commodity production) and the private (unpaid) labour of wives in the home. 'In this form, male supremacy, which long antedated capitalism, became an institutionalized part of the capitalist system of production'. Without it capitalism could not develop.

This split is related to a second split: between our 'personal' lives and our place within the social division of labour. 'Work' and 'life' were separated; proletarianization split the outer world of alienated labour from an inner world of personal feeling'. Women were cut off from men, made inferior: for their labour — housework, child-rearing — was devalued: unpaid, done in isolation 'from the socialized production of surplus value'[5]. The housewife emerged, alongside the proletarian worker. Her tasks came to include 'responsibility for the "human values" which the family was thought to preserve'[6]. The housewife and mother was supposed to maintain the realm of personal relations. Without the housewife, the proletarian workforce was unable to emerge.

The general line of Zaretsky's argument and historical thesis says something important about the Sutcliffe family, which in many ways could be described as archetypal: as having inherited, almost to the point of caricature, Victorian and Edwardian structures. John Sutcliffe's admiration for his patriarchal grandfather, served by his women at the head of his table *or* his office; his insistence upon letting everybody know who was master in his own home; his suffering at the hands of his own topsy-turvy parents (Ivy Sutcliffe, in steady employment at the factory, while his father dallied); his reliance upon his wife to bring the children up, and his complaints about his sons being 'mother's boys', as if she had been solely responsible for the way they grew up, all confirm the double split Zaretsky is describing. The father is the boss, the breadwinner; the mother is the housewife, housebound. The father has to do with a large social world, and gives his best to it (the cricket, the football, the choir, being popular); the mother deals with personal matters. The crisis occurs for him, an acute crisis, when, his wife having gone out to work and begun to have a social life (going to pubs), she also starts having an affair. Her sexual freedom seems to go hand in hand with her having become, however modestly, a wage-earner. In other words, seen from a socio-economic angle as well, Peter Sutcliffe inherits a doubly split model from his father: 'home' and 'the street' have to be kept separated at all costs.

The family grew to be of particular importance to proletarians gradually emerging from the worst stages of poverty because it was 'the place where subjectivity could come into being, the only space that proletarians "owned". So the proletariat came to share the bourgeois ideal of the family as a "utopian retreat" '[7]. For John Sutcliffe, as for millions of men in the late 19th and early 20th century, who finally got a wage high enough for their wives and children not to need to go to work in the mills or the mines, keeping the wife, 'respectable' Kathleen Coonan, at home (unlike his own 'common' mother), meant social elevation and the possibility of home values. His son Peter wants to go one better. Strangely, that means altering the pattern: having a wife with a profession, a wife that goes out to work. The meaning of 'home' is also modern — the leap the younger Sutcliffe attempts to make is indeed considerable: it means the power (money) to get hold of private property, objects of consumption, food, clothing, domestic articles and, indeed, a house that will be carefully decorated. 'We didn't go in for a family, more for material goods', was one of Sutcliffe's lucid statements to Dr. Milne[8]. A double strain is thus brought about: the husband loses his visible form of control over his wife; she is not bound by four walls, she is a wage-earner, his visible equal; but also, home is emptied of content, or personal value. For a man as damaged in his sexual identity as Sutcliffe, the need to symbolically demonstrate his power over women, and the meaning of home, is excruciating: I have noted how the most intense period of the killings corresponds to Sonia beginning work, and the buying of the house in Heaton.

In a book on Labour and Virtue[9], Katherine Blunden argues that middle-class men, or men aspiring to middle-class status, caught between the new dream of social promotion brought about by expanding capitalism, and fear of regression, of ruin, which the continuing existence of labouring masses confronts them with, need to be reassured. Their women are given that role. Initially, their being 'locked up' within the home, housewives, tells them apart from working-class women who may move in and out of prostitution. Female virtue appears to be connected with inactivity — the lack of a job. This had been verified in Sutcliffe's experience by what had happened to his mother. Now the old nightmare that Sonia was a prostitute too was given new form. Her job as a teacher *both* meant social promotion for him and the threat of regression. He was exorcising that threat by killing women in her place —showing that it was *others* who were in the 'pit' — working-class prostitutes.

Sutcliffe was indeed totally caught between classes. For he was also working-class, and though his eventual job as a long-distance lorry-driver had status and independence, it still was a working-class job; he was subject to a boss, working with machines, with his hands, and he had no security — driving offences might take his licence away. As was about to happen when he was arrested. His sheltered truck cabin, 'up above everything', twice five feet over the ground, which made him feel 'right powerful', was about to be taken away from him. But 'home' gave him none of the standard recognition:

> Typically, the working-class man views the world of the family in a different light to other social relationships. Whereas at work he is individually powerless, at home he has personal influence and recognition. He goes out to work for others (the wife and family) partly on condition that they, in return, reaffirm his patriarchal status. Without the material benefits of food, sex, relaxation, and the psychological benefits of emotional support — there would be no point to his working at all . . . what is fundamentally at stake in the working-class family is a man's 'conjugal right' to reproduce the *authority* he faces at work. Because the insistence on domestic

'harmony' is, at root, a defence of male supremacy, the balance of man's identity hangs upon the demarcation of domestic responsibilities . . . And because, in its origins, the sexual division of labour is irrational, such confrontation encounters deeply unconscious barriers of resistance.[10]

This is what a working-class man instinctively feels. But Sonia rules the roost. Mick tells his brother he should assert himself:

'He wouldn't say owt at all to her, you see, but I just said, "Well, that's up to you, but I'm just going to tell her what I think, and you should do bloody same."

'If owt wanted doin', he'd do it for 'er, but then she'd have something else for 'im straight away. I'd say, "C'mon, we're going out for a bloody pint; we're going for a drink," which would get her goin' straightaway. "He's not going anywhere. He's doing this, and when he's finished he's doing that and that . . ."'[11]

What is extraordinary is that this is not just what Mick Sutcliffe thinks, and says. Burn quotes him without bothering to verify the facts — so recognizable are the attitudes, and the language, that they appear as authenticity itself. Sonia passionately refuted these claims: that for example she forced her husband 'to start decorating the moment he came home tired from work (when in fact I decorated the entire house myself)', accusing Burn of 'religiously reproducing persistently their coarse expressions'[12]. But it's not just Burn. Dr. Milne stated in Court, as mitigation of Sutcliffe's acts, that Sonia 'readily admits that she had been at times temperamental and difficult and . . . that she has frequently teased and provoked her husband.' A prison warder quoted as a witness said that she 'completely overwhelms and dominates him.' The Attorney-General asked, '(Was Sutcliffe's) behaviour because he was having a rough time after his marriage? Was his wife . . . behaving impossibly so that he dreaded coming home?' These comments, made, as

Elizabeth Wilson stresses, by normal men — 'sophisticated, highly educated men in positions of power and influence'[13], shows how pervasive is the defence of male supremacy in the domestic circle, so pervasive and so irrational, as Tolson says, that a wife's 'nagging tongue' can be regarded as a sufficient motive for multiple murder.

Violence to Women

This largely explains Sutcliffe's 'good conscience': his secret conviction that he was doing something proper. Something *manly*. The fact is that England is full of sophisticated, highly educated men who claim that it is natural for men to be aggressive — rather than 'outgoing', expansive, lustful. War, as Hélène Cixous says, is only to be expected. As in this:

> Male sexuality, because of the primitive necessity of pursuit and penetration, does contain an important element of aggressiveness . . . we know in our hearts that each one of us harbours within *himself* the same savage impulses which lead to murder, torture and war.[14]

A telling 'himself', which excludes women from the readership of this passage by Anthony Storr and from humanity altogether. Yet Piers Paul Read quoted it (approvingly) in his *Observer* article on Sutcliffe's trial. Sutcliffe was in good company. No wonder he thought 'God' was with him.

The Dobashes, investigating violence against wives, argue on the contrary that 'the use of violence is a learned response, learned in the company of others (an adolescent gang, a family) . . . Men are socialized into aggression' they contend, 'taught directly or indirectly that it is an appropriate means of problem-solving and of demonstrating authority in certain situations.' This is coupled with 'a set of beliefs and standards regarding the appropriate hierarchical relationship between men and women in the family and the rightful authority of husbands over wives'[15]. Their claim is backed by telling historical data.

They agree with the French historian Petiot that from the fourteenth to the sixteenth century onwards, there is a slow deterioration in the position of wives in the household, leading to the husband being finally established 'as a sort of domestic monarch'; and with Stone's claim that the strengthening of the *state* in England included the parallel destruction of the power of aristocratic kinship and the fostering of the power of the husband and father within the conjugal unit: 'Kings are compared to fathers in families' (so said King James I, 1609). 'Thus the state and the nuclear family were inextricably intertwined and mutually supportive'. The influence of the patriarchal family upon the development of other institutions has been noted by both Phillippe Ariès, in *Centuries of Childhood*, and by Foucault in *Madness and Civilization*. The order of the family became moral — and political.

This was reinforced by two factors: the rise of capitalism, bringing about the division of labour described by Zaretsky: the separation of the domestic and commodity modes of production, resulting in the devaluation of domestic work (unpaid and housebound). And the rise of Protestantism, investing the head of the household, the father, with 'much of the authority and power of the priest'. For Luther and Calvin, God and Biology agreed to place women in a position of subordination and obedience. (Luther actually argues that women's narrow shoulders and broad hips qualify them for housework, while men's broad shoulders and narrow hips qualify them for outdoors activities). The chastisement of wives was legitimate as a means of enforcing submission. In the sixteenth and seventeenth centuries and even after, 'flogging was used throughout society as a means of controlling the powerless: children, women, and the lower classes'. Through-out the Reformation there was *public* chastisement of 'nagging wives'. This disappeared in the course of the nineteenth century. That the 'ideology' survives is clearly shown by the remarks about Sonia quoted above. Tacit (or explicit) consensus within the community that a man was within his right if he used force against his wife as long as he did not exceed certain limits survived throughout the seventeenth, eighteenth and nineteenth centuries. The state and the community chose not to intervene in the relationship between husband and wife. It took a long time for legislation to be established. The first rejection of the chastisement of wives was in 1829; but as late as 1915 a London police magistrate declares that 'the husband of a nagging wife . . . could beat her at home provided the stick he used was no thicker than a man's thumb'[16].

John Sutcliffe slaps his wife across the mouth after having seen her talk to men in a pub. Trevor Birdsall, who was with Sutcliffe *twice* when Sutcliffe went out to attack women, used to beat his wife Melissa although she had lost one leg. She had bruises to show. Sutcliffe kept silence about Trevor's domestic violence. Trevor kept silent about Sutcliffe's street violence. (Burn 105).

For a long time Anna Rogulskyj was not considered as one of the Ripper victims because the slashes across her back and abdomen were thought to have been made with a cuban heel. She had a Jamaican boyfriend: it was thought he had punished her in the appropriate manner for infidelity.[17]

> 'Me and Jane, when we were right little, we used to bath together, an' he'd just put this chrome towel-rail on wall — he didn't do right many jobs in the house, but one of them he had done was that. Anyway, as Jane were getting out of bath she slipped and grabbed hold of it to save herself and pulled it off. And we were terrified, we wouldn't come out of bathroom, even though it were an accident. An' he went berserk'.[18]

Thus Carl, about his father.

The Dobashes give substance to Séverine Auffret's distinction between two *kinds* of violence, which 'biological' arguments ('it is *natural* for lions to eat antelopes; it is *natural* for male antelopes to be aggressive in their pursuit of females'), and 'idealist' arguments of the Hegelian kind (the 'Master and Slave' dialectic, used by Simone de Beauvoir as a model for *The Second Sex*) tend to obscure and ignore. We do not mean the same thing when we talk about the violence of a spontaneous cock-fight, and the violence of a war. 'Political war, sexual violence, for mankind, do not spring from instinct nor from the soul, but are a specific human activity inscribed in history. The institutionalizing of violence may *use* the data of primary aggressiveness, it does not derive from them'. When children fight for a ball, or for play, the fighting is still connected with pleasure and goes no further. When a gang of kids decides to attack a Jewish boy, or go 'Paki-bashing', their violence has become an *act*, with a socio-economic, institutional basis[19]. Sutcliffe's violence is of the second kind. To claim that there is an unbroken link between that, and primary aggressiveness, is to side with, to defend, institutionalized violence. We have suggested how many people in power were, and are, prepared to do that.

Industrial Tools: Mastery over Machines.

The 'Superman' ideal of masculinity harboured in Sutcliffe's 'deranged' mind also comes from a complex historical formation. The conflict between the individual and society was given a new meaning by the expansion of Capital. Zaretsky argues:

> On one side the objective social world appeared, perceived at first as 'machinery' or 'industry', then throughout the 19th century as 'society' and into the 20th as 'big business', 'city hall', and then as 'technology' or 'life', as the domination of the

proletariat by the capitalist class became more difficult to perceive. In opposition to this harsh world that no individual could hope to affect, the modern world of subjectivity was created'[20].

Our culture is pervaded by a notion of the conflict between the individual and society: it can be found in Freud as in Weber. It is described as 'the human condition'. In the 19th century, the Romantic tradition,

> 'conjured up a series of figures who allegedly stood apart from society on the basis of their own personal uniqueness: the hero, the virtuoso, the mystic, the world traveller, the Wandering Jew . . .'[21]

This includes, of course, the artist. But also, as Rimbaud would say, 'the great Criminal, the great Accursed One, the Supreme Scientist'. Criminality can be the way to Value, to self-assertion. The convict and the artist are brothers.

In many ways, the pranks of the Sutcliffe family and their friends can be seen as an attempt at protest against social exploitation. Mick's forays onto the council rubbish tip are not just for money (any more than his smashing of shop-windows is for looting, or his father's burglaries are for profit: the profit, if there is one, is a bonus). Mick's job is to dig ditches for the council. If he boldly steals from that same anonymous council, if he comes back home on Christmas night with boxes full of shirts his father has perhaps helped to weave at the textile factory where he works, he is retrieving his pride, his 'manhood'. He may be at the lowest end of the spectrum, labouring for the drainage of society's waters (as Peter labours at the waterworks, or at the cemetery) but he's also shown that same diffuse society that he does not care a damn for its 'order' by laying his hands on what it values and protects: goods for consumption. Peter is saying the same when he steals from corpses. When he harangues and insults the body of a woman magistrate, he is also expressing a symbolic, heroic rebellion — but already, more twisted and deviated than Mick's.

It is clear that these acts have to do with the assertion of masculinity. Juliet Mitchell quotes the foreman of a bacon factory who claims that, while the men grumble, women allow themselves to be shifted from job to job: 'Now a woman, you can move her as much as you want, and she'll never complain, she'll just get on with whatever she's told to do'.[22]

Not so a man, haunted as Sutcliffe was by heroic or demonic dreams of manhood. 'He told me he was interested in the powers of black magic', his friend Fitzgerald told Beattie. 'He said there were various forces in the world we would never understand, but . . . he would make contact with them and tap them.' Of that ilk is Tennyson's Kraken, used as a model for the warning in the truck cabin:

> Below the thunders of the upper deep;
> Far far beneath in the abysmal sea,
> His ancient, dreamless, uninvaded sleep
> The Kraken sleepeth . . . (until)
> . . . In Roaring he shall rise and on the surface die.

As Dracula, 'lord of the Un-Dead', sprang upon Yorkshire from the Whitby graveyard where he lands, so Sutcliffe/Zapolski leaps from Bingley cemetery. Dracula descends with his 50 coffins upon the city of London. His family name is *Sz*ekelys, and the *Sz*ganys execute his orders. 'We *Sz*ekelys', the Count says, 'are right to be proud, for in our veins runs the blood of many courageous races which fought, like the lion, for lordship.' 'Lordship': readers of Freud, at this point, might remember 'Signorelli'[23]. 'Lordship' was also what Zapolski promised Sutcliffe.

Dracula comes from the fictitious Carpathians, described by the young solicitor who visits him as a kind of 'horseshoe' in which, as in an imaginary 'whirlpool', all the known superstitions of the world are gathered. Sutcliffe also, in his dream of being a man whose latent energy would 'rock the nation', is like a whirlpool in which all the Romantic criminal superstitions of the West seem to be gathered. A look at what the Sunday Times 'Insight' team called 'The Geography of

Terror', the map showing where the crimes took place, indicates Sutcliffe's homes (Bingley, Bradford, then Heaton) and place of work (Clark's, Shipley) to be like the eye of a hurricane, wreaking havoc in its eddies. Stopping short on symbolic borders: Haworth, the Brontë's place, north. Rural York, east. Sheffield, the steel city, south, where the arrest will occur[24]. Symbolically too, the man seems to have been successful in his killings in the places which are the birthplaces of the first Industrial Revolution: Bradford, the city of woollens; Manchester, the city of textiles. A textile factory is the place where John Sutcliffe works and where Peter had his first job.

Sutcliffe's attempt to descend upon Sheffield, move as it were from the places of the first Industrial Revolution to the second, makes sense in this perspective. You could also say it was inevitable, because of his fascination with motors. A whole series of heroic models combine Man with the Motor to produce Superman. The term, 'Bachelor Machines' has even been coined by Michel Carrouges[25]. 'Bachelor' because man, ignoring woman, mates with the machine. Many such machines (as in Kafka, Jarry, Roussel) are torture machines; others are masturbatory. They have haunted the nineteenth and twentieth century imagination, from Poe to the Dadaists and the Surrealists. They represent machines as 'male' — excluding female — and an imaginary attempt to gain mastery, by harnessing the machine and making it take the place of all that is 'other' (in eroticism, in religion, in power-structures).

There also are anthropomorphic examples of 'Bachelor Machines'. *Frankenstein,* at least in its popular version, could be regarded as one. For Frankenstein is trying to harness the forces of modern science. He is also trying to by-pass the female reproductive system by producing a man. And he uses the dead to do this. His 'monster' is a strange combination of the 'monstrous' (the Kraken, the Id element, the welling up of deep repressed forces which mean perhaps, among other things, as Mrs. Gaskell suggests in *Mary Barton,* the industrial proletariat) and a new Adam, but this time machine power. The Hulk, more than all the other figures of 'doubles' (Thor, Warlock, the Werewolf, Spiderman, and many others) in the comics Peter Sutcliffe was so fond of reading as a child[26], is the modern heir to *Frankenstein*. All the more impressive as he is innocent, his duplicity, the accidental result of spontaneous creation. Gentle Bruce Banner, a physicist, has been caught in the zone of a nuclear explosion. He does not die, nor, lucky fellow, does he get cancer. He acquires the uncontrollable ability to turn into a 'Green Goliath', a giant of superhuman and invincible strength whenever anyone makes him angry. Though presented as a curse, excluding him from intercourse with women, his double nature is ideal. His violence, being uncontrollable and not of his doing, is as unblameable as it is unstoppable. He takes on and defeats the whole of the US army, the navy too if need be. Thus he combines absolute power with absolute goodness. For David (Bruce Banner) is kindness itself. Hulk-Goliath, though filled with, and fulfilling, all the aggressive drives of the 'Id', by some wonderful turn of events, however, never kills anybody (the trains he overturns never have any passengers on them), and he only harms 'baddies'. His 'Dr. Jekyll and Mr. Hyde' nature performs miracles indeed. Thanks to him, the supreme threat of the machine, nuclear explosion, is encountered and harnessed. Violent drives are not only uncontrollable (no need to keep yourselves reined in, kids) *and* innocent, they turn out to be good in the end. Anger and violence, especially when combined with machine power, are given full licence.

'Better let him sleep?' the note in the truck asks.

Hulk has fists 'like a sledge-hammers'. Which Charles Atlas promised to his disciples.

Hulk is the (chance) victory of an individual over the most abstract of oppressors, the supreme form of modern technology[27]. The modern worker is at the mercy of technology; 'reified'[28], fragmented by the 'machine' that employs him. In *A Seventh Man* John Berger strikingly illustrates how the tools can take possession of a man:

> He begins to watch his arm, as if it were being moved
> by what it is holding instead of by his shoulder. He
> thinks of water pumping his arm. The moving pieces
> shift his eyes, the air breathes his lungs. In places
> liquids ooze out of the machine . . . He knows that
> what he is doing is separate from any skill he has . . .
> He has been told that the factory makes washing
> machines.[29]

Sutcliffe embodies both the Hulk, the man who, discovering his
power with body-building, then with the aid of motor-bikes and
motor cars, has come to wield the hammer and the screwdriver
against the 'baddies' who do not count, and the vulnerable
employee who can be told off by his boss, who can lose his
driving licence. In odd moments of lucidity, he almost realizes
that the 'machine' has taken him over: that far from being his
master, he is its slave. Though Bruce Banner summons the
Hulk to the rescue of his frail self, the 'monster' may be
uncontainable: 'I was shouting in the car. I set off back and
was changing up and down the gear-box. Eventually I got back
home, locked the car in the garage and went to bed. I felt a great
sense of achievement at that stage'.

I have remarked earlier that Sutcliffe uses his bullworker
and his motors to construct an artificial masculinity.

The tools he uses for killing are also sexual and industrial.

Fetishism

When I say 'fetish' here, I refer to two well-established
concepts. The first is from *Capital*, where Marx discusses how
the use-value of an object can become so subsumed by its
exchange-value that it takes on a 'fantastic' character, that its
social and physical dimensions are made 'ghostly'. A relation
between things takes the place of a relation between men. A
table ceases to be a table made by craftsmen from wood, to be
eaten at, etc: its value becomes static — effaces its 'thingness'.

The second meaning is from Freud, in particular in a late essay, 'Splitting of the Ego in the Process of Defence'[30]. He is discussing the case of a patient who in early childhood must have been subjected to a psychic trauma. A little boy of between three and four was threatened with castration by his nurse who had found him masturbating. The threat was ascribed to the father. The threat had a full effect upon the child who had seen female genitals. But instead of giving up the satisfaction of the instinct, he 'created a substitute for the penis which he missed in females — that is to say, a fetish'. He effected 'a displacement of value — transferred the importance of the penis to another part of his body', — namely, to his toes. His fear of castration also took the form of a fear of being 'devoured' by the father. The creation of a fetish enabled the little boy not to choose between satisfaction of the drive and the demand of reality. He rejected reality, refusing to accept any prohibition, and recognized the danger of reality, trying to divest himself of the fear by means of the displacement. 'But everything has to be paid for in one way or another, and this success is achieved at the price of a rift in the ego which never heals' and becomes 'the centre-point of a splitting of the ego.' However, the 'anxious susceptibility' about 'either of his little toes being touched' suggests that the fear of castration was what had 'found the clearer expression'.

Sutcliffe had an anxious susceptibility about his socks (which he insisted on washing himself, because of his problem of smelly feet) and shoes. The number of times in which the word 'foot' occurs in his testimony at court is striking. Why for instance does he say of his position in the grave he was digging when he heard the 'voice' that he had 'his feet about five foot' underground? Wouldn't it be more usual to say that his head was at ground-level? In that same testimony, he also stresses how on one occasion a policeman had on his notebook in front of him, a replica of the boot-print that had been found near two of the corpses, but that he failed to see the sole of that same boot which Sutcliffe was wearing and that he showed him as he climbed back into his lorry. This inability of the policeman to *see* the boot was of course taken by Sutcliffe as a sign that his mission was to continue. The 'father' having taken no notice of the fetishized penis does not mean to 'remove' it. Conversely, it must be remembered that Sutcliffe stopped attacking women in 1969 after he had been found equipped with a hammer and screwdriver by a policeman. And he will start owning up to being the Ripper to the police questioning him in Sheffield after a young policeman with a spirit of initiative remembers that upon being arrested in a dark alley in the company of Ava Reivers, Sutcliffe had asked to go and 'relieve himself'. The policeman goes back to the spot where Sutcliffe went. He finds a hammer and screwdriver hidden under a tank. Then more tools are found hidden in the toilet-tank of the police station.

I have discussed earlier the possibility of a traumatic scene having occurred between little Peter and his father — or of a general sense of 'threat' having been generated by John Sutcliffe's documented violence. What is striking is the permanence of 'foot' episodes in Sutcliffe's history, and their transformation — all very much supporting, especially in the light of Sutcliffe being diagnosed as a schizophrenic, Freud's description of a 'splitting ego' connected with fetishism. He learns to walk by means of a leather boot reinforced at the heel and the toes; his father, when he is ten, buys him some football boots and fails to interest him in playing football, though he calls him a 'natural'. The Charles Atlas method proposes to make his fists (not feet) into 'sledge-hammers'. But then, Mick Sutcliffe claims that once your adversary is down, you've got to kick him as hard as you can: the one rule is to 'win' (ie, fists can double up as booted feet). I have recounted some of the episodes in which Sutcliffe is described as either having booted 'an old 'un', or proposed to go and give one of the 'bags' (a punching bag?) a good 'kicking'. Steve Close claims that one of Peter's gravedigger's pranks was to play rugby with a skull, running 'the full length of the school playing field, climbing up the goal-post to leave it perched on top'.

In Sutcliffe's attacks tools became the substitutes of feet: as if the 'displacement' which Freud talks about moved from the

body (the foot) to socks and finally to industrial fetishes. One of
the intermediaries may be the Durex offered by Sutcliffe to
Sonia (his 'sock' will shoe another, but it still will be worn by his
girl). Whether this is true or not, it is striking that in some of the
early attacks he uses a sock stuffed with a brick, or a sock filled
with gravel. That particular sock tears upon impact, and 'what
was in it fell out'. The father's watch had had the glass of its face
broken upon impact against the door when he hit his wife. His
pocketful of currants (as Eliot would say, nastily, of the Smyrna
merchant) had scattered when he escaped from the house he
had been trying to burgle, and he had been caught. The
hardness of that 'sock' is flawed. Something harder must be
substituted for it. Cars. Engineering. He hit old Bishop on the
head with a mallet. 'Sledge-hammers'. Hammer is the answer.
And then that too doubles up. Cars. Fiddling with motors.
Screwdrivers. Hammer and screwdriver: balls and penis. Let's
sock it to them. 'Let's go down Lumb Lane for a jump, then give
the pro a kicking instead of paying'[31]. He jumps with both feet
on the bodies of some of his victims. Lumb Lane. Lump.
'Lumpf', little Hans says about faeces. Is there an *anal* element
in these attacks, always from the *back*, 'let's *sock* it to them', the
back of the head?

Lump: Yvonne Pearson is killed by means of a lump-
hammer.

A lump sum of money. The first prostitute will not give him
his five pound's change for the ten-pound note she's retained.
The new five-pound note remains inside Jean Jordan's bag, it
leads the police to him, nearly gets him caught. Five pounds, ten
pounds: five, ten toes? Making sure one is 'all there'? That the
contents haven't been spilled?[32]

Fear of castration seems all pervasive. Under its pressure,
the fetishism, and the disavowal of reality, assume such
proportions that it is as if displacement and continuity made for
total, symbolic meaning. Contagion at any rate seems to be the
order of the day. Even as I am trying to read the data, I find
words like 'Lumb' (Lane) *become* 'lump' and 'lumpf' and 'jump'
and 'lump-hammer' and 'lump-sum'. The reader of this

scenario becomes the schizophrenic, reading the message on Zapolski's grave. The terrifying thing is that you can't get out of this by saying that it's all mad, and therefore untrue: it is true in the sense that it has happened, and been allowed to happen. Sutcliffe's severe state of sexual disturbance produced an almost wholly 'artificial' access to masculinity. He lives in a world in which a prostitute can be associated with a parcel of guts, in which killing can be associated by football fans with 'scoring', a 'ball' with a 'head', natural male aggressiveness with rape, fists with hammers, masculinity with power over someone weaker[33], — and in which women's humanity can be erased for the sake of using them as 'the other'[34]. The object or the place can be used for the sake of a demonstration, used as destroyable nature, a surface on which an inscription can be scrawled. Or the herd of pigs into which the evil demons that have taken possession of a man can be expelled.

Detectives, attempting to determine which type of weapon exactly had been used to attack the bodies of the victims were placed in rows in a Yorkshire slaughterhouse, armed with every kind of tool (sculptor's, surgeon's, carpet-fitters, etc.) and spent hours (or was it days) ripping at the flesh of pigs, pigs' skins being reputed to be, of all animal skins, the one that bruised most like human flesh[35]. 'Cannibals have called human flesh "long pig" ' is the remark with which Beattie introduces his own 'chamber of horrors' story.

What is worrying about this is that the quest for the murderer places the detectives in the position of the killer — imitating his acts — but also, establishing types of substitution similar to his. Women become nothing but corpses, become assimilated with animal corpses. The bodies are there to be prodded by tools. A 'phantasmagoric' aura of cannibalism floats over the whole thing. Men's scientific (forensic) or engineering tools *relate to each other* above the denied naturalness of the victims, animal or human, their pain, the waste of life. 'As soon as a wooden table emerges as a commodity, it changes into a thing which transcends sensuousness . . . it stands on its head, and evolves out of its wooden brain grotesque ideas . . .'[36]

Fetishism is at work in the detectives as it is in the killer.

'Value . . . does not have its value branded on its forehead; it rather transforms every product of labour into a *social hieroglyphic*. Later on, men try to decipher the hieroglyphic, to get behind the secret of their own social product'[37].

Fetishism is at work not only in the tools which Sutcliffe uses for killing, but, in a less acutely displaced form, in the way he arranges the bodies of his victims. Irene Richardson was having a period and wore two pairs of pants. Sutcliffe lifted the skirt, removed the tights only on the right leg. He removed one of the pants and pushed it right into the foot of the removed tights. He then covered the body with the woman's coat, so as to conceal it entirely except for the feet. He carefully arranged the boots on the thighs.

Tina Atkinson's body is 'staged' in a similar, although less elaborate, way. Sutcliffe removed the trousers she was wearing, but only one leg of the pants and tights, and only one boot. Tampering with the feet is constant: he undresses Helen Rytka's body, only leaving the socks on, and throwing the shoes far away. He leaves Vera Millward's body dressed, but removes the shoes and carefully arranges them on top of her. Barbara Leach's body also gets displayed in a special way, feet against the wall: according to Beattie, the arrangement must have taken about half an hour. For a murderer risking detection every minute, this care must mean something. Dr. Bandara's shoes and bag also get thrown away.

The pants pushed into the leg of the tights strike me as a displaced violation, as well as an attempt to make the victim appear ridiculous: the stuffed leg is a rag-doll, a stuffed pillow, a grotesque equivalent to the tampon, displayed over her like a label. The empty shoes, neatly placed on the thighs, parody her sex and mock the 'tidy little girl' which Sutcliffe himself may hate being when he removes his own boots before coming in at home, placing them side by side at the door. The displacement in Irene Richardson's case may be greatest because, the woman having her period, her femininity asserts itself in a way that Sutcliffe cannot directly deal with. In other cases, with mounting violence, as if the depth of the hatred became uncontrollable so that it ran away with other urges, to make the murdered body 'signify' something, so that those who will find it 'read' and decipher the meaning which has been inscribed — in other cases, there is a direct violation: of an atrocious kind, but always by means of a *substitute* for the penis, a fetish whose function is to deny that femininity exists. A piece of wood is pushed into Emily Jackson, a piece of broken glass into Jayne MacDonald, a screwdriver into Josephine Whitaker. These gestures prolong others, whose significance is the same: to expose feminity as 'obscene'; and to negate that he (or anyone else) can have any relation to it except unnaturally, through artificial holes punctured by means of industrial tools into the 'wrong' places. He does not strip the bodies of his first three victims (which might connote desire, or curiosity); he pushes the bras up and the trousers or pants down, punching holes in the back and in the abdomen. This may also, not on the level of what he means to show, but on the level of the 'drives' that have taken possession of him, signify his hatred of the female womb as I have suggested when discussing Melanie Klein's theories. And that element becomes stronger as his fury becomes worse, his slashing bolder.

But he did keep repeating to the police as to his family or the doctors, that he wanted 'to show how obscene prostitutes are'; that they were 'littering the street' and he wanted to 'clean up'. Wounding them repeatedly, and arranging their bodies so as to make them appear ridiculous, un-sexy (stripped all the wrong way, the reverse of what a strip-teaser would do to attract desire). To make them abominable was his way of destroying femininity, out of his own culture-induced hatred of himself as potentially feminine. He *was* the bitch: he had to denounce and desecrate 'her' elsewhere, so as to rid himself of the plague that she was. He lacerates them with a screwdriver, like voodoo effigies, or as a child might rain pin-pricks into a doll that for him or her (for a while at least) is made to figure the persecuting world that cannot otherwise be kept at bay.

His attacks pass on a disease. A kind of contagion is at work.

Sutcliffe is described as having always lived with his back to the wall as a child, afraid of being approached from the back, fearful of human contact, sexually timid and with a speech defect. All his surviving victims, skulls crashed in some cases 'like a smashed eggshell'[38], now live a haunted and damaged life, terrified of men, back to the wall, their sexual life often in ruins.

But on another level his attacks passed on, or showed up another kind of disease. The one that Marx is talking about when he says that 'exchange-value' transforms the 'products of labour' into 'social hieroglyphics' that men try to decipher afterwards. Sutcliffe's victims were *not* 'obscene'. The 'obscenity' was in his own sick eye. He inscribed obscenity upon them (the way an image might be inscribed on a piece of gold to make it into a coin) by displaying them and wounding them in such a way as to make them legible as such. By defacing them, 'labouring' at them with tools which industry uses to mould and subdue nature, he was placing them outside culture, outside the walls of the city. By making them appear grotesque, he was also placing them outside nature. Stuffed under an old sofa, in a piece of wasteground, horsehair pushed into her mouth, her poor body battered by a lump-hammer, left to rot undiscovered for a month, Yvonne Pearson could indeed appear like Abomination, the 'plague' upon the city. No human being would want to identify with her.

The trouble was that Sutcliffe's *text* was read as he meant it to be read. All the accounts I have seen of the discovery of the bodies of his victims insist upon the horror of the 'sight' he had left. 'It made even hardened detectives blanch', or, 'the superintendent in charge said that he had been almost paralyzed with numbness', or, 'the sight that awaited the police was such that . . .' About Yvonne Pearson, Cross's comment is: 'it was a humiliating end for a girl who saw herself as a cut above many of her fellow prostitutes.' Even though elsewhere, he, and others, make attempts to dissociate themselves from the distinction between innocent victims and prostitutes[39]. That one should feel grief, or pity, any of the fellow-feeling that would go to the victims of a terrorist massacre, does not even seem to be envisaged. How would the journalists have written about those bodies if they had been children's? 'It was a humiliating end for a little boy who saw himself as a real "toughie".' Doesn't that make you want to puke? Why doesn't it when you're reading about Yvonne Pearson? Would the fans have chanted, 'Twelve-nil', would adolescents have worn T-shirts saying, '12-Nil', if a child-murderer had been sought? How would Yvonne Pearson's body have been dealt with if she had been Indira Gandhi — or President Reagan or the Pope? Well, we saw, didn't we?

Twelve

Prostitution

(The Status of the Merchandise: Divided; For Sale; and Silent)

Black Goats, White Sheep: The Victorian Inheritance

It is evident that what made Sutcliffe's killings possible, and gave them their meaning, is the status and image of prostitutes.

Criticizing the 'inhibiting' effects of Acton's 1857 book on Prostitution[1], Judith Walkowitz points out that 'the effort to relate prostitution to existing social structures was undermined by a compulsive need to build defences against the social reality under investigation':

> To investigate seriously those questions, the researcher would have had to view these women outside the realm of pathology, as neither pollutants nor the polluted, but as poor women who were integrated into a complex sexual economy.[2]

Looking at the reactions elicited on many sides by the Yorkshire Ripper case, it is staggering to notice how close we still are to Victorian attitudes. Judith Walkowitz makes precisely this point in her examination of the 'Jack-the-Ripper' case: 'For the Ripper story has continued to provide a common vocabulary of male violence against women, a vocabulary now almost one hundred years old'.[3]

I see four main ways in which Sutcliffe's attitudes express

Victorian ideologies — ideologies which are still very much with us today.

1. All serious writers on prostitution[4] make the point that it is extremely fluid, a 'transitory state', that there is no clear demarcation between a prostitute and a non-prostitute. There is much casual prostitution; temporary prostitution too, especially among working-class women who are hard up. All nineteenth century commentators agreed that it was a 'rational economic choice'. It still is.

> . . . prostitution was the inevitable result of the appalling working conditions and low pay of women in domestic service, in the sweated trades, notably dressmaking and millinery, and in the factories of the north.[5]

Journalists writing about Sutcliffe's victims resort to terms like 'professional' or 'semi-professional' to try and express the differences between the women. Black, or half-black. The reality is much more complex. Wilma McCann and Irene Richardson occasionally resorted to prostitution, doing so more and more as, left alone to fend for their children, they needed money. Emily Jackson went with clients regularly in the evenings with the support of her husband who would drive her to 'The Gaiety', a modern pub on the outskirts of Harehills in Leeds, and wait for her. He let her do it because she liked it. Jean Jordan did it occasionally without the support of her boy-friend: she would go on a 'jaunt', sometimes thumbing a lift to her native Scotland. A solitary escape. Helen Rytka and her twin sister, orphans who had been fostered, tried to work. The one had a job at a sweet-factory in which she netted about £20 a week, the other was at art college. They then decided they could make plenty through prostitution, thus being able to live together and perhaps save for a better future. Helen wrote poems. The possibility of returning to studies some day was there. Vera Millward, a Spaniard who'd come after the war to work as a maid, began to resort to prostitution after the death of her husband when she found herself unable to cope financially with her five children. They were taken from her and put with foster parents. She then started living with a West Indian, and had more children, fell ill. Her boy-friend was unemployed. She resorted to prostitution again. Ava Reivers, a Jamaican, went out on a regular evening stint; Marcella Claxton, also a Jamaican, went out with boyfriends, not with clients. Anna Rogulskyj, though never into prostitution, was still treated by the police as 'suspect' because she drank and swore and had had several boy-friends. Teresa Sykes, though an unmarried mother, was treated as OK because she lived with her father. Margo Walls had no man-friend; she lived with her widowed mother. Jacqueline Hill had a fiancé; she was a student.

All these women were out in the streets at night.

Sutcliffe saw them all as 'black'.

In his case the need to label, to inscribe prostitution upon the bodies of women by means of murder, sprang from a fear of indifferentiation — fear of 'his' women being working-class, falling into the 'pit' of underprivilege — and sex. Why do the police, and the Attorney General who tried to move the jury with the 'really tragic case' of the 'innocent victim' (Jayne MacDonald) as if the others had deserved to die for being prostitutes, and the journalists for whom the only shade of distinction is 'semi-professional', also need to present the world of women as *either* black *or* white?

2. The 'Jack the Ripper' murders in 1888 helped the respectable classes, obsessed with fears of class conflict and social disintegration, especially in the wake of 'Bloody Sunday', (Nov. 18, 1877, when London's working people tried to enter Trafalgar Square and were forcefully repressed by the police), focus their anxieties on the East End of London. The Whitechapel area, where the murders occurred, came to symbolize 'social unrest born of urban degeneracy':

> Part of London's declining inner industrial rim,
> Whitechapel stood at the edge of the vast East End,
> London's proletarian centre . . . To middle-class

observers, Whitechapel was an alien place, a centre of cosmopolitan culture and entrepôt for foreign immigrants and refugees, whose latest wave consisted of poor Jews escaping the pogroms of Eastern Europe in the 1880's.[6]

Whitechapel was seen as 'a moral landscape of light and darkness, a nether region of illicit sex and crime.' Many similar things could be said about the Yorkshire Ripper case.

It occurred during the period in which recession began to make itself felt, to scar and depress the industrial North in particular. 1974 happens to be both the date of the first petrol crisis in the wake of the Yom Kippur war, and that of Sutcliffe's marriage. He begins to kill in 1975. Social unrest attendant upon unemployment and racial tension erupted in Brixton and also all over the country, including Leeds Chapeltown area where many of the murders had taken place, in July 1981, shortly after the end of Sutcliffe's trial. I do not have the data that would enable me to do more than note the coincidence, but I do remember feeling that the impending violence I had felt about me at the time of the Ripper killings had at last found its proper target. I offer this for what it's worth. It certainly should be explored in the light of the relation between 'Bloody Sunday' and the Jack the Ripper murders. What is striking is that both Chapeltown and Manningham Lane (the Bradford red-light area) have much in common with the Whitechapel area, including the way in which they are perceived. Cross, being a Leeds man, is clear-sighted about the almost universal misunderstanding of the characteristics of Chapeltown which journalists from all over the world found it convenient to foster: it was portrayed 'as a modern equivalent to the original Ripper's East End slums' (themselves melodramatized by the press at the time), rather than

> what close examination shows it to be — a multi-racial suburb of considerable (albeit faded) elegance, leafier than most other parts of Leeds, with shops and cafes to cater to a range of ethnic cultures.

And, very low down on the list of characteristics, a fairly high proportion of prostitutes.[7]

Moving to the Victorian mansions of Chapeltown had meant social elevation for 19th century Jewish immigrants. Between the 1830's and 1850's they moved out further to the countryside, and precisely as in London's East End, they left behind a large number of

> Jewish businesses and shops, some of which continue to thrive. Although a Jewish working-class community of mostly old people survives in Chapeltown (again, just as in the East End or the Lower East Side) most inhabitants today are poor Commonwealth immigrants and very poor whites, many of whom are Eastern Europeans who settled in Leeds after the War.[8]

All that Sutcliffe needs is solitude. He does kill sometimes in run-down alleys and pieces of waste ground. He also kills in pleasant and pretty places; children's playing fields, parks, campus grounds, genteel gardens. A mythical contagion, however, is made to spread from the one to the other, a sense of the overwhelmingly seedy, violent, dark, industrial North. Perhaps it enables the rich South to feel complacent: that sort of thing only happens in Yorkshire. Male violence is displaced onto one extreme northern example. It can be ignored elsewhere. The dangers of social unrest can be forgotten while people experience 'fear and loathing'[9] of the victims. Chapeltown or Manningham Lane — prostitutes — Ripper murders. Conveniently located, both socially and geographically, they are left to get on with it. Meanwhile, they are providing an entertaining though gruelling circus for the rest of the country.

The fact that Chapeltown and Manningham Lane should hold such a high proportion of immigrants — the Bradford area with an overwhelming Asian population ('the country people and peasants who jetted from the East to a new life in the bosom of Empire'[10]), the Leeds district even more mixed, with people from Eastern Europe (Poles and Czechs and Ukrainians) as well as from Asia and the West Indies — symbolically reinforces a point that has already surfaced: that Sutcliffe was killing also to differentiate 'his' women from working-class women/prostitutes. Sonia was Czech. They live at Garden *Lane*, Heaton. Lumb *Lane*, Bradford, the prostitute area, Sutcliffe always refers to as 'the' lane. A further source of confusion. . .

3. Discussing the rich and entangled story of early middle-class feminist crusades against male vice and in defence of prostitutes, Judith Walkowitz argues that the feminists became entrapped in the 'social purity movement', which had a strong Evangelical strain. The campaign orchestrated by Stead, with misguided data on a mistaken platform, created a public furore that led to the passing of the Criminal Law Amendment Act of 1885, which had pernicious effects. It formed the basis of legal prosecution against male homosexuals until 1967.

> It drove a wedge between prostitutes and the poor working-class community. It effectively destroyed the brothel as a family industry and centre of a specific female subculture; further undermined the social and economic autonomy of prostitutes; and increasingly rendered them social outcasts.[11]

The social purity movement, although middle-class in origin, spread to the working classes. Social purity helped the working man 'bolster (his) authority as (a) responsible patriarch' through, in exchange, submitting to 'a certain domestic ideology':

> In general, sexual respectability became the hall-mark of the respectable working man, anxious to distance himself from the 'bestiality' of the casual labouring poor at a time when increased pressure

was being placed on the respectable working class to
break their ties with outcast groups.[12]

Every word of this is true of Sutcliffe's drive for respectability
and social ascent. The 'casual labouring poor' who are to be
made into 'outcasts', for him, were made to take on the specific
image of the prostitute. The religious vocabulary that is
implicit in his description of prostitutes as unclean, as a plague,
as litter, and that is manifest in his sense of mission of being an
Old Testament exterminating Angel, evidently has its roots in
the Victorian Evangelical movement.

'Social purity', Judith Walkowitz shows in her description of
the consequences of the Amendment Act, is 'reactionary'. It
obviously has its contemporary equivalent in the USA, with the
Moral Majority movement, one of the powerful offshoots of the
'New Right'. Passed 'ostensibly to protect women', Sylvia
Pankhurst remarked of the White Slavery Act of 1912, it 'is
being used almost exclusively to punish women.' This was also
what was triggered by the Jack the Ripper murders.

The people who mobilized over the murders were 'almost
exclusively male'. 'An army of West End men, fascinated by the
murders and bent on hunting the Ripper, invaded the East
End. Meanwhile, a half-dozen male vigilante committees were
set up in Whitechapel . . . These male patrols were organized to
protect women, but they also constituted surveillance of the
unrespectable poor, and of low-life women in particular.'

> . . . the message of social purity to men was mixed: it
> demanded that men control their own sexuality, but
> it gave them power to control the sexuality of women
> as well, since it called upon them to protect their
> women and to repress brothels and streetwalkers.
>
> (During the Ripper episode) men ostensibly out to
> hunt the Ripper harassed some women on the streets
> while husbands threatened wives with 'ripping'
> them up in their homes.[13]

Yallop has six pages recounting awful incident after awful

incident in Yorkshire between 1975 and 1981: some reveal an alarming degree of fascination with the new 'Ripper': hoaxers confessing or reporting 'bodies' to the police in countless calls over five years; children at parties playing 'Cops and Rippers'; massive sales of 'Ripper alarms' in northern cities and a whole array of gadgets: necklaces with whistles attached, and a stink pen called 'Rapel' for women to place inside their pants. Others suggest the types of 'imitations' which Judith Walkowitz mentions. Yallop details four cases of violent rape in which the aggressor boasted of being 'The Yorkshire Ripper'. He also recounts how in May 1979 two vice squad police officers arrested a woman for soliciting, then forced her to have intercourse, threatening to kill her if she didn't and to 'make it look like a Yorkshire Ripper job'.[14] Conversely he quotes a speech by the Vice Chancellor of Leeds University warning 'all women students' not to be 'out alone after dark' under any circumstances, urgently requesting 'the cooperation of all students.' That meant, and it was as good as an order, that male students were to see female students home. The protection of the 'good women' was to be ensured by men — while 'bad' women were exposed to vice squad officers.

Meanwhile, Sutcliffe would regularly see the secretary from Clark's home to protect her from danger in the streets. Or his wife. Or his sister. Then he went out to kill Barbara Leach. Was he giving a lead, or following one? 'The message of social purity . . . called upon (men) to protect their women and to repress . . . streetwalkers.'

The police regulated prostitution in Bradford, using women as 'live bait', afraid that if the killer didn't strike again, he would never be caught. How dangerous that was, was demonstrated in January 1980, when a woman who had been violently attacked by a man was helped by other prostitutes:

Sitting watching were policemen in a car who made no effort to intervene. When one of the women ran screaming to the police car for help, they told her that they had been instructed not to move, that they were there to collect car numbers. The attacker got away.[15]

(The Ripper episode) covertly sanctioned male antagonism toward women and buttressed male authority over them. It established a common vocabulary and iconography of male violence, papering over class differences and obscuring the different material conditions that provoked sexual antagonism in different classes[16].

Social space was segregated: the women indoors, the men patrolling the streets, private detectives or improvised detectives like Yallop looking for signs, out on a trail. Little boys had a song, Yallop recounts; 'folk' was springing anew from the cobblestones: he calls it a 'modern nursery rhyme':

Ripper, Ripper.
Hunt. Hunt.
Ripper, Ripper.
Cunt. Cunt.[17]

Man the hunter and woman the goose. Naughty naughty geese that won't stay in the penfold.

4.   I felt a Cleaving in my Mind —
As if my Brain had been split —
I tried to match it — Seam by Seam —
But could not make them fit.[18]

Her womb from her body. Separation. Her clitoris from her vulva. Cleaving. Desire from her body . . .
Death from the city. Wilderness from the city. The Cemetery. The Garden . . .
The errant from the city. The ghetto. The ghetto of Jews. The ghetto of Moors. The quarter of prostitutes . . . The underworld. The underground. The sewer. Space. Divided.
'Where he begins'[19]

The Great Crusade, led by Josephine Butler, one of the foremost 19th century feminists, attacked the Contagious Diseases Act (1864-1868) which provided for the sanitary or medical inspection of prostitutes in designated garrison towns. The treatment of prostitutes under the Acts epitomized a pervasive and underlying misogyny. 'Sirs', declared Butler, 'you cannot hold us in honour so long as you drag our sisters in the mire.' The campaign was radical. It drew thousands of women into the political arena for the first time:

> They rejected the prevailing social view of 'fallen women' as pollutants of men and depicted them instead as victims of male pollution, as women who had been invaded by men's bodies, men's laws, and by that 'steel penis', the speculum.[20]

It objected to regulating women's bodies by means of a metal tool and, while the clients go unmolested, looking into women's wombs. Wasn't Sutcliffe confronted by precisely that 'Victorian' image when he visited the wax works in Morecambe, the room with all the women's torsoes cut open, the egg-shaped holes with the exposed foetuses in them, larger and larger as the months are supposed to go by? In order to see what the anatomy figures show, you would have to cut open eight or nine dead women with dead foetuses inside them, at different stages of pregnancy. The figures both ignore that the life of the foetus depends on women's wombs being closed, not being prised open in any way, and assert that women's bodies *are* subjected to 'tools', science, engineering. The first Jack the Ripper was supposed to be a surgeon. I have suggested what complex significance Sutcliffe's 'tools' had. But there again, the way in which not just in Victorian times but in our day, still, gynaecological units or the police can treat women, a gross and lurid caricature of which was presented by the wax works, 'told' him that he was, in some way, 'licensed'[21].

The Division of Women

He had put liberation back 100 years, Yallop says, describing how, in the end, women cancelled all but the most pressing engagements: church services in the evening were either cancelled or brought forward, fathers drove daughters hundreds of miles back to colleges and universities rather than put them at risk after dark. Even 'feminists might have been boiling inside, but many would not go out alone after dark',[22] or phoned each other as soon as they got home.

Helen Rytka had a safety system: her twin sister and she would take the number of the car with which each went in turn, then wait twenty minutes for the other to come back. Her sister being late, Helen had thought she had time for a 'quick one' and went with the dark bearded man with the soft voice and gentle manner.

Feminists found themselves pushed into adopting the same safety measures as prostitutes before them. Helen Rytka's system, after all, would have worked if she had not made an exception. But it took a long time for the feeling of sisterhood, for that 'identification' with prostitutes which Josephine Butler's movement in many ways achieved, to assert itself. For women only marched after Barbara Leach's murder: the murder of a student. They carried placards saying, 'Women Demand Curfew On Men' and 'Cut Off Male Power', and a 'Women's Right to Self-Defence Campaign' had originated in Bradford after the murder of Josephine Whitaker. Yallop is a fairly unsympathetic witness. Yet he has a point when he says that women's muteness at the time of the previous murders was suspect: 'Was it only when they felt personally attacked that they could respond?'[23]

In 1888, during the Ripper manhunt, 'feminists were unable to mobilize any counter-offensive against the widespread male intimidation of women.' Josephine Butler, with what seems to have been her remarkable clear-sightedness, 'did express concern that the uproar over the murders would lead to the repression of brothels and the subsequent homelessness of women; but these were isolated interventions . . .'[24]

The clock has not gone back a hundred years. The contemporary women's movement did organize patrols against the threat. As consciousness progressed and debates gathered momentum, articles brought them to light[25]. A prostitutes' rights group protested at the trial with slogans reminding the public that prostitutes were mothers too, and that the Ripper had orphaned 23 children: '70% of prostitutes are mothers.' Essential things were being said: 'Women are not responsible for men's crimes'; 'Attorney General condoning the murder of prostitutes'. Hardly anyone took them in.

But they were being said. And very much to the point too is the enormous amount of work, written and done by actively supportive centres and groups on the *related* issues of rape, pornography, wife-battering, and on the connection between marriage and prostitution. They throw light on the same structures as those the Sutcliffe case illuminates. When Rosalind Coward says that 'pornography enforces a split in the way women's sexuality is represented — between the "wife" and the "goer"[26]', she is talking about precisely the type of 'division' of women, 'housewife' or 'harlot', white or black, 'decent' (Sutcliffe's term) or 'polluted', which patterned Sutcliffe's crimes. There have been many lucid attacks, both of the double standard (so clearly illustrated by John Sutcliffe and so insanely pursued by his son), and of the way in which prostitution has the function — paradoxically — of preserving marriage, providing an outlet for monogamous men's frustrated desires:

> Innately, it seems, women have sexual attractiveness, while men have sexual urges. Prostitution is there for the needs of the male hunchback — no one asks how the female hunchback manages . . . No one worries about the needs of women who might have 'cravings' and desires . . . The cravings of men

constitute . . . the overt, socially recognized
problem.[27]

Our society is able to believe that male sexuality
differs fundamentally from female sexuality, not only
because of the way sexual desire has been socially
constructed, but also because of the way modern
'scientific' *knowledge* has been socially constructed
. . .[28]

There is something difficult, of a peculiar nature, in issues
which, like violence to prostitutes, and the division of women,
involve women's sexuality[30].

Every woman is, potentially, a prostitute. If you are
underprivileged, hard up, prostitution is a continuous temptation. It gives you the finance, it may also give you the
fun, the freedom, the bits of luxury, the sex you need: as Yvonne
Pearson, Tina Atkinson, Mrs. Jackson and Ava Reivers in
different ways seem to have done. If you are middle-class,
prostitution is doubly your 'border'. You move close to it
whenever you decide to become 'sexed'. To attempt to attract,
to wear signs of attractiveness, to engage in sexual encounters
outside the bounds of marriage, or regular coupling. Husbands
(like John Sutcliffe) who feel threatened by their wives'
sexuality call them whores. Conversely, when a woman acts
respectably, prostitutes become her counterpart. She can be
decent *because* they exist. She is their exploiter. They give 'her'
man the satisfaction her respectability denies them.

How do you define a prostitute? The money? If so, how come
that people like Sutcliffe and his friends thought it was a good
'joke' to pay a prostitute with blows? Any woman he thought
was a bit loose became to him 'a scrubber'. 'He loathed tarts —
paid or unpaid', said Carl[31]. The Reading police who were
filmed by Thames television interviewing a woman who had
complained of rape accused her of being 'one' because they
made her 'confess' that she had had sex with 'more than one
man'. 'How many', they said to her, 'show us with the fingers

of your hands, both hands? Only one?' Is it being a 'professional' that counts (the occasional tending not to figure in statistics)? Doing it as a full-time source of income? Does getting favours, political clout or prestige, a social position through sex, count? (inside or outside marriage). I can remember a charming Belgian woman I met in Greece, with whom I was admiring a snake-shaped gold bracelet, hinting to me that I was an idiot if I couldn't get my husband to buy it for me. I fail to see what is the difference between her and Yvonne Pearson buying herself nice clothes out of handsome payments from businessmen, except that Yvonne Pearson didn't have tenure and had to work a hell of a lot harder for it. But at the same time, yes, there is a difference. There is, in prostitution, something in excess of the merchant system, which has to do with its fascination, its appeal. Something also which has to do with the crossing of boundaries. And the establishment of boundaries, enabling 'virility' to assert itself by means of a line of demarcation between, and inside, women, a line nonetheless rigid for being a shadow line. Sutcliffe's murders had to do with the inscription of that line.

Wherever you go, whoever you are, the cleavage is there. At the time of the murders, as a 'sexed' being, *I* was the prostitutes that were being murdered. As a 'respectable' wife-and-mother, I was also what Sutcliffe meant to 'protect', for whom he cleansed. Whichever way I turned, I was 'in' it. Up to my neck? As you all were, sisters. And brothers.

And yet there is a sense in which Sutcliffe's acts can be related to other types of persecution.

Racism for instance. Or religious fanaticism. The good, the bad. White or black. Protestant or Catholic. Prostitute, or non-prostitute. Are there not underlying fascist elements in Sutcliffe's killings?

If you examine the racial or 'national' origins of his victims, you notice that 13 were 'English'; one Polish/Irish, married to a Ukrainian, two Scottish, two West Indian, one West Indian/ Italian, one Malay, one Spanish: all first generation immigrants. Three of the women were also living with West Indian immigrants. So what? you may say. Out of 21 victims, (I am including Ava Reivers), 10 or 11 were 'prostitutes'. To charge £5 a time, you must be pretty low down the social ladder. Go and wander through Chapeltown or Manningham Lane, and note the high proportion of 'foreign' or 'coloured' people. No wonder the proportion of immigrants among Sutcliffe's victims is so high — more than a third, whereas the towns of Leeds and Bradford have an immigrant population well below 10%. You could even say that it is because Sutcliffe held no 'racist' opinions that he 'went' with coloured women. And treated them just the same way as English women.

Precisely. Because Sutcliffe looked for women in the parts of towns where they could most easily be attacked. Perhaps even because he was not a 'racist', his murders have a racist impact: he mainly murdered 'foreigners'. His percentage holds the same secret logic as the percentage of dead black soldiers during the Vietnam war. His cleansing of the streets is *also* getting rid of immigrants.

And yet, he married an immigrant. And his brother-in-law (the man married to Sonia's sister) was, if what is reported is correct, an Asian . . .

His murders also *look like* social exploitation. He kills prostitutes, office-cleaners, shop-assistants, clerks, secretaries, students . . . the social level rises as his own social ascent makes him more confident, he aims 'higher'. But none of the victims is rich, none of them a 'professional' woman in that other sense of the word. Students? Yes. Lecturers like myself? No.

To climb. Does that necessarily mean to exploit?

But more than racism, and social exploitation, Sutcliffe's killings resemble anti-semitism.

I was looking for similarities between all these, till a friend pointed out to me a crucial difference. The 'racist' regards the 'nigger' or the 'bicot', the Arab worker in France, as *naturally* his inferior. As sub-human, 'animal'. Beating him up is punishing him for not having kept his place. Whereas the anti-semite, the Nazi, implicitly acknowledges the humanity of the Jew, but decides that he is 'evil' and must be destroyed, so that a moral, perhaps a metaphysical, certainly a *cultural* order should be maintained. Ku Klux Klan members and 'Paki-bashers' do not want to exterminate their victims. They know it is far too useful to have a sub-proletariat. They are making 'examples', they are showing who is 'master', in the face of a social or economic threat. The Nazi would readily destroy down to the last Jew so that society at large should be purged from a 'corrupt' element.

The killer of prostitutes is closer to the anti-semite. He believes that his mission is moral, almost religious. Also, you can tell whether a man is black or white at one glance: there is something about *visibility*. You cannot tell whether a person is Jewish or not, unless he/she is dressed in particular costume. Any more than, unless you have ways of knowing, you can tell whether a man is Catholic or Protestant in the streets of Belfast. The signs by which you can tell that a woman is a prostitute are equally tenuous, 'mystical', as Sutcliffe's frequent mistakes showed. Jacqueline Hill was condemned because she turned to adjust her skirt.

Carl says that he did ask his brother in Armley jail 'what he had done it for.' Sutcliffe replied that there were 'dirty slags' littering the streets: he was only cleaning out a little. His tone was so casual, it was as if he had been 'talking of the weather, or a programme on the telly.' Carl didn't know what to say, so he said, 'I never liked prostitutes either.' Peter said, 'Exactly' and changed the subject[32].

'I don't like prostitutes' — 'I don't like Jews.' Not that there is what you could call a 'collusion' between Sutcliffe and Society. But he felt enough of a 'patriarchal' consensus around him, in all the forms I have described, for him to believe that he was working for 'order', 'cleaning up'. He panicked at the revelation that Jayne MacDonald was not 'one': a conscientious Nazi might have felt the same upon discovering that he had by mistake sent a loadful of pure Aryans to the gas chamber. Then the thought comes: 'Newspapers lie; God cannot make mistakes; she must have been a prostitute.'

Religious fanaticism, of course. Sometimes when the Old Testament God orders a mopping-up operation against his enemies, he really means, 'wipe them out', down to the last head of cattle.

The Merchant System

There *is* something specific about the murder of prostitutes. Is it that they are the 'place' where gold and pleasure, the two forces which, according to Balzac, draw Desire in the capitalist world, meet?

It is striking that Sutcliffe only began to attack women after his encounter with the first prostitute. True, there were the other two fiascos I have discussed which helped precipitate the murdering drive. But didn't he feel *licensed* to kill because 'sex' had entered into a fatal combination with 'money'?

Sutcliffe felt humiliated, outraged by that first encounter. It is worth pointing out that he had done nothing wrong. Is it a sin not to have an erection? Especially for a woman you don't like, whom you've gone with out of a sense of duty? Is it a sin to be robbed? Funny society that heaps coals of fire on the head of a man who does not have a 'hard-on' and does not drive a 'hard' bargain, but which chuckles admiringly if that same man kicks and robs a woman.

And yet how had Sutcliffe been robbed? You could argue that from the moment when the prostitute delivers the goods — gets undressed, caresses the man, is ready to copulate — she has 'earned' the man's money, whether the man is capable of taking the goods or not. Sutcliffe's prostitute might have been wrong not to give the *change* back. She may have thought that the extra fiver was as compensation for the client being unable to help himself. At any rate, it would be ridiculous to blame her for applying the hard criteria she had to live by. But using this vocabulary shows how fetishized the whole relationship between prostitutes and clients is — how a relationship between people becomes a 'ghostly' relation between things. To 'take' connotes a communication, an exchange; but it denotes possession. It suggests that the man who 'takes' has something at the end, when you would think he's rather 'lost' something – his erection, semen. There has been pleasure. He only 'takes' his pleasure, or the woman, if she has no pleasure, or he is doing it against her will. The money part of the deal compensates for his being the only one who has pleasure. The fiver corresponds to the woman's absence as a real partner. It pays for her availability, her lack of demand for pleasure. It pays, not for the man's release — otherwise the woman would be doubly the receiver: of the man's semen, and of his money — but her submission to his desire. In that sense, Sutcliffe's prostitute had delivered the goods. When there is a mutual pleasure, the scene is set for the exchange between Midnight Cowboy and the ageing tart: they have both had a jolly good time, and each is waiting for the other one to pay.

Sutcliffe therefore was 'robbed', not in terms of the *act*, but in terms of culture's valuation of the act. He had come to buy the proof of his virility. That proof was being doubly denied him: he felt no desire for the woman, could not manage an erection and she retained his money.

Exploring the connection between 'feminization' and death, Hélène Cixous sees it as part and parcel of the hierarchization of opposites which allows the masculine principle as 'active' to dominate over the feminine 'passive' one. Masculine desire, she argues[33], has been constituted from lack or loss: it depends on the Law of Return. Man appropriates; he brushes with death (as during orgasm) in order to come back to himself somewhat aggrandized, having gained 'a supplement of masculinity, a surplus of virility, authority, power, money or pleasure.' This is why 'the other' (woman's body) is necessary. This is why it must be colonized and conquered: 'It is necessary that she recognize him and by recognizing him, during the moment of fulfilment, that she disappear leaving him a profit — or an imaginary victory'[34]. Thus female passivity is considered as a necessity in a man's partner, but lethal if it threatens to contaminate him.

If Hélène Cixous is right, then prostitution further

exacerbates the relation to debt, that is the fear of indebtness, with which virility is always associated on account of the way lack (the fear of castration) structures it[35]. The sense of freedom, of relief, which the man gets from the prostitute, has to do with his 'payment' liberating him from all sense of 'debt' (gratitude, love, etc). But the payment, the whole monetary dimension of sex in prostitution, also consecrates the 'indebtness'. It makes a symbolic structure actual — even more inescapable.

And so, Sutcliffe finds himself doubly feminized: he has had no return for his money, gained no confirmation of his masculinity, failed to be recognized as active, and has been left 'indebted' on that count. But also, the money which should have freed him, of which he should have been the master, has been witheld from him. Keeping his change (a fiver *equivalent* to the fiver he meant to pay her), the prostitute has actively placed him in the feminine position, the conquered, the mocked, the passive. She has made him into a symbolical equivalent of herself.

No need to recall that prostitution such as we know it is bound up with the modern merchant system: 'In non-monetary societies such as those of Africa', Ned Polsky writes, 'prostitution appears unknown before European contact and/or urbanization, and erotic depictions do not have the pornographic functions they have in monetary economies'[36]. What is significant here is that the prostitute, because she is *paid* for *sex*, enters into a ghostly set of exchange with money. She *is*, like money, branded. Her erotic value is advertised by the cost of the clothes she wears. Beattie opens his *Yorkshire Ripper Story* with an account of Ava Reivers pacing up and down the street, tightly wrapped in her £200 rabbit-fur coat. As we're told she charges £10 a time, we quickly calculate that it took twenty 'shots' to buy the coat. Her very display of attractiveness, which signals it is for sale, is also what marks her out for the police or the 'respectability' crews. Branded, written about in a particular way. For the likes of Beattie, what matters about Ava Reivers is how much she costs, and that she's about to be murdered. That's what makes her interesting. Branded, as the actuality of a piece of silver, or paper, entirely disappears under the 'value' that the stamp of the sovereign confers on it.

Well then — the 'circulation' being already so complete — perhaps another kind of circulation can enter into it: what if 'money' — a 'brand', after all — became blows? a fiver — a bunch of fives — socking it to her . . .

That way, instead of being 'had', Sutcliffe will be the one by whom women are 'had': divided into 'good', and 'bad'; their passivity displayed; they are paid for all the 'evil' of which they are the cause. Owned, conquered, like the dead from the graveyard — as nature is by machines. All it takes is — well, money? — Murder.

Thirteen

Silencing Women

Not content with laughing at Sutcliffe with the other men at the garage, his first prostitute had come and 'banged' on the roof of his car.

While everyone else agreed to call him the 'Yorkshire Ripper', the name the *Yorkshire Post* had coined for him and which was adopted by the media, Sutcliffe, in discussions with his friends called him 'The Headbanger'. So at least John Johnston, Sutcliffe's best mate at Clarks, claims (Cross 167).

There may be reasons why the name 'Yorkshire Ripper' should have been so universally adopted, some of which I have already touched upon in the previous chapter: it displaced the actuality and frequency of the violence against women onto 'nature' (and irrepressible beast of prey), the mythic past (a Victorian 'Jack the Ripper') and a remote industrial North. It stripped the phenomenon of its reality. Why Sutcliffe should have preferred the name of 'headbanger' is not quite so evident. It certainly reveals the gap there is between the myth and the actuality of murders.

'Headbanger'. The adolescent 'headshaking' dance term is taken from some deranged patients' practice to beat their heads rhythmically against a wall. The reclaiming of the word is already defiant, would-be suicidal, a pun. You dance as you would express the utmost despair, regardless of the damage you do to yourself. You refuse the sense, the will to live, that the grown-ups are offering you. Your solitary head mimicks a sexual beat. In some Scottish towns, a 'headbanger' can be the madly-daring, eccentric boss that would lead a gang of youths to victory.

Sutcliffe's choice of the term places his own vision of his acts inside the tradition of jokes of his days as a gravedigger. Laddish pranks. He is punning yet further than the initial adolescent pun. For it is not his own head that this new 'headbanger' bangs: it is women's heads. That he could coin such a pun does show how sick his humour was, but what is interesting about it is that it also reveals quite a lot about his unconscious motivations.

The strength of the revenge motif. It is as if he were eternally punishing women for the banging of his car by the first prostitute, with all it signified in terms of the threatening activity of women, his wife and mother included. His own *identification* with women: he hits their heads as if he were banging his own. Above all, the term shows that his primary, his controlled violence was directed not at the womb (which the term 'Ripper', suggests) but at the head.

The head: the seat of thought. The seat of language.

I fell you with a hammer-blow. Shut up.

It is all to do with speech: who can speak, who can't, who *should*.

His father when a child had to pass messages between his own father and mother: they wouldn't speak to each other for years. His father left his mother and went to live with a mute.

Peter had a stammer as a child, would blush when spoken to. He copied other people's talk. 'He was like a sponge, always picking expressions up from other people'[1]. It would take him years to arrive at that controlled, soft Yorkshire voice.

Sonia's father, when cross, would not speak to his daughters. He sent verbal messages via his wife.

She grows up caught between two languages. The one at home, the other at school. She finds it hard to communicate and to make friends.

When she goes back to Peter after the Italian, she gets impatient with him. Tries to control him.

The woman's 'banging' on his car. The sound of a motor. An explosion. A sledge-hammer. She laughs at him. Outrageous noises.

For a long time he has tottered on the threshold of speech. He keeps tottering on the threshold of subjecthood.

Silence! Speech is not speech: animal noise, parrot chatter, railing, nagging, laughter. Singing bitches, I cannot solve your riddle, for your riddle is in me too. Only by silencing you for ever can I reach that manhood you taunt me for lacking. I am the headbanger. I mock you as I strike. It's a prank. A mission. The unconscious, or the superego, speaks. I give myself away as I speak. I recognize my own madness, my own perverted bachelor drive. And so I have to do it again. And again. I burst out of your smashed skulls, as Athena rose fully armed from Zeus's head, which Hephaestos, the smithy-god, has split open with his tools. I become Man in the process. But then I dissolve again.

It could all be regarded as a monstrous freak, if all along the line the 'system' had not been so keen to sponge on Sutcliffe.

He thought women were either 'innocent' or prostitutes. So did the majority of the public, the judiciary, the police. Sutcliffe only got caught when the proportion of 'innocent' victims became larger than that of prostitutes, sliding up the social scale: he was becoming subversive.

He thought prostitutes were responsible for everything. He loaded it all on to their backs. What were respectable papers like *The Times* doing when they were selecting headlines for their report of the trial? 'The Woman who laughed.' 'Prostitutes were responsible for everything.' 'We couldn't agree and make it up.' The emissary goats which the media found were all female. The reporters were all male (so were the judge, attorneys, barristers, psychiatrists, superintendents, etc. Who says we live in a world in which women are equally represented?) It was the fault of the first prostitute, the mother's fault, (she should have remained virtuous), Sonia's fault (she should have kept her mouth shut). I have heard many people argue that 'Sonia was cleaning the house: he was cleaning the streets,' thinking the observation profound, and not realizing the wit was exactly the one *dictated* by Sutcliffe. It was even implied that the sister had done it. I have recounted already how Maureen was asked to pose for one of the tabloids and made to look like Myra Hindley. The assumption is that she is the one who'd *really* been doing it all the time. There is a twist to that story. Sutcliffe angered his fellow-prisoners while on the Isle of Wight by systematically defacing the papers, cutting out the Page Three Nude in the *Sun* newspaper. A system had been set up whereby Sutcliffe could have symbolically murdered his own sister as 'litter', to clean her and the likes of her from 'bad' women, while she was made to look as if she'd been the one who'd done the murdering. A neat ploy, which makes the woman *both* the victim of righteous murder, and the perpetrator of vile murder. A deeply schizophrenic ploy, and of the media's own making.

I have also noted how women were silenced throughout the arrest and trial: from Ava Reivers, told to shut up because the police weren't interested in her (a little sympathy might not have gone amiss: the woman had been on the verge of being murdered), to the survivors, the families of the victims, and the wife. None of the survivors had their description of their attacker believed. Yet two of the photokits produced turned out to be extremely accurate. Marcella Claxton's most informative account was virtually disregarded, on account of her low IQ (and her being black?). No such calculation was made when it came to collecting Mick Sutcliffe's story. Yet it is pretty obvious that his IQ is not of the highest. None of the survivors was called to testify. None of them netted much of the big money the papers were paying for stories (Ava Reivers excepted), while the family of the murderer made a pretty packet — and the male friends did quite well[2]. The police followed suit. The Chief Constable in charge, Ronald Gregory, went on to 'cash in' on the deaths by publishing his memoirs in the *Mail on Sunday*. He was 'reputed' to have earned £50,000 (*The Times*, July 1, 1983)

There is worse. While living women were being thought unworthy to testify, *hysteria* was inflicted on the bodies of the victims by the Attorney General. Brandishing the screwdriver that had been used to perforate Josephine Whitaker's uterus, he made it 'testify' against the perpetrator. He tried to show by an appeal to the 'gut-reactions' of the jury, that the murders were 'sexual'. It was as if two men, the murderer and the Representative of Order, had been fencing with each other, while the silenced body of the victim was the battlefield — the white page, with the red seal of 'Manhood' on it. Only the wounds, the obscene and deviated mouths opened by male tools, spoke. For the killer, they said, 'obscenity'. For the prosecutor, they said 'sex'.

The only recognized female assertion, in that context, was the mothers' attack on 'cheque-book journalism'. The Queen had the good taste to support it. This was followed by suits against the Sutcliffe estate, some of which were won in High Court[3]. But the Sutcliffe estate is worth little: there is the house in Heaton, probably mortgaged, half of which belongs to Sonia. What redress is there in the law — what compensation payable? Still, if a surgeon in a hospital, or a drug company, had made a mistake, enough would be found to make life, financially at least, bearable.

Meanwhile, faced with the hue and cry about cheque-book journalism, the respectable paper which had offered Sonia a six-figure sum for her story, hastily withdrew its offer.

The Silence of Sonia

And so she never sold, never told her story. She has denounced the lies; she was treated like a murderess at the police station where she was taken to see Peter after his arrest, with a police woman in her cell following her into the shower.[4]

She has all the more merit in having remained silent while her story has been told with unremitting coldness or downright hostility, by a series of men — doctors, journalists, biographers — not to mention the Sutcliffe family.

Surely there is something exemplary in that silence? Is it that the only way she can retain her dignity, her self-respect is by not returning blows — not speaking back — not requiring sympathy, placing herself in the situation that has been that of the victims: denied as speaker, denied as subject? The irony is that this is indeed the choice. If she speaks she'll be treated as a grey eminence, the actual murderer. If she stays silent, she becomes one of the victims. It is as if there was no way to break out of the awful dichotomy.

There is something tragic about Sonia's fate. The fate of an immigrant girl whose every effort to dig herself out of the pit has turned against her — turned into murder.

It is not known why she went back to Peter after going out with the Italian. Perhaps her father put his foot down, not liking the flashy young foreigner. Perhaps the Italian went away. Perhaps she was touched by Peter's steadfastness, yielded to his entreaties. Perhaps she found that she was deeply attached to him.

But what is certain is that she returned *angry*. The family say that it is then that she ceased to be silent and withdrawn, and that she made a bid for 'control' of Peter. Fought for him. Their account suggests that Sonia was both resentful and frustrated. 'Alright, you've got me back, I'll stay with you. But you don't fulfill me. I don't like you a lot. If you want me here you can jolly well do what I want. It's the least you can do.' She would tell him to shut up. Dress the way she liked. 'It was do this and do that.'

Then she goes off to college in London, alone in a student's hostel, under a lot of pressure to succeed. Her sister who lives nearby has just got married, is a successful pianist. She, Sonia, is the inferior one, the unloved, the neglected one. Barefoot. Her Prince Charming offered her a Durex to go with the Italian. Or perhaps it was the Italian that was Prince Charming, the white sportscar that was the coach. Now it's a pumpkin, and Prince

Charming is lost. When she breaks down, she thinks she is Cinderella.

(She hates ashes. She hates dirt. She'll have to keep cleaning. Cleaning, she digs herself up and away from the fireplace.)

She wants a bigger teddy bear. Peter visits her every weekend. He won't let her go out with anyone else. She's internalized her father's austere ambition. She wants to get on, to succeed.

But she's frustrated. She becomes a potter. Cold women do not like clay and mud. Sonia likes clay. Cinderella did not like mud. 'Take off your boots before you come into the house.' Yet she likes mud, the mud you finger and mould. She's been cut off from access to her own desire. She's split. And she wants a bigger teddy bear.

She cannot bear the pressure of exams, her father's demands, the demands her sister's success places upon her. Girls who cannot bear exam pressure become anorexic.

Sonia loses weight. Drastically. She breaks down. Has to go into hospital.

She's been branded. She is a victim. She is a martyr. She's got stigmata. Being female is being a victim. She wants success. She wants power. Election. There's Peter. He's offered her a Durex. Secret contempt in her heart perhaps. She clings to him. There is only him. At least she can vent her frustration on him, punish him for the misery she feels. She lashes out at him.

He cannot give her what she wants. But he's like her. Divided like her. Alone like her. He too wants to get out of the pit. She deeply resents him. She also loves him.

Together they may make a go of it.

In Garden Lane, Heaton, she cleans compulsively. Decorates. Everything spick and span. They get a dog. Cannot stand the dirt it makes. Get rid of it.

She miscarries.

Life will not come to them. Neither a rich sexual life, nor babies. Alright. She does not want life. Does not care much for cooking, anyway. She'll have a beautiful home. Cleanliness. Things. She'll save up. One day, they may go for the good life. Peter is under a lot of strain. She is under strain too. Has been working as a night nurse at weekends (those Saturdays when Peter murders[5]). But Peter is under worse strain. He might lose his driving licence. Where would his job be then? He's fainted twice. She's had to give him mouth-to-mouth ressuscitation. They'll sell up. Get free from all that pressure. Go for the good life, yes, buy a cottage in the country, grow their own stuff. She'll work as a full-time potter. She'll go on bettering herself.

When the police come to tell her why they've arrested Peter and that he's confessed, she is watching a Teach-Yourself-German programme on the TV. She turns off the sound, keeps the picture. As the policemen speak, she goes on trying to decipher the foreign words, the educative words, mouthed on the box by foreign lips.

She thought she had received the stigmata.

Her violence is turned inwards. She hurts herself. She breaks down. She is the one who suffers the damage. Or so she thought. True, she needed the relief of lashing out at Peter at times. She thought that was alright. She would have broken down otherwise. And it was his fault, after all . . .

Stigmata. St Francis of Assisi?

But also Jocasta. When she's finally understood about Oedipus, Jacosta quietly goes to her chamber and hangs herself.

'A strangled woman swinging before our eyes', the Chorus says.

Oedipus blinds himself with one of her brooches.

Sutcliffe blinds Jacqueline Hill.

'Perturbed' or 'incomplete' man *exports* his trouble. He defines another being as 'feminine', pierced through. Vows that she will neither speak nor see.

Is our 'system' perturbed then, that it vowed that women would do neither?

Fourteen

The Police Enquiry

The time it took to catch Sutcliffe, and the number of errors made by the police, caused the then Home Secretary, William Whitelaw, to order a full investigation. The results were published in February 1982. The mistakes were acknowledged. Nobody was blamed, and no disciplinary measures were recommended. The Chief of the West Yorkshire Police, Superintendent Gregory, braved the journalists and considered himself so little responsible that he went on to write his memoirs, part of which were serialized in the *Mail on Sunday*. Public outcry over more money being made out of crime stopped the publication of his book.

In a sense no particular individual was to blame. It was the whole system, its lack of *will* to catch the killer, that had to be indicted — or else, it had to be said that it was all due to a series of unfortunate accidents.

Cross is quite good at outlining the mitigating circumstances. The West Yorkshire Police had suffered from a series of administrative reorganizations that had much impaired co-ordination and efficiency. In 1974, Whitehall had forced the County Police to merge with the City Police. The enormous branch had then been cut in two, South Yorkshire Metropolitan Police, centred on Sheffield, and West Yorkshire Metropolitan Police, centred on Leeds and Bradford. A police officer at the time had complained to the *Yorkshire Post,* claiming it would take five years for things to fall into place. Facing the mobile and clever killer, there is an enormous, grinding machinery, in which rivalry is rife.

The first detective to enquire into the case was Inspector Hoban, who, besides holding a bravery award, seems to have had a good mind, and has every reporter's good word. He immediately connects the murder of Emily Jackson, the second acknowledged victim, with that of Wilma McCann he had been called in earlier to investigate. The only clues at that time are the wounds (inflicted by a knife on Wilma McCann, and a Philips screwdriver on Emily Jackson), and the strong print of a rubber-boot with heavy-ribbed sole on Emily Jackson's thigh and on the sand around her body. It comes from a Dunlop Warwick size 7 (8 at the most). Hoban thinks that the crimes are the work of a 'psychopath' who feels a deep hatred for such women.

In the summer of 1976 (Emily Jackson died in January of that year), Hoban is forced by promotion to leave his 'beloved Leeds'[1]. He is succeeded by Det. Chief Supt. Jim Hobson. The change at the top cannot have increased the cogency of the thinking about the crimes. The murder of Irene Richardson, in February 1977, leaves one further clue: perfect tyre prints, 'cross-ply', two 'Indian Autoway' at the front, and one Pneumant at the back; from 4' 1½" to 4' 2½" apart. But once the list of cars which this description could fit has been established, the Inspector's discouragement is complete: 26 possible makes, with registration numbers from 1962 to 1970. 100,000 'possible' cars – many more if the tyre print had slipped by even ½".

More useful information comes to be added, at this point the attack on Marcella Claxton (8th May 1976) comes to be regarded as having been made by the same man. She has produced an accurate description of the killer and of his white saloon. Also, the sheet covering Tina Atkinson's body (she was the only woman murdered in her own room, in April 1977) shows the same boot print as that on Emily Jackson.

Jayne MacDonald's death creates much of a stir: sixteen years old, 'clean and fresh as a flower', her father said — he died of grief a year after her murder. She was a supermarket shop-assistant. Assistant Chief Constable George Oldfield joins the murder squad. Police operations become more intensive. There are 679 door-to-door enquiries; 3,300 statements are recorded, in particular by prostitutes. They yield no new clues. Some valuable ones, however, are provided by the attack on Maureen Long, in the summer of 1977. The partial print of a blood-stained hand is found on a piece of ceramic from a broken sink. Maureen Long produces an accurate description of her aggressor, and talks of a white Ford Cortina Mark II with a black roof. By this time, 304 full-time detectives are working on the case. The police have interviewed 175,000 people, taken 125,000 statements, and checked 10,000 vehicles. George Oldfield (the third man on the case) asks for a psychiatric profile of the killer. He is told he should search for an 'over-controlled aggressive psychopath', not unlike the Boston Strangler, who had turned out to be 'happily married and the father of two children'.

It is, however, Jean Jordan's murder that will lead the police closest to the killer. Detective Chief Supt. Jack Ridgeway, from Manchester, warns the Leeds police of the discovery of the famous £5 note. It is nearly new, number AW51121565. Through some irony, both 1 and 5 recur three times. Ridgeway arrives, accompanied by 30 detectives. There is a little bungling: according to Yallop it took them 12 days, 15-27 October, to obtain vital information about where the new notes had been distributed. The police also lost their way from Manchester to Baildon, near Bingley, where their headquarters was set up: 'it was symbolic of the entire exercise: lost handbag, lost time, lost policemen'[2]. But Ridgeway discovers that the notes had been distributed by the Midland Bank to its Shipley and Bingley branches, and those to a number of firms that employed altogether 8,000 men. Of course there was the possibility that the note had been spent straightaway, and thus passed on ... 5,000 men were interviewed, then the

Manchester detectives went back home.

One of the companies they had concentrated on was W.H. Clark (Holding) Ltd., Canal Road, Shipley. They had questioned the men, among others a Peter William Sutcliffe, from Garden Lane, Heaton. Nothing had drawn their notice, and Mr. Sutcliffe's wife had confirmed his alibis.

Marilyn Moore, who survived her attack on 14 December 1977, provided the most accurate description corresponding with that already given by Marcella Claxton. The photokit issued at the time closely resembles Sutcliffe[3]. But Marilyn Moore describes a maroon saloon, probably a Morris Oxford; the car was a red Corsair. Sutcliffe frequently changes his cars, and nine months later, he gets a grey Sunbeam Rapier. But the front tyre prints correspond to those found by the body of Irene Richardson: the killer transfers his tyres from one car to the next. Nobody I have read comments on this, yet there seems to me to be something weird there: the killer is faithful both to his boots and tyres.

March 1978. Two letters, signed by a man who calls himself 'Jack' are received by the police. They mention 8 murders, which includes that of Joan Harrison, killed in Preston in 1975 (which Sutcliffe will swear he had nothing to do with) — but not the murder of Yvonne Pearson, whose body has not yet been found and which at first will not be attributed to the Ripper, her being battered to death not fitting with the established method of killing.

Two new murders (Helen Rytka, Huddersfield, and Vera Millward, Manchester) fail to provide new clues. The ferocious violence of the wounds to the abdomen however make the police add to their list of motives: vengeance for frustrated fatherhood. By September 1978, the Yvonne Pearson murder is linked with the Ripper as are the attacks on Anna Rogulskyj (Keighley, 1975), and Olive Smelt (Halifax, 1975). Those on Maureen Long (Bradford, 1977) and Marilyn Moore (Leeds, 1977) are also confirmed as being by him. But the attribution of the Joan Harrison murder to him will help to mess up the trail.

There were grounds for associating that murder with

the others. A Preston prostitute, an alcoholic also addicted to morphine and up to eight bottles of cough medicine a day, the wretched woman had paid the warden of the hostel where she was staying 'in kind' for the right to have a bath — and had been murdered later that same night of November 1975. Her bag had disappeared and was only found 7 months later. It had been thought that theft had been the motive. The circumstances of her death were retrospectively examined when various unsolved murders or attacks were being connected with the Ripper. She had been hit from behind, possibly with a hammer. The tights and pants had been removed from one leg only; the boots had been carefully placed on the thighs, as had been the case with Irene Richardson. The killer had jumped so savagely on her that her sternum had perforated her liver (as with Yvonne Pearson). Finally, he had bitten her breast: the print had revealed a gap between the top front teeth. A similar bite will be found on the body of Josephine Whitaker. To make matters even more confused, Sutcliffe will, when questioned after his arrest, deny that he bit Josephine Whitaker. Perhaps because it was too intimate, too 'sexual' a gesture for him to be able to own up to it. But the denial certainly opens the question of whether Sutcliffe was not also lying when he denied having killed Joan Harrison[4]. Joan Harrison's killer had copulated with her before killing her. There may even have been anal intercourse. But Sutcliffe kept insisting that there was nothing 'sexual' between him and his victims. The only victim with whom he had sex was Helen Rytka, because, he explained, that was the only way he could conceal what he was doing (he had already hit her on the head, but she was not dead) from two taxi-drivers who had arrived on the scene. When the police questioned him after his arrest in Sheffield, the only accusations that moved him were those concerning Jayne MacDonald and Joan Harrison. It is known that he felt remorse for the death of the 16-year-old. Can it not be that he denied the Harrison murder because the sexual character of the encounter repelled him? His very vehemence might be a sign of his guilt.

The theory is convincing. Good if it were true. If Sutcliffe didn't do it then Joan Harrison's killer is still at large. Worse, the 'fetishistic' structures which I analyzed earlier, in all their rampant misogyny, are not so exceptional as it appeared. The semen and saliva samples found on Joan Harrison's body are those of a 'B-secretor'. It was a lucky blood group for the detectives; group B is rare anyway, and secretor even rarer (it means that minute particles of blood can be found in the saliva): only 6% of the population belong to that group. Sutcliffe *was* group B. But he was a non-secretor.

The author of the letters signed 'Jack the Ripper' was a 'B-secretor'. (The saliva that had stuck the envelopes had been analyzed). His third letter reaches the police headquarters shortly before the murder of Josephine Whitaker. The new murder confirms some of the 'true' data: same boot prints as those found near Emily Jackson and Tina Atkinson; the description of a man seen with Josephine Whitaker shortly before her death tallies with that given by Marilyn Moore, the man with the 'Jason King' moustache. There are new data too: traces of milling grease and tiny metal particles are found in the wounds, suggesting that the man has engineering or mechanical connections (which Sutcliffe did). But the new, 'true' data are going to combine with 'false' ones and send the police astray, owing to the clues left by the Harrison murder and those produced by the letters of the self-styled 'Jack the Ripper'.

All his three letters had been posted in Sunderland near Newcastle. The first on 8 March, five weeks after Helen Rytka's death; the second, sent to the editor of the *Daily Mirror,* one week later, 13 March 1978; the third, on 13 March 1979. The first two had already led George Oldfield, under pressure to show some progress in the enquiry, to declare that the police were 'nearer' than ever, although the Helen Rytka murder had produced no new clues. But the third letter shows the same traces of milling oil and metal particles as are going to be found in Josephine Whitaker's wounds. There is no doubt that the coincidences are eerie: not only do the two killers behave with the same fetishistic hatred of women, but they are in a similar trade and betray the same type of emotions: for the author of the letters makes tearful excuses about the Jayne MacDonald murder.

Three months later George Oldfield receives a tape, also posted in Sunderland. The Ripper team then decide to go for massive publicity. Oldfield summons the media to the Police Academy in Wakefield, on 26 June 1979, and lets them listen to the cassette. It will be played everywhere, on radio, TV, on football grounds, in working-men's clubs. The formidable campaign, code-named 'Project R' publicizes both the voice and the handwriting, advertising a special number where people can ring if they think they've identified either. Between the launch of the campaign and Sutcliffe's arrest, the police receive 878,796 calls, all of them misleading, many of them 'larks'.[5]

Detective Chief Supt. John Domaille is entrusted with the formation of a new squad, The Dirty Dozen, to re-examine all files. Enquiries mount up, costing 3 million pounds, and so much energy and tension that George Oldfield, exhausted by worry, overwork and chain-smoking, has a massive heart attack. He is forced to take temporary retirement. Mobile exhibitions, 'multi-lingual road-shows' travel from pubs to clubs to commercial centres and even to village greens. Newsagents are made to distribute two million copies of a four-page brochure giving a short account of the murders and reproducing samples of the supposed 'Ripper's' handwriting, and an extract from the cassette. Posters claiming, 'The Ripper would like you to ignore this. The man next to you may have killed twelve women', designed by the Poulter agency, are plastered over 6,000 boardings[6]. By 1980, the police have interviewed 250,000 people, written 23,000 statements, visited 26,000 houses, and checked 175,000 vehicles. 'Project R', overwhelmed by files and documents, gradually sinks into chaos.

Computers had been installed in the red-light districts of West Yorkshire, South Yorkshire, Humberside and Manchester in 1978. They register 2 million vehicles[7] and, among others,

Sutcliffe's car close on 50 times. But a large number of these belong to people who have to regularly cross these areas to travel to work. When questioned by the police, Sutcliffe claims he is travelling to work. Furthermore, the police (approved by William Whitelaw, who has visited the Ripper rooms and wants to be sure that the public's right to maximum privacy is ensured) are full of scruples about questioning the men whose cars have been spotted in the red-light areas: they don't want them to get into trouble at home. They are full of tact, 'concerned only with eliminating them as suspects'. We have seen that the same scruples did not apply when prostitutes were being used as bait. So enquiries are not set up with quite the spirit of diligence that might be needed. Also it gets to being well-known where the cameras are. Barbara Leach is murdered just outside the Bradford red-light area . . .[8]

The media don't exactly collaborate with the police either. Papers have been asked not to reveal some vital clues (such as the engineering connection). The Bradford *Argus*, annoyed about having been kept out of an important briefing, go ahead and publicize the list of the supposedly most secret details[9] — including the shoe size and the blood group.

This may be the reason (as well as his reported hatred of the name of 'Ripper') which makes Sutcliffe, who lives in Bradford and reads the local press, on his next two 'missions', strangle or attempt to strangle his victims. Having failed to kill Dr. Bandara, he returns to his proven method, attacking Teresa Sykes and murdering Jacqueline Hill. No doubt of his watchfulness and cunning, of the care he takes to keep his clothes out of view of his wife and to clean them himself, of how he deals with his own cars. But there is no doubt either that 'luck' is with him. And that the police are phlegmatic about catching him. Not just in the tact they show to him as a visitor to the red-light district when they question him. Not half an hour after the murder of Jacqueline Hill, an Iraqi student finds her bag on the pavement of Alma Road, where she has first been hit. He takes it back to the student hostel, and two hours later, one of his friends, Tony Gosden, notices that there is blood on it. A third student instantly phones the police and Tony Gosden searches the bag to see whose it is. When the police arrive, the students ask them to go and check if Jacqueline Hill is in her bedroom. They refuse, choosing to consider the bag as 'lost property', fill out forms and depart, having only given a cursory glance at the spot where the bag has been found. Jacqueline Hill's body lies a few metres away, where it will not be found until the next morning. Nine precious hours have been lost. A new 'Super Squad' arrives. Jim Hobson heads it but it will be chance, and the initiative of a young policeman, that will get Sutcliffe caught.

Two striking points arise from the arrest. First, that it isn't the West Yorkshire police, in whose area the majority of the murders have been taking place, but the South Yorkshire Police (Sheffield) that catch Sutcliffe. Likewise, the only enquiry that had nearly led to Sutcliffe, the one about the £5 note, had been conducted by the Lancashire Police. Secondly, even after the Sheffield Police think they've got the man and 'phone their West Yorkshire colleagues to tell them so, they're told, 'we've already questioned the man; you can let him go.' Earlier, a young West Yorkshire Detective-Constable, Laptew, had gone to interview Sutcliffe at his home in September 1979. He had noted that his Sunbeam Rapier had been spotted in the Lumb area of Bradford no less than 36 times. He found a great deal to be suspicious about in the interview and following his hunch, found that in 1969 Sutcliffe had had a conviction for going out 'equipped to steal' (though nothing was said about the hammer). Laptew's report was only seen nine months later and routinely marked 'to file'[10] It is as though the place that had produced him, where he killed, did not want to, or could not *see* him. *The Sunday Times* Insight Team described the seventeen lives of the hunted man; better than the proverbial cat. Sutcliffe was nearly caught (as by the taxi-drivers, with Helen Rytka), and disturbed or chased eight times. Nine times he was questioned by the police, and they let him go. Once he met Maureen Long in the centre of Bradford, and she failed to recognize him. Four times he was questioned about the £5 note, once because of his 'engineering' job after the discovery of milling oil and metal particles on Josephine Whitaker's body, three times because of the frequency with which his car was spotted in the relevant areas. Two of these times, Sonia gave him an alibi. On the third, Laptew filed a keen-sighted report . . . Once, as I have already reported, Sutcliffe was wearing the very boots whose sole-prints the questioning policeman had on his pad in front of him.

It is, of course, easy to show retrospective wisdom, and there is no doubt that Sutcliffe was exceedingly cunning at covering his tracks. Yet the build-up of inefficiency, chaos and ill-luck is such that one must ask whether something else was not at work. The police were in the process of bringing in Scotland Yard, at the end — although, as some local people wrily commented, Scotland Yard in their own time had failed to catch 'their' Ripper.

Precisely. Perhaps it wasn't Scotland Yard that was wanted. Perhaps it was someone with the ability to think imaginatively.

The Purloined Letter

Poe's story, 'The Purloined Letter', has as its subject a gentleman detective; a Frenchman called Dupin.

The tale is as follows: There are a King and a Queen. One day, the King enters the Queen's apartment while she is reading a letter. It is not explained what the letter is about, nor who has written it. What is clear is that the letter is compromising. The Queen does not want the King to see it. As the best defence against detection, she places it casually in full view, wrong side up, on the piano. The King notices nothing; but the Minister who has entered with him and who is the Queen's enemy, sees and understands the Queen's gesture. Casually, he takes a letter from his own pocket and substitutes it for the Queen's letter. He knows the Queen is powerless, for were she to protest she would draw the King's attention to that very letter she wishes him not to see. From then on, the Minister is in possession of the Queen's letter and has the power to blackmail her. The Queen, acting secretly still out of fear of being found out by the King, asks the Chief of Police to find the stolen letter. But despite an extensive and intensive search of the Minister's apartment and of his office, the police find nothing. They go through the books of the library page by page, even unscrew the legs of the chairs to see if they are hollow: all to no avail. At his wits' end, the Chief of Police asks Dupin for help. Dupin then calls on the Minister on some trifling but plausible pretext. He spots the Queen's letter, displayed in full view, on a letter-rack — but turned inside out. He arranges another visit during which the Minister's attention is called to the window to witness a disturbance Dupin has arranged. And while the Minister is looking out, he substitutes a fake letter, with outside markings identical to those the Minister has used to disguise the Queen's letter, for the stolen one. He then sells the Queen's letter to the Chief of Police.

With their TV cameras in the red-light districts spotting millions of cars, the thousands of calls received in answer to their publicity campaign, their computers sifting masses of data, their dozens of thousands of door-to-door enquiries, it was as if the police, in the Ripper case as in the Poe story, had searched every inch of the ground — gone through the books of the library page by page, as it were — but failed to see the evidence, the inverted letter, even when it was fully displayed. Even when Sutcliffe placed his sole under the very nose of the policeman who had a photograph of it under his eyes, the policeman did not see it.

The French psychoanalyst Jacques Lacan has written with his customary — phenomenal — resourcefulness about the Poe story. Some of the points he makes are relevant to the analogy I am drawing. The letter is purloined, prolonged, he says. It travels from person to person in the course of the story. From the Queen to the Minister, from the Minister to Dupin, from Dupin to the Chief of Police. The letter is like the signifier (you do not know its 'signified' ie you do not know what the letter is about, why it is compromising for the Queen). And the signifier is moveable. It repeats its effects. Whoever possesses it is affected by it. The holder of the letter is in a *feminine*, a *passive*, position. The Queen is powerless to stop the Minister from stealing her letter. The Minister, once he has the letter, is vulnerable to theft as well. What he has done to the Queen can now be done, and is done, to him. Dupin parts from the letter for money, Lacan suggests, in order not to become 'feminized' in his turn. Money breaks the spell which ownership of the letter passes on. The letter *is* feminity. It is contagious, like the castration that passes from Zambinella to Sarrasine in the Balzac story which I discussed earlier.

The police were searching for a criminal whose personality would fit the myth of male violence that was being projected around the murders. What they should have been seeking was 'femininity', a moveable and dangerous *signifier*, so dangerous that Sutcliffe killed out of hatred for it, the 'impotence' he felt himself threatened with. Like the police in the Poe story, in their search of the Minister's premises, who never look at the letter-rack which is tucked inside the mantelpiece, in-between the legs of the chimney, the police in the Ripper case cannot see the fetishistic signs that Sutcliffe leaves about: the empty boots, or shoes, placed on the thighs of the victims, in one or two cases pushed in between the thighs. The boot-print, the tyre-prints, the Dunlop 7 pressed as it were under the policeman's nose. They cannot see either in the smallish, soft-spoken, polite, respectable man with a good job (he is number one driver at Clark's) and a mortgage and a nice house in a nice area, the mad male killer, and Public Enemy No. 1, the embodiment of 'working-class Evil' which they, as representatives of Order, are trained to seek.

Computers on Rue Morgue

Alas, there was no Dupin to imaginatively project himelf into the Minister's situation, as the Minister had with the Queen, so as to 'see' the inverted object. Not until very late, anyway. But there are computers.

The police and reporters say in defence of the use of computers on an unprecedented scale that it was, after all, a computer that helped catch the killer. One of the policemen who had apprehended Sutcliffe in Sheffield with Ava Reivers asked on his 'walkie-talkie' for Sutcliffe's number plate to be checked on the centralizing computer: the number turned out to be false, and Sutcliffe was arrested in the first instance for having stolen a number plate.

It remains true, nonetheless, that, as Cross says, 'while the computer would give on the one hand, it would take away with the other. It was as if the enquiry was presented with too many facts and figures . . . The more sophisticated the questions asked of the computer, the greater would be the police work-load in checking the information provided'[11]. To make matters worse, when it came to checking on the vehicles spotted in their millions by the cameras in the red-light districts, a whole new programme had to be devised 'because the language used on the Police National Computer was totally different from that used on the D.V.L.C. computer at Swansea'[12]. But it also seems that the police could only do its sums the wrong way round.

Thus, having decided that the letters and cassette from Sunderland were genuine, George Oldfield established five criteria by which the killer could be found. Any suspect not corresponding to the five points could be eliminated:

1. The man had been born between 1924 and 1959.
2. He was not coloured.
3. His shoe-size was under 9.
4. His blood-group was B.
5. He had a 'Geordie' accent.

The first four clues were correct. The fifth was false. The first four were based on evidence found on the bodies; the fifth was uniquely based on the cassette. But an accent being the first, or one of the first things, to be perceived when a suspect is being questioned, Sutcliffe was several times eliminated on account of his soft Yorkshire voice. And none of the survivors who had produced accurate descriptions of their aggressor had mentioned a Geordie accent.

Oldfield, Hobson, Gregory, etc. all decided to believe that the cassette was from the real murderer (this being supported by the attribution of the Joan Harrison murder to the killer) — despite the following facts:

1. The third letter announced that the next victim would be an 'old slut' from Bradford or Liverpool. 19-year-old Josephine Whitaker was murdered in Halifax.

2. The hoaxer boasted, 'I'm not daft, I don't live in Sunderland, I only post my letters from there.' But the West Yorkshire Police asked the Sunderland Police to concentrate their search on Wearside, linguists having traced the man's accent to that area.

3. The Northumberland police conducted an extraordinary search (even a church warden suffering from angina and a man in a wheelchair were questioned . . .). In Castleton they visited 11,000 houses. They ended up fairly sure that they had questioned the author of the letters, and that he was not the killer (he had secure alibis for the nights of the crimes[13]). That meant that the killer did not necessarily have a Geordie accent. Furthermore, two expert linguists from Leeds University, Lewis and Ellis, conceived serious doubts as to the genuineness of the accent, and communicated these doubts forcefully to the West Yorkshire police. They had also established that the author of the letters had copied the style of one of the books written on 'Jack the Ripper', and that the details which the hoaxer had produced to make his letter appear authentic, far from being known to the police alone, had all, at one point or another, been revealed by the press. A 'nutter' who had followed the reporting closely would have known everything the hoaxer revealed. Despite all this, the West Yorkshire Police continued their publicity campaign and clung to the North East hypothesis. Lewis gloomily predicted to Cross at the time 'that the effect of the one million pound publicity campaign would be to guarantee that the Ripper was *not* caught'[14]

The police's five-point addition sticks. But in other circumstances, they seem unable to analyze or programme the data:

1. The computer that was tracing the owners of vehicles recorded to have gone through the various red-light districts may have come up with millions of cars. But it is not said how analytic the programmes were. How many times did a car have to be registered for its owner to become suspect? What hours of passage were considered relevant? Until his November 1980 attack on Teresa Sykes, Sutcliffe never attacked before 8 pm, and most of the time after midnight: wouldn't this have enabled

the police to eliminate cars travelling to work and back? Sutcliffe, a long-distance lorry driver, would have worked irregular hours: did his trips, though, necessarily take him to Lumb Lane and Chapeltown? In how many of the relevant red-light districts had a car to be spotted before its passage became significant? If such criteria had been applied, wouldn't the numbers have been more manageable?

2. As Laptew's visit to the Sutcliffe home shows, a number of car owners with frequent sightings *were* interviewed. But what efforts were made to connect such interviews with the other data which the police had collected? They had tyre prints, descriptions of various cars given by the survivors (someone whose cars corresponded even remotely with these would have been worth testing closely), boot print, shoe size (that was easy to check. Besides, Sutcliffe still owned the famous Dunlop boots; a look at his boot collection would have sufficed . . .). It was also supposed that the owner of the Dunlops did a lot of driving, the sole being depressed at the top, where the right foot rests on the accelerator (and Sutcliffe was a lorry driver)[15]. It was also thought that the man had a gap between his front teeth (which Sutcliffe did[16]). There was the palm print found near Maureen Long. There were the traces of milling oil and metal particles. There was the known blood group B. Laptew did have the intelligence to seek for some modes of corroboration and to file a report outlining grounds for suspicion. But why was no blood test carried out at any stage when Sutcliffe was being questioned? Why no shoe verification?

3. The same questions arise about the enquiry into the £5 note. It is true that at the start the number of possible recipients of the note was formidable (8,000). But further work by the Manchester Police had reduced the list to 300 by the 3rd time they return to Clark's. The fourth time, two men only from Clark's are taken for questioning and Sutcliffe is one of them. His mates say that one of the policemen had said, 'that's the bugger!' and that Sutcliffe was white as a sheet. Yet Sutcliffe is released because Sonia gives him an alibi. I think Sonia acted in good faith. She was often at work on the relevant Saturdays and no doubt trusted Peter's accounts of his evenings. Twenty

evenings over 5 years are not easy to remember. And on the evenings relevant to the Jean Jordan enquiry, Peter and Sonia had been moving into their new house, giving a housewarming party: how could she suspect that after he'd driven the guests home, and she had gone to bed, Peter would have driven over the Pennines? But what stops the policemen from taking a blood sample, a boot size — from doing an identity parade? There are survivors who have produced descriptions, who might remember if they saw the man . . . None of this was done. To put it mildly, as Mr. Colin Sampson, the new Chief Constable of the West Yorkshire Police, did in his report into the handling of the 'hunt' 'it begs the question as to whether detectives always knew what was required of them. Were they briefed properly? There seems to have been a lack of persistence and follow-up in respect of the interviews with Sutcliffe[17].'

4. The same comments apply to the use of Sutcliffe's previous conviction in 1969. Only Laptew bothered to make the connection. And the report was not even complete, since it omitted to mention the hammer and screwdriver.

5. All these connections should have been 'added up'. What's more, why was the Joan Harrison murder never subtracted from the total sum of attacks? What bound this murder to the Ripper hunt was that the semen and saliva test had revealed a 'B Secretor', and that the saliva test on the envelopes containing the hoaxer's letters showed up the same group. Traces of semen must have been found on the bodies of two other victims: the killer had masturbated on the back of Wilma McCann (as near the felled Marcella Claxton), and had had intercourse with Helen Rytka. Sutcliffe was *non*-secretor. 'Dr Patrick Lincoln, of London University's medical school, an international expert on blood-group typing, states that confusion between a secretor and a non-secretor of any blood group is impossible[18].' If so, how could the connection continue to be made?

The police capacity for deduction or induction was not exactly brilliant.

What got Sutcliffe caught was that a young policeman had an *idea*.

When he was being questioned with Ava Reivers in Sheffield, and it turned out that his Rover had a fake number plate, Sutcliffe had excused himself for a moment. He had taken his jacket, in which he had rolled up his hammer and knife and hidden the tools underneath an oil-tank. He is only accused of the theft of a number plate; but Sergeant O'Boyle, despatched by the Ripper Squad, keeps him overnight. For the first time (it is his tenth interview with the police) there is a blood test, and it turns out it is group B. Hearing this, Sergeant Ring, one of the two policemen who had apprehended him, decides to go back to the place of the arrest. He remembers that the man had asked to 'go for a pee' behind the stone porch near which his car was parked. He walks round the porch, finds the oil-storage tank, shines his torch on the ground by the wall, and finds a ball-pen hammer and a knife. It is after being told about this discovery, while the police are pressing him about the attack on Teresa Sykes on bonfire night (for once, Sonia has not verified his alibi, remembering that he had only come in at 10 p.m.) that he owns up: 'I think you are leading up to the Yorkshire Ripper — Well, that's me'[20].

While computers were churning out millions of data, enquiries were made in their thousands, files piled up chaotically, pigs were being slaughtered wholesale to identify the murder weapons, the killer's gestures reproduced etc. etc., no *reading* of the evidence was attempted.

When one man — Sergeant Ring — projects himself imaginatively into Sutcliffe — imagines that the killer's tools (the male organs) can be removed, deposited in a sheltered corner (in the camouflage of the mother's skirt?) — when he conceives subconsciously that the masculinity he's dealing with is artificial — that the object that is in fact being sought is 'femininity' — then, like Dupin, he sees the 'purloined letter'. Sees the powerlessness that hides under the storage tank — the powerlessness that inflicts a curse: devour, or be devoured.

Inside the fake letter he puts in the place of the real one, the one he's taken from the Minister, Dupin writes two ironical lines from a seventeenth century French play. They are about

Atreus and Thyestes, the evil brothers. Atreus served Thyestes the flesh of his own children for a meal.

'They' would make mince-meat out of him. He made mince-meat out of *them*.

Was Sergeant Ring well paid?

Superman, or one 'with something missing'?

When, in January 1980, Sutcliffe is questioned for the fourth time about the £5 note, he is asked to produce a sample of his handwriting. The police want to see if it resembles that of the 'Jack the Ripper' letters. It doesn't, but if they had compared it instead with that of a poem sent 4 months earlier to the Sheffield *Star*, (on 6th September 1979, four days after the murder of Barbara Leach), things might have been different. They would have seen that the capitals of that poem were by the same hand that wrote the notice displayed in Peter Sutcliffe's lorry, warning people to 'let him sleep'.

That message proclaims Sutcliffe's desire: to be a 'man whose latent genius if unleashed would rock the nation, whose dynamic energy would overpower those around him.' To be the Kraken, the Hulk. But precisely because it displays itself so openly, and because its 'literary' terms seem excessive, therefore humorous, nobody takes it seriously. Likewise, at Clark's, because he is a bit weird and has been questioned so often by the Police, Sutcliffe is jokingly called 'the Ripper'. It is indeed the purloined letter, there for all to see, but invisible because it is so blatant. And because it is the wrong side up. Sutcliffe is a model employee; he does have trouble keeping time, but he is efficient, highly skilled at finding his way (he has lots of maps in his cabin), the oldest-serving driver. He's even been chosen to pose at the wheel of 'Wee Willie' as an ad for the firm.

The police are confronted by two types of documents. The letters and the cassette posted in Sunderland bear all the hallmarks of truth. They are a hoax. Sutcliffe's poem to *The Star* seems to be a hoax. It is truthful, but according to a truth that nothing in the 'system' can recognize.

The third letter from Sunderland (with a deleted section in

the middle, containing clues the police did not want to reveal)
went as follows:

> Dear Officer,
> Sorry I haven' written, about a year to be exalt (sic),
> but I hav'nt (sic) been up North for quite a while. I
> was'nt (sic) kidding last time I wrote . . . That was
> last month, so I don't know when I will get back on
> the job but I know it won't be Chapeltown too
> bloody hot there maybe Bradford's Manningham.
> Might write again if up North.
> Jack the Ripper
> PS Did you get letter I sent to Daily Mirror in
> Manchester

All the signs that would be ascribed to the 'typical' criminal are
here: poor spelling, poor punctuation, limited vocabulary,
coarse language ('bloody'). Low literacy, in short. The tone is
direct, flat — like the 'uneducated', accented 'Geordie' voice of
the tape:

> I'm Jack, I see you are having no luck catching me. I
> have the greatest respect for you, George, but, Lord,
> you are no nearer catching me than four years ago
> when I started. I reckon your boys are letting you
> down, George. They can't be much good, can they?

Sadly, it is easy to see why the police would have been so ready
to accept the authenticity of the letters and tapes. It's not just
that the low literacy and accent connote 'working-class',
keeping criminality where it is thought to be, but it is also that
the vocabulary, the attitudes, reflect and confirm those the
police recognize. The author speaks of the 'job'; he talks of
George's 'boys', who are letting him down. It confirms a
patriarchal structure. The head of the squad is the father, he
counts on his boys, he'll tell them off if they let him down.
Father and sons are at one in their struggle against Public
Enemy No. 1.

There is more. The hoaxer names himself. Calls himself

'Jack', the name given to the killer by the media. It is as if he had sent one of the photokits as a photograph of himself. He demands attention (did you get my letter to the Daily Mirror?). Above all, describing himself as the *author* ('I'm Jack', I sign the letters, I speak this cassette) he also makes a bid for authorship of the murders according to the criteria of representation. I, the Author, have done the act, since I own up to it. He also recognizes George as his reader, his hearer, the rightful recipient of his messages. As his adversary perhaps, but one who, being hailed as such, finds himself confirmed in the role he wants to play. The field has been chosen, the duel can start. Good against Evil, Saint George against the Dragon. George Oldfield listens, fascinated, almost lovingly leaning over the tape; listens to the voice which is challenging him from the depths of hell. Ah, but the voice betrays its origins. Find out where hell is, comb it street by street. And you will find Satan. Satan lives in Wearside. He must do. For I, George, the head of police, am confirmed as a subject by him, Jack the Ripper, the myth sprung anew from the urban hell on our borders.

The poem to *The Star* is of an altogether different kind. To start with, it's a poem. It is literate. Rhyming couplets. Carefully written, like the work of a model schoolboy (Sutcliffe as a youth kept beautiful accounts), right on the lines, with

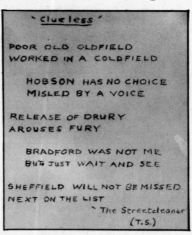

'Clueless'

POOR OLD OLDFIELD
WORKED IN A COLDFIELD

HOBSON HAS NO CHOICE
MISLED BY A VOICE

RELEASE OF DRURY
AROUSES FURY

BRADFORD WAS NOT ME
BUT JUST WAIT AND SEE

SHEFFIELD WILL NOT BE MISSED
NEXT ON THE LIST
'The Streetcleaner
(T.S.)

neat, alternating symmetrical spacing and alignment. It's in the tradition of the 'nonsense' poem. An enigma connoting a degree of scholarly attention: the title underlined, in between quotation marks, as is the signature; both in ordinary type, contrasting with the capitals of the text. The capitals themselves may be to disguise the hand — to make the text more legible — or do their five tiers hark back to the five tiers of Zapolski's grave, with *their* capitals?

What does 'Clueless' refer to? The poem itself, or the author of the poem? If it is the poem, then it means that nothing in it is going to give the author away (either as author or as murderer). Indeed, the author never appears as subject; never says 'I'. Signs with a 'war-name', impersonal, 'pure', 'the Street-cleaner'. Even the initials that follow, T.S., either duplicate 'The Streetcleaner', or are a code: Pe*t*er Sutcliffe? Trevor Sutcliffe (Sutcliffe calls himself either Dave or Trevor when he picks up a woman)?

If 'clueless' refers to the author, it can hardly mean 'daft'. Sutcliffe knows perfectly well he is clever, cunning; the poem itself is a clever ploy. Those who are 'clueless' in that sense are rather the potential readers of the poem — the police whom the poem goes on to describe as totally off the scent, the readers who will be none the wiser for reading this. It is as if the 'lessness' of the title was meant to afflict those who come into contact with the poem. 'You will be none the wiser for having read this', it implies.

Five couplets. The number five again. Ten lines. Ten fingers? No punctuation. Each couplet seems to have little connection with the others: like the apparently 'random' accumulation of the murders?

> Poor old Oldfield/worked in a coldfield/Hobson has
> no choice/misled by a voice.

The two Superintendents in charge of the enquiry, Oldfield and Hobson, have gone wrong. They are not addressed directly, as by the hoaxer ('I have the greatest respect for you, George'), nor are they called by their first name, invited to an intimate test of strength. They are formally, mockingly, contemptuously referred to. Undermined by a pun, a joke on their names. 'Old Oldfield': your name defines you; you're working an old mine, an uneconomic pit; you're not just far from warm, you're plain cold. As for you, Hobson, like the Hobson of the play, you've got no choice; the tape has led your enquiry astray. Only I say this in such a muted form that you won't understand what I mean. I know that the 'voice' which is making you bark up the wrong tree is really God's, indirectly protecting me.

Why Oldfield and Hobson should be laughed at is self-evident. Why Drury, who had nothing to do with the Ripper hunt, should figure in the third couplet is less clear. Beattie explains that the reference is to Ken Drury, ex-Commander of Scotland Yard Flying Squad, sentenced to eight years' imprisonment for corruption, and who, at the time the poem was sent to the *Star*, has just been released after serving only 26 months. What is less clear is whether the 'fury' which this early release provoked was that of the public at large, or simply that of the pure, the good, 'streetcleaning' citizen who is writing the poem. The latter is the more likely. Drury's tampering had been with vice, prostitution; although his case affected London, his corrupt permissiveness could be seen as part of the 'litter' whose accumulation called for even more exterminating zeal from the man with a mission.

There are other reasons why Drury could have been added. He completes a fallen trinity of Bad Fathers: old, incompetent, mistaken and also corrupt. Thus the system built by the hoaxer's message, in which the police represent Order and the killer the enemy of society, is reversed. The supposed representatives of order are useless and wicked. Against them the true Defender of Order rises, Zorro-like; his deeds of darkness do the job which the police are incapable of doing. Remember John Sutcliffe's indignation against Albert, the policeman who had had an affair with Kathleen. 'A fine to-do when we have to be protected from people like you, who ought to protect us . . .' Well. The Angelic Son, with his sword of fire, has taken over. He swoops upon the towns:

> Bradford was not me/but just wait and see/Sheffield
> will not be missed/next on the list.

The cunning and inconsistency are complete. The first three couplets, though 'mocking' were 'truthful' in their way. The couplet about Bradford refers to the killing of Barbara Leach, which had occurred four days earlier. Sutcliffe had killed her. So the only piece from the poem which the police might have a chance of recognizing (they are obviously not going to recognize the parodic descriptions of the first three couplets), the only 'clue', is disguised by a lie. The next couplet is half-truthful: Sheffield will not be missed, but there will be murders or attacks in other places before Sutcliffe decides to strike there: so it was not 'next on the list.'

The poem is truthful in its negations. Here speaks a voice without a subject, a voice without a proper name. Four of its propositions are negative, or imply a negation ('cold field', 'no choice', 'not me', 'not be missed'). The language is meant to subvert, undermine and mislead. It is the voice of lack. A voice forever arrested at the sphinx, the riddle stage; forever unable to step over the border of truth, of manhood. A voice so filled with loathing for what it sees as its own feminine indifferentiation that it kills, and kills again. To punish 'femininity' for the 'something missing' in him.

What fascinates is that it carries all sorts of unconscious meanings in its undertow. For instance, 'clew' or 'clue', according to the Oxford English Dictionary, means 'a globular body; a ball; a ball of thread or yarn. That which guides and threads a way through a maze.' 'Clueless' then could be an admirable description of the lack of coherence, or palpable sequence, in the poem. But if clue means 'ball', it could also mean 'ball-less'. Impotency.

Likewise, 'drury' or 'druery' used to mean 'love, especially sexual love'. Following the suggestion, 'release of drury/ Arouses fury' takes on a new, a startlingly apt meaning — a meaning made possible by the fact that all words being in capitals, 'drury' is as readable as 'Drury'; names may be nouns.

Indeed, to pun, 'Oldfield' can be read also as 'old field'.

It may be objected that as none of these meanings can be 'meant', and a lorry driver being unlikely to write poems with the help of the Oxford English Dictionary, the speculations are idle, pushed too far. But there is something about the Sutcliffe case, especially as relates to language, that consistently produces over-meaning — as if the under-belly of the language had taken over and begun to proliferate on its own. Thus, if one takes the second line of the first three couplets, they turn out to be remarkably true about Sutcliffe himself, though again he cannot have meant them to be: Worked in a coldfield (Sutcliffe did work as a gravedigger) Misled by a voice (he heard God's voice coming from the grave) Arouses fury (what happens to him when he gets primed to 'do it').

And since 'Bradford' ('was not me') means, not just, 'the city of Bradford', but, 'the killing of a girl in Bradford', it even looks as if Sheffield had suggested itself as a place to strike (especially after the punning on 'Oldfield' and coalfield/coldfield) on account of its name: She . . . ffield. The feminization of the cities is certainly striking, coming after the 'list' of the three 'fathers'. 'Next on the list'. Don Juan can defy the Commander; his list is about to get even longer.

'The Streetcleaner' sees himself as a defender of Order, a Vigilante Hero. He takes the place of the derisory Fathers. His irony deflates them, shows them to be powerless, castrates them. 'Just wait and see': the new God keeps the cities better policed than the old Titans. One can hardly be surprised that the police did not want to see such a letter. To them, it was the Medusa stare.

On the occasion of Christmas 1984, the West Yorkshire Police sent a 'Best Wishes' card to Sutcliffe in the psychiatric hospital where he is at present. 'We felt that Mr. Sutcliffe might help us with some of our enquiries', was the explanation given when Mrs. Hill and other relations of the victims expressed their outrage. Presumably they meant that he might own up to some more of the unsolved murders.

Notes

Part One

One

1 David A. Yallop, *Deliver Us From Evil*, Macdonald Futura, 1981, p. 349.

2 'Notice: *The Grammar of Ornament'*, *Fortnightly Review* 1, 15 May 1865, pp. 124-5. My thanks to Claire Howard for drawing my attention to this piece.

3 Yallop, op. cit., p. 318.

4 Epigraph to *Blow Your House Down*, Virago, 1984: '. . . if you look long into an abyss, the abyss also looks into you', Nietzsche, *Beyond Good and Evil*.

5 Gordon Burn, *'Somebody's Husband, Somebody's Son'; The Story of Peter Sutcliffe*, Heinemann, 1984.

Two

1 Burn, op. cit., p. 221. The 'all-male company' were 'playfully punching each other and hugging each other and pumping each other's hands'. All male writers on the topic pick up the sporting analogies. Describing Sutcliffe's account at court of his God-given mission, Yallop writes, '. . . the Yorkshireman in the witness box is reminiscent of Boycott in top form battling against Lillee and Thompson bowling at half-pace' (= the Attorney General).' Op. cit., pp. 354-5.

2 Cross, *The Yorkshire Ripper; The In-depth Study of a Mass-Killer and His Methods*, Granada, 1981, pp. 23-5. Yallop has a list of 11 'unsolved'

murders or attempted murders in the same period, op. cit., p. 324.

3 Yallop, p. 351. The title of his book is *'Deliver us from Evil'*.

4 For Cross and Yallop see ref. above. John Beattie, *The Yorkshire Ripper Story*, a Quartet/Daily Star Publication, 1981.

5 Ref. above.

6 Judge Boreham, summing up for the jury, said that Dr. Milne's citing of Sutcliffe's 4 years as a gravedigger in Bingley cemetery as partial confirmation of his claim is 'very much like claiming to have swum the Channel and your friends doubting it and taking them and showing them the Channel as proof. Well, it doesn't prove much, does it?' Quoted Yallop, p. 360.

Part Two

Three

1 For instance, the repeated paradox which makes *awareness* of the impending threat make it come about. First the parents, Laius and Jocasta, and Oedipus himself, later, are told by an oracle that the boy will kill his father and marry his mother. They do something to prevent it from happening, and this is precisely what permits it to happen. It is the formulation, the bringing to consciousness, of the incestuous and murderous nature of desire that brings its fulfilment about through attempts to avoid it (perhaps this is what Freud will come to in *Beyond The Pleasure Principle*). Secondly, if we are to regard the Oedipus story as 'the' myth of human knowledge (solving the riddle of life by a discovery of 'origins') one must ignore that transgression and despair are part and parcel of the process of self-knowledge that it presents. Oedipus gets to know himself, thus experiencing horror and blindness, because he's continuously *erred* in the pursuit of goodness. It's because he and his parents have tried so hard to avoid breaking the supreme taboo that they have broken it — that they discover how irresistible transgression is — that they come to know 'the horror' of life.

2 See in particular the two essays, 'Some Psychological Consequences of the Anatomical Distinction Between The Sexes', (1925) and 'Female Sexuality' (1931), which have led to so much controversy (Karen Horney, Melanie Klein, and more recently, Luce Irigaray — *Ce Sexe qui n'en est pas un* — Sarah Kofman — *L'Enigme de la Femme* — not to mention Lacan's *Encore*, some of Cixous's essays, and Juliet Mitchell's *Psychoanalysis and Feminism*).

3 Hélène Cixous, 'Le Sexe ou la tête', *Cahiers du Grif*, 13, 1976 (Oct.); tr. as 'Castration or Decapitation', *Signs* 7, 1981, 41-53.

Four

1 Burn, 243-4.
2 Yallop, 351-4.
3 Cross, 248.
4 Beattie, 152-3.
5 Burn, 232.
6 'Sleeping Beauty': see Hélène Cixous's discussion of this in 'Le Sexe ou la tête'. op. cit. and in *La Jeune Née*. I translate from the essay: 'Woman, if you look out for her, you have a strong chance of finding her always in the same position, that is, in bed . . . always in relation to a bed (there is a pun on 'lit'/'il', bed/he): sleeping Beauty is drawn from that bed by a man because women cannot wake up for themselves, as you know, they need the intervention of men. She is raised from her bed by man who comes in order to lay her down on another bed so that she can give birth ad infinitum as in fairy tales.'
7 R. Jakobson, 'Two Aspects of Language and two Types of Aphasic Disturbances', *Fundamentals of Language,* Mouton, 1971, p. 69. The essay is extraordinarily relevant, as it classes aphasic disorders into 'metaphoric' and 'metonymic'. Obviously, Sutcliffe was not an aphasic. Yet his 'reading' disturbance is clearly of the 'contiguity', 'metonymic' order described by Jakobson.

Five

1 A great deal is known about Sutcliffe. The family, the friends, the neighbours, were interviewed by scores of journalists between the arrest and the trial. Four books (ref. above) have been written on the case. There are variants, some due to error, others due to the witnesses changing their stories according to who they were talking to. I have tried to get the 'facts' as accurate as possible. The chase after 'perfect' accuracy is however a mad one, since, for instance, while *all* reporters agree as one that the body of Wilma McCann was discovered by a milkman at 7.41 am (not 7.40 or 7.45), there are several disparities in everything else concerning the victims. The book I have used most in relation to the Sutcliffe family themselves, whatever reservations I have about it, is Burn's, as he is the one who 'double-checked' things most thoroughly, and he spent two years 'researching' the Sutcliffe's in Bingley.
2 Burn, 17-19.
3 Burn, 23-4.
4 According to Cross.
5 Burn, 29.

6 Burn, 31.

7 Lee Comer, *Wedlocked Women*, Feminist Press, 1974, p. 13.

8 Andrew Tolson, *The Limits of Masculinity*, Tavistock Publications, 1977, pp. 23-40.

9 By witnesses and biographers alike.

10 Burn, 32.

11 Id.

12 There is much in Lawrence in the way of attempting to 're-define' masculinity that one should be grateful for. I am thinking in particular of 'Love in the Haystacks'.

13 *The Times*, 12 May 1981. My italics.

14 The phrase used by Piers Paul Read in one of his *Observer* articles on the case.

Six

1 The question is so huge I would not know where to start listing books on the subject. Perhaps I could simply send the reader to Freud, the *Introductory Lectures* and the case history of 'Little Hans', for instance; and to something like Sheila Rowbotham's *Woman's Consciousness, Man's World*, or the selected bibliography at the end of Tolson's *The Limits of Masculinity*, op. cit.

2 Tolson, p. 46.

3 Cross, 49.

4 Burn, 21 and 58.

5 This, and other details about the Szurmas from Burn, pp. 64-65.

6 Tolson argues that unlike the lower middle-class, in which the image of patriarchal authority is based on moral dignity and 'respectability', 'working-class families maintain collective memories of poverty and physical insecurity . . . And working-class masculinity is characterized more by an immediate, aggressive style of behaviour than a vision of personal achievement'. Op. cit., 28.

7 Quoted by Burn, 5. The details here are also from him, pp.4-9.

8 Id, 30.

9 Id, 56.

10 Id.

11 Id, 69.

12 Id, 184.

13 Id, 16-17. Cross has a different story. He says that John Sutcliffe suffered from a mysterious skin disease, an allergy, that got cured once he moved out of the bakery into the textile mill. Heat had had something to do with it.

14 Burn, 17.

15 Id. 80.

Seven

1 Burn, 54 and 51.

2 For these anecdotes see Beattie, 118-9, Cross, 51-4 and 57, Yallop 326-7.

3 Richard Wolheim, explaining Freud on *Jokes and Their Relation To The Unconscious*, in *Freud*, Fontana/Collins, 1971, 100.

4 Id, 105.

5 Freud, *Standard Collected Works*, VIII, 179.

6 On this see Séverine Auffret's *Des Couteaux contre des femmes; de l'excision,* Ed. des femmes, 1983, the chapter strikingly called 'La cruauté des glucides'.

7 Couldn't it be that Sutcliffe pierced the eye of his last victim because in doing so he was going yet 'one further', doing a supremely daring thing, accomplishing the ultimate violation — as well as attempting to deny his victim's humanity?

8 Burn, 54. What does Burn *think* is happening, what is *he* saying when he narrates such episodes? Would to God he'd say. For his unquestioning use of John Sutcliffe's own language makes him sound like an 'adoptive' son. 'Bull's eye' is the expression he borrows from John Sutcliffe as an image for getting at the truth. In the light of what precedes, why I find this alarming may be clear.

9 Burn, 185.

10 Beattie, 122. ' "Let's go down Lumb Lane for a jump, then give the pro a kicking instead of paying" ' (to friend Ken Johnson).

11 Freud provides a sliding scale in jokes, from the more 'innocent' to the more 'tendentious'. See *Jokes . . . , Standard Collected Works*, op. cit., vol. VIII.

Eight

1 Burn, 77.

2 Burn, 52-53.

3 Id, 66.

4 Quoted by Beattie, 119.

5 *Studies in the Psychology of Sex,* Philadelphia, Davis, 1918, vol. III, pp. 109-110. Anecdotes abound as to Sutcliffe's shyness and 'modesty'. His fellow gravediggers say he would never strip to work in the summer heat; that he would never look a woman in the eye, etc. 'He seemed to look through you, not at you' is what some of the women who knew him as a young man say. One Carol Jones, whom he 'dated', speaks of his 'gentlemanly' behaviour and his 'cold' kisses. Beattie has a story by one Margaret Tovey who claims that when she

was 15 she had every kind of sexual relation with Sutcliffe but the 'normal' one: when the affair ended she was 'still a virgin' (Beattie, 121).

6 Freud, 'Notes on a Case of Paranoia Running Contrary to the Psychoanalytic Theory of the Disease', *Standard Collected Works*, Vol. XII, pp. 62-63. See also Freud's discussion of the 'negative Oedipus complex' in the Wolf-Man case in *The Ego and the Id*, ch. III and for a discussion of religion and paranoiac delusions, 'The Future of an Illusion' and *Civilization and Its Discontents*.

7 Burn, 81.

8 Id, 184.

9 See H. Segal on *Klein,* Fontana, 1979; also Juliet Mitchell's *Psychoanalysis and Feminism.*

10 'Some Theoretical Conclusions Regarding the Emotional Life of the Infant' in M. Klein *et al., Developments in Psycho-Analysis*, the Hogarth Press, 1952, p. 199.

11 'Notes on Some Schizoid Mechanisms', op. cit., P. 292.

12 'The Theory of Anxiety and Guilt', op. cit., p. 276.

13 'Notes on Some Schizoid Mechanisms', p. 293.

Nine

1 Burn, 72.

2 *The Times,* May 16, 1981.

3 See detailed testimony in *The Times,* May 14, 1981.

4 *The Times,* May 16, 1981.

5 Dr. Milne said he had great experience in the field. He had dealt with about 200 'sick' criminals in his career.

6 *The Times,* May 13, 1981.

7 Robin Holland, married to one of Sutcliffe's sisters, said to Beattie (p. 122): 'Prostitutes were always on his mind. I became so sickened that I stopped going out with him'. Other friends, (Ken Johnson, David Boldy, the Barker brothers and Trevor Birdsall) as well as his brothers have confirmed this, and told Burn and Cross how frequent Sutcliffe's visits to the prostitute districts were.

8 Burn, 114-115. I spare the reader further description.

9 Burn, 116.

10 Freud, 'The Loss of Reality in Neurosis and Psychosis', 1924, Pelican *Freud*, vol. XX, pp. 221-224.

11 Tolson says in an 'Althusserian' perspective: '. . . within a social formation . . . there are two kinds of defining structures: not only social institutions (school, legal system, mass media, etc., constituting a "State Apparatus"); but also "general ideologies" (located in types of ritual, and language). Social consciousness is as much structured

by the "codes" of a general ideological discourse, as it is by institutional boundaries and rules of behaviour.' Op. cit., p. 140.

Ten

1 Freud, 'Some Neurotic Mechanisms in Jealousy, Paranoia and Homosexuality' (1921), Pelican *Freud* X, p. 202.
2 All details from Burn, pp. 86-88. Confirmed by Cross and Beattie.
3 Burn, 95-97.
4 Id. 88.
5 Burn, 90-2.
6 *The Times,* May 7, 1981.
7 Cross speaks of two miscarriages (p. 169); Burn mentions one (p. 139).
8 See Cross for detailed account, pp. 158-162.
9 Freud, Pelican *Freud* X, p. 217, 'Neurosis and Psychosis'.
10 Burn, 92.
11 Quoted in Dr. Milne's report read at the trial, *The Times,* May 7, 1981.
12 Id.
13 'The aetiology . . . of a psychosis . . . consists in a frustration . . . of one of those childhood wishes which are forever undefeated . . . (In a psychosis the ego) lets itself be overcome by the id and is thus torn away from reality. A complication is introduced into this apparently simple situation, however, by the existence of the superego, which . . . unites in itself influences coming from the id as well as from the external world, and is to some extent an ideal model of what the whole endeavour of the ego is aiming at — a reconciliation between its various dependent relationships.' Freud, 'Neurosis and Psychosis' op. cit., p. 216.
14 All these collated dates thanks to Cross, 118.

Part Three

Eleven

1 R.E. and R. Dobash, *Violence Against Wives: A Case Against the Patriarchy,* Open Books, London, 1979, pp. 23-24.
2 Yallop, pp. 282-3.
3 Kate Millet, *Sexual Politics,* 1971; Juliet Mitchell, *Woman's Estate, 1971;* Shulamith Firestone, *The Dialectic of Sex,* 1970. See also Sheila Rowbotham, *Woman's Consciousness, Man's World,* 1973, Michelene Wandor, ed., *The Body Politic,* 1972, and the work of Jan Pahl and Jalna Hanmer on women's centres and community work. Also Juliet

Mitchell and Ann Oakley eds, *The Rights and Wrongs of Women*, 1976.
4 Eli Zaretsky, *Capitalism, the Family and Personal Life*, Pluto Press, 1976.
5 Id, pp. 29-31.
6 Id, p. 64.
7 Id, 61-2.
8 *The Times*, 7 May, 1981.
9 Katherine Blunden, *Le Travail et la Vertu. Femmes au Foyer: une Mystification de la Révolution industrielle*, *essai*, Paris, Payot, 1982, p. 179.
10 Tolson, op. cit., pp. 68 and 70.
11 Burn, 169.
12 Sonia Sutcliffe, article in *Guardian* 'Diary', op. cit.
13 E. Wilson, *What is to Be Done About Violence Against Women? Crisis in the Eighties*, Penguin, 1983, p. 57.
14 Id, 58.
15 Op. cit., p. 23. Anthony Storr was quoted in Piers Paul Read's *Observer* article of 24 May 1981.
16 Dobashes, op. cit., pp. 49-57 and p. 74.
17 Cross, 13.
18 Burn, 81.
19 Séverine Auffret, *Des Couteaux contre des femmes; de l'excision*, Paris, Ed. des femmes, 1983, pp. 83-89.
20 Zaretsky, op. cit., 57.
21 Id, 59.
22 Juliet Mitchell, *Woman's Estate*, Penguin, 1971, p. 129.
23 See Freud, *The Psychopathology of Daily Life*.
24 *The Sunday Times*, 24 May, 1981.
25 Michel Carrouges, *Les Machines célibataires;* see also the texts accompanying the catalogue of the 1975 exhibition, Alfieri.
26 Cross, 45.
27 'More and more the labour process appears to be governed by neutral, scientific laws such as centralization, efficiency, the imperatives of technology, etc. . . . Rather than encountering the capitalist class, the proletariat is faced by abstract, scientific laws and countless, immediate oppressors.' Zaretsky, 71.
28 Tolson, p. 58. Next passage also quoted by Tolson: 'In the eyes of his employer a man is not seen as a human being . . . but as a unit in the cost of production'. In all this, of course, the primary reference is to Marx; also Lukács, 'Consciousness and the Reification of the Proletariat', in *History and Class-Consciousness*.
29 John Berger and Jean Mohr, *A Seventh Man*, Penguin, 1975, p. 99.
30 Freud, *Standard Collected Works*, op. cit., vol. XXIII, pp. 275-278.
31 Beattie, 119 and 122.

32 'We know from dreams what liberties "unconscious mental activity" takes with numbers. If, for instance, the number five occurs in a dream, this can be invariably traced back to a five that is important in waking life. But whereas in waking life the five was a five years' difference in age or a company of five people, it appeared in the dream as five banknotes or five fruits. That is to say, the number is kept, but its denominator is changed according to the requirements of condensation and displacement'. Freud, *Standard Collected Works*, vol. XIX, p. 89, 'A Demonological Neurosis'. See also 'Dreams and Folklore', id., vol. XII, 186. Sutcliffe is reported to have often kept his wage-packet intact, unbroken, and boasted about it to family or acquaintance — like the Douglasses, the family of the girl Tessa he was 'courting' in Glasgow. The Duke of Wellington figures on the reverse side of the five-pound note (at the back of the Queen), with canons and horses, seen from the *back*, going to the battle of Waterloo.

33 Much work has been done by women on 'pornography': Andrea Dworkin, *Pornography: Men Possessing Women;* Susan Griffin, *Pornography and Silence,* to quote some of the best-known; see also Rosalind Coward, 'Pornography: the Opposing Feminist Viewpoints'; *Spare Rib*, Issue 119, June 1982, pp. 52-3.

34 Simone de Beauvoir, *The Second Sex.*

35 Beattie, 139-140.

36 Marx, *Capital*, vol. I, Penguin ed., pp. 163-178.

37 Id.

38 Cross, 14.

39 Cross, 108.

Twelve

1 *Prostitution Considered in Its Moral, Social and Sanitary Aspects in London and Other Large Cities; With Proposals for the Mitigation and Prevention of Its Attendant Evils,* 1857 revised 1870.

2 *Prostitution and Victorian Society; Women, Class and the State,* Cambridge University Press, 1980, pp. 46-47.

3 'Jack the Ripper and the Myth of Male Violence', *Feminist Studies,* vol. 8, No. 3, Fall 1982, p. 569.

4 Besides Judith Walkowitz, see Frances Finnegan, *Poverty and Prostitution; A Study of Victorian Prostitutes in York,* Cambridge UP, 1979; Kate Millet, *The Prostitution Papers,* Paladin, 1975; Ellen Strong, 'The Hooker' in Morgan, Robin, ed., *Sisterhood Is Powerful: An Anthology of Writings From The Women's Liberation Movement,* NY, Random House, 1970; Jeffrey Weeks, *Sex, Politics and Society: The Regulation of Sexuality since 1800,* Longman, London, 1981. Also Barbara Taylor, *Eve and the New Jerusalem,* Virago 1983 and Eric Trudgill, *Madonnas and*

Magdelens: The Origins and Development of Victorian Sexual Attitudes, Heinemann, 1976. For a summary of questions posed by prostitution and a good basic bibliography see E. Wilson, op. cit.

5 Elizabeth Wilson, op. cit., 101.

6 'Jack the Ripper . . . ' op. cit., pp. 544-547.

7 Cross, 78.

8 Id., 79-80.

9 'Jack the Ripper . . .', 552.

10 Cross, 8.

11 J. Walkowitz, 'Male Vice and Female Virtue: Feminism and the Politics of Prostitution in Nineteenth-Century Britain', *History Workshop Journal,* Issue 13, Spring 1982, p. 84.

12 Id, p. 87.

13 Id, 88.

14 Yallop, 275 (incidents recounted 270-8).

15 Id, 277.

16 Judith Walkowitz, 'Jack the Ripper . . .', 563.

17 Yallop, 275.

18 Emily Dickinson, 1896; quoted by Susan Griffin.

19 Susan Griffin, *Woman and Nature; the Roaring Inside Her,* Harper and Row, 1980, pp. 94-6.

20 See both E. Wilson, 'Prostitution: Economic Violence', pp; 97-116 and J. Walkowitz, 'The Politics of Prostitution', op. cit. pp. 80-1.

21 Not such a caricature: one only has to think of the treatment of many rape victims by the police.

22 Yallop, 287.

23 Id, 270.

24 J. Walkowitz, 'The Politics of Prostitution', p. 88.

25 Mandy Merck, 'Looking at the Sutcliffe Case', *Spare Rib,* July 1981, 16-18; Wendy Holliday, 'I Just Wanted to Kill a Woman': Why?; the Ripper and Male Sexuality', *Feminist review,* 9, Autumn 1981, 33-40; Nicole Ward Jouve, 'Le Fossoyeur du Yorkshire, gardien de l'ordre?' *Des Femmes Hebdo,* 50, June 1981.

26 Op cit., *Spare Rib,* June 1982.

27 Mary McIntosh, 'Who Needs Prostitutes? The Ideology of Male Sexual Needs', in Smart, Carol and Smart, Barry, *Women and Sexuality and Social Control,* Routledge and Kegan Paul, London, 1978, pp. 54-55.

28 E. Wilson, Op. cit., pp. 109-110.

29 J. Walkowitz, 'The Politics of Prostitution', p. 90.

30 On some of the contradictions see S. Heath, *The Sexual Fix,* Macmillan, 1982.

31 Quoted by Beattie, 134.
32 Beattie, 133-4.
33 Catherine Clement/Hélène Cixous, *La Jeune, Née*, Paris, Union générale des Editions, 1975, p. 61.
34 My translation, with the help of I. de Courtivron's own translation in 'Weak Men and Fatal Women: the Sand Image', *Homosexualities in French Literature*, ed. George Stambolian and E. Marks, Cornell UP, 1979, p. 225.
35 See Hélène Cixous, 'Castration or Decapitation', op. cit.
36 'On the Sociology of Pornography' in Ned Polsky, *Hustlers, Beats and Others*, Anchor Books, New York, 1969, p. 186, See also the testimonies about American Indians and the Arapesh in New Guinea gathered by E. Wilson, op. cit., 75.

Thirteen

1 Burn, 60.
2 Trevor Birdsall was asked on 6 May 1981 by the Attorney General whether he had entered into any agreement with a newspaper. He had received £500 plus unspecified amounts to repay bills and London expenses maintenance money from *The Sunday People*. His girlfriend had contracts with *The People* for £2,000. Ronnie Barker had received £700 from *The Sun* for photographs of Sutcliffe's wedding, and was expecting other payments for photographs from *The Sunday People*. These figures according to Burn, 236; he says that Olivia Reivers had received £1,000 from *The Daily Star* and was expecting more; also, that *The Star* virtually sequestered the Sutcliffe brothers, hiding them from the rest of the press in various hotels, buying them expensive clothes and plying Mick with drink so that it turned him into a complete alcoholic. The *Daily Mail* hotly pursued John Sutcliffe, closely followed by the *Yorkshire Post*. Sonia and her parents were besieged and hounded by crowds of reporters, but refused to 'deal'. Burn, 236.
3 Mrs. Irene MacDonald won her suit for damages for the loss of her daughter Jane on Jan 14, 1982; some of the survivors (Marilyn Moore) also won their cases.
4 See Sonia's report to the *News of the World*, (which specified that they had *not* paid her any money): she was kept at home and questioned without having the chance to talk to her husband and know the truth from him; the police refused to give her any information, even to let her read a paper, while they were talking to the press (which they should not have done prior to the trial); she was kept in a cell with a policewoman, had to keep the door open while she took a shower, was not allowed to phone home, and the whole police

station was filled with a sense of 'jubilation'. She claims that her
house was cold (which led a policeman to compare it to a 'morgue')
because she was expecting to go straight to the police station when the
police came to collect her. (June 7, 1981).
5 She had been doing short notice 'relief' work at the Sherrington
nursing home in addition to her supply teaching. This is what kept
her out of home on Saturday nights. Burn, 175.

Fourteen

1 Cross, 33.
2 Yallop, 138-9.
3 See the 'Insight' team article, *Sunday Times*, 24 May, 1981.
4 See above.
5 Beattie's figures, culled from the GPO revenue for the Leeds
number 646411. All figures given here are approximate as none of the
four books on the Ripper Case produce the same. I have chosen those
that were either repeated, or seemed to have been best checked.
6 Beattie, 86. Same source for the next set of figures. Cross says that
the publicity campaign cost £1 million, but in fact very much less
because a lot of people gave work free. Burn repeats the £3 million
figure. He talks of 27,000 house-to-house searches, and 22,000
statements taken.
7 Other sources say 5 million.
8 These details from Cross: 'Senior officers . . . stressed that when
armed with the delicate details of an individual's visits to the red-light
districts, they were concerned only with eliminating a man as a
suspect. The information was treated confidentially, and to this end,
discretion, tact and diplomacy had to run hand-in-hand with the
detectives' more usual characteristics of suspicion and vigilance'.
9 This according to Yallop, 232.
10 Burn, 180. Confirmed by the other books.
11 Cross, 153.
12 Id, 234.
13 Id, 138 and 147-8.
14 Id, 149.
15 Id, 235.
16 Whether this was on account of the bite found on Joan Harrison's
body (a murder Sutcliffe did not commit — which makes Joan
Harrison's murderer even more of a 'double' of his) — in which case it
was a 'mistaken' but truthful clue(!) — or because a bite had also been
found on Josephine Whitaker's body — is not sure as some reports
mention this and others not. I must note here, in the light of the
Melanie Klein theories I mentioned earlier, that such a bite tallies

with the aggressiveness against the 'bad breast' — against the body of
the mother.

17 *The Times*, Friday July 1 1983.
18 Cross, 236.
19 Id, 208-9.
20 Id, 208-212.